Pathways to Excessive Gambling
A Societal Perspective on Youth and Adult Gambling Pursuits

CHARLOTTE FABIANSSON
University of Western Sydney, Australia

LONDON AND NEW YORK

First published 2010 by Ashgate Publishing

2 Park Square, Milton Park, Abingdon, Oxfordshire OX14 4RN
52 Vanderbilt Avenue, New York, NY 10017

Routledge is an imprint of the Taylor & Francis Group, an informa business

First issued in paperback 2020

Copyright © 2010 Charlotte Fabiansson

Charlotte Fabiansson has asserted her right under the Copyright, Designs and Patents Act, 1988, to be identified as the author of this work.

All rights reserved. No part of this book may be reprinted or reproduced or utilised in any form or by any electronic, mechanical, or other means, now known or hereafter invented, including photocopying and recording, or in any information storage or retrieval system, without permission in writing from the publishers.

Notice:
Product or corporate names may be trademarks or registered trademarks, and are used only for identification and explanation without intent to infringe.

British Library Cataloguing in Publication Data
Fabiansson, Charlotte.
  Pathways to excessive gambling : a societal perspective on
  youth and adult gambling pursuits.
  1. Gambling--Social aspects. 2. Gambling--Social
  aspects--Australia. 3. Teenage gamblers. 4. Gambling
  industry.
  I. Title
  363.4'2-dc22

Library of Congress Cataloging-in-Publication Data
Fabiansson, Charlotte.
  Pathways to excessive gambling : a societal perspective on youth and adult gambling
  pursuits / by Charlotte Fabiansson.
     p. cm.
  Includes bibliographical references and index.
  ISBN 978-1-4094-0431-6 (hbk) 1. Gambling. 2. Gambling--Social aspects. I. Title.
  HV6710.F35 2010
  363.4'2--dc22

2010003869

ISBN 978-1-4094-0431-6 (hbk)
ISBN 978-0-367-60269-7 (pbk)

Contents

List of Figures	*vii*
List of Tables	*ix*
Acknowledgements	*xi*

1 Introduction   **1**
1.1 Background   1
1.2 Overview of the book   4
1.3 What is gambling?   8
1.4 Gambling in a historical perspective   11
1.5 Why is gambling a problem?   15

2 Gambling Research and Gambling as a Recreational Pursuit   **17**
2.1 Gambling research   17
2.2 Youth gambling research   22
2.3 Introduction to leisure   31
2.4 The youth construct   33
2.5 Youths' leisure environment   35
2.6 Gambling as a recreational activity   37

3 Global Gambling and Regulation of Gambling   **41**
3.1 Global gambling   41
3.2 Gambling expenditure   49
3.3 Gambling regulation   51
3.4 Responsible gambling   63
3.5 Promotion of gambling   71
3.6 People affected by gambling   73
3.7 Conclusion   76

4 Gambling in Australia   **79**
4.1 Introduction   79
4.2 Local clubs' role in the community   83
4.3 Adult gambler profile   87
4.4 Gambling prevalence in Australia   91
4.5 Gaming machine gambling in New South Wales   101
4.6 Conclusion   106

vi   *Pathways to Excessive Gambling*

5   Youth Gambling   **109**

5.1   Introduction   109
5.2   Research methodology and design   110
5.3   Youths' gambling experiences   112
5.4   Gambling for money   114
5.5   Non-age restricted gambling   115
5.6   Age restricted gambling   119
5.7   Summary of older youths' gambling experiences   127
5.8   Youths' gambling intensity   129
5.9   Youths' arrangement for gambling payments   131
5.10   Youths' spending structure   131
5.11   Conclusion   136

6   Adults' Excessive Gambling Pathways   **141**

6.1   Introduction   141
6.2   Research methodology and design   142
6.3   Introduction to gambling   148
6.4   Age of independent gambling   151
6.5   The first gambling win   153
6.6   Factors inspiring gambling propensity   156
6.7   Pathways to problem gambling   159
6.8   Cultural gambling traditions   161
6.9   Monetary cost of gambling   163
6.10   Reasons for seeking help   164
6.11   Gambling's impact on personal and public life   167
6.12   Social isolation   170
6.13   Gambling as part of other personal and social issues   173
6.14   Conclusion   177

7   Concluding Discussion   **181**

7.1   Introduction   181
7.2   Gambling in the global society   186
7.3   Young people's gambling   187
7.4   Adults' gambling   191
7.5   Gambling pathways   193

8   Has Gambling Research a Future?   **197**

List of References   *201*
Index   *223*

List of Figures

4.1	Total clubs and hotels electronic machine gaming pre-duty profit in New South Wales between 1999 and 2004	103
4.2	Aggregate gambling expenditure for the whole of Australia and NSW 2005–06	104
5.1	Youths' reactions to losing money on gambling activities in per cent	135

List of Tables

1.1	Other examples of high lotto wins	2
3.1	World lottery sales by region in 2004–2007	41
3.2	International comparison of the number of horse races held and horse racing prize money in 2006	44
3.3	Countries with the highest number of (electronic) gaming machines – casino-style machines 2006	47
3.4	Total installed base of gaming machines by region in 2004, 2006 and 2008 by numbers and per cent	48
3.5	AGMMA's win and lose table – the randomly calculated hypothetical percentage of return of total amount staked that players might experience	67
4.1	History of gambling in Australia	80
4.2	Gambling turnover, participation rate and number of businesses in Australia 2005–06 (Australian dollar)	83
4.3	Social and demographic characteristics of all people, gamblers and non-gamblers 1999 in per cent	89
4.4	Estimated number of gambling businesses in Australia by state/territory, 2004–05 and number of venues with gaming machines in Australia by state/territory 2005–06	93
4.5	Estimated number of gaming machines in Australia by venue type 2005–06	93
4.6	Gaming machines per 1,000 adults and per adults in Australia by state/territory 2004–05 and 2005–06	94
4.7	Summary: Aggregate and per capita gambling expenditure in Australia by state/territory 2005–06	96
4.8	Proportion of HDI spent on all gambling forms in Australia by state/territory between 2000–01 and 2005–06 in per cent	98
4.9	Gambling taxation revenue, gambling tax as a proportion of total tax revenue and gambling expenditure as percentage of gambling tax revenue in Australia by state/territory 2004–05 and 2005–06	99
4.10	The clubs and hotels with the highest electronic gaming machine pre-duty profit in New South Wales local government areas (LGA) the period February/March 2004 to January/February 2005	105

5.1	Young people's experiences of buying raffle tickets by age and gender	116
5.2	Young people's experiences of betting on games by age and gender	118
5.3	Young people's experiences of buying lotto tickets by gender	120
5.4	Young people's experiences of participating in casino table games by age and gender	122
5.5	Young people's experiences of playing Keno by gender	123
5.6	Young people's experiences of betting on sports by community and gender	126
5.7	Summary of age limited gambling games by age groups in per cent	128
5.8	Gambling activities most frequently played and most fun to play	130
5.9	Average spending on gambling activities during an evening by age groups and gender in per cent	132

Acknowledgements

I am indebted to all those who have helped me over the years with my research and the development of this book. I would like to thank my colleagues, family and friends who have provided me with encouragement and pertinent comments on earlier drafts of this book. I would also like to thank the young people who took part in the research and gave valuable information about being young in the twenty-first century in rural and regional Australia and the high schools that so generously gave me access to their students. I am grateful to the multicultural problem gambling support organisation that collated people's stories about gambling pathways and elucidated the adversity they experience as a consequence of excessive gambling. I enjoyed my discussions with the multicultural support organisations; these gave me insights into migrant daily life in Australian communities. I thank representatives from local governments, community leisure and youth support organisations that took the time to enlighten me about community life and the challenges young people encounter in their everyday lives and in recreational pursuits and I am grateful for the representatives from local community clubs who explained the history and philosophy of their community engagement. I have welcomed the editorial suggestions and reviews I have received and I would like to express my sincere thanks to the publisher and the commissioning editor for making the book a reality.

Chapter 1

Introduction

1.1 Background

Gambling has always fascinated people. Throughout the ancient world and right up to today, gambling has been openly supported in some cultures, while in others, treated as a distraction from important work. In ancient and historical Egyptian, Greek and Roman writings, references to gambling can be found. Archeological excavations have uncovered not only tablets referring to gambling, but also implements associated with gambling. In China, such implements have been discovered dating back as far as 2300 BC; in Egypt ivory dice made before 1500 BC have been found and a tablet referring to gambling was found in one of the pyramids of Giza. By 3000 BC astragals (knucklebones) and card games were played. The card game 'primero' was played in Egypt; it is the predecessor to modern poker and an early European card game. To be a spectator at chariot races and play dice were the games for the common people, while horse and dog racing were reserved for royalty and the noble groups of the society (Ashton 1968).

In the twenty-first century gambling is still a common and popular activity. Horse racing, lottery products, gaming machines and casino table games have been developed from ancient gambling forms and gambling traditions and gambling has gained a social recreational status in some societies. The recreational status of gambling is central to the main arguments of the book, the way recreational gambling has become integral to the social milieu, where governments and community groups have utilised people's interest in gambling to collect money for community projects. Lottery systems are used to raise money for health and community projects where the available public funds are insufficient to the purpose, thus people and their communities are provided with facilities that would otherwise be beyond the funding scope of the public purse. Additionally, governments gain substantial revenue from taxation of gaming profits, thus it has become an indispensable income source.

Furthermore, gambling has proliferated, growing from a local, community based and personal activity into a global anonymous phenomenon where the gambler can gamble from anywhere in the world. In societies, where gambling is legal and has gained a social recreational status, it is widely promoted in the mass media. Advertisements of gambling products are directed at the individual, emphasising how a big win would change his or her life and create a carefree future. These gambling advertisements can be seen and heard most days in mass and other media.

In Australia in July 2009, the Powerball lottery stake reached A$80 million and in the previous month the Lotto lottery stake was A$90 million. These winning stakes were the hitherto highest lottery stakes of any Australian lottery game. In the days leading up to the draws, both lotteries were given extensive mass media publicity, which enticed more than the usual regular customers into buying Lotto and Powerball tickets. By Australian standards, these winning stakes were exceptionally high, but not when compared with other jurisdictions or global lottery systems. In Italy (August 2009), the right numbers in the SuperEnalotto finally was won giving the winner or winners €146.9 million (£128.3 million; US$211.8 million) (other examples, Table 1.1).

Table 1.1   Other examples of high lotto wins

Prize	Lottery	Country	Month Year	Comment
€126m	EuroMillions	Spain	May 2009	Largest single winner in any lottery to date
P347.8m	Philippine Lotto	Philippine	February 2009	Asia's largest prize
€25m	State Lottery	Netherlands	July 2008	Tax free lump sum
€100m	SuperEnalotto	Italy	October 2008	Largest Italian prize
€16.2m	National Lottery	Ireland	July 2007	Biggest single winner and jackpot (Ireland)
US$390m	MegaMillions	United States	March 2007	World's largest jackpot
€37.6m	National Lottery	Germany	October 2006	Largest German prize and single winner
US$365m	Powerball	United States	February 2006	World's largest single ticket winner
€180m	EuroMillions	France and Portugal	February 2006	Europe's largest jackpot
€115m	EuroMillions	Ireland	July 2005	n/a
US$363m	The Big Game	United States	May 2000	Later renamed Mega Millions
£42m	National Lottery	United Kingdom	January 1996	Largest UK prize

Source: Based on data found at www.usamega.com/archive-052000.htm; www.timesonline. co.uk/tol/news/world/europe/article6274441.ece; news.bbc.co.uk/1/hi/world/europe/4746057. stm; news.bbc.co.uk/1/hi/uk/4676172.stm; news.bbc.co.uk/1/hi/world/americas/4740982.stm; www.sisal.it/se/se_main/1,4136,se_Record_Default,00.html; www.gelderlander.nl/algemeen/ dgbinnenland/3405786/Jackpot-van-25-miljoen-valt-in-regio-Den-Haag.ece.

Introduction 3

What is often lost in the hype of a large lotto win are the odds of picking the winning numbers. Irrespective of the method used, if the numbers need to be in the right order or if the numbers are picked from a different set of numbers, the chance of winning is in the range of one in 13,983,816 (for picking six numbers out of 49 numbers), one in 76,275,360 in for example the EuroMillions lottery (picking five numbers between one and 50 and two lucky star numbers from a pool of nine numbers) or larger depending on the distinctive rules used to pick the numbers.

Gambling stories reported in the media most commonly have an element of the sensational and range across stories about people who have won large amounts of money or gambled away millions of dollars on casino tables, electronic gaming machines or at the horse track, whether they used their own money or embezzled money. There is less perceived newsworthiness in stories of the excessive small-scale gambler who gambled his or her whole monthly salary in one session. The money lost is generally not in the hundreds of thousands, but it is the family's entire available funds, until the next payday or welfare cheque. For the gambler's family it is a devastating situation when there is no money for food, clothes, bills or even school excursions – but it is hardly newsworthy.

Gambling thus has many facets. This book examines gambling as a social recreational activity in local community settings – the type of gambling in which people from all walks of life participate, from the seemingly innocuous introduction of young people to gambling with family and friends through to the adult excessive gambler who requires professional counselling. It covers the regular gambler who plays on gaming machines, this is the gambler who patronises local community gambling venues, but is rarely mentioned in the media. These gamblers are neither big winners nor losers, but constitute the core group and the biggest group of gamblers at community clubs. They are more likely to play with smaller amounts, tens, hundreds or maybe single figure thousands of dollars per session; they are numerous and might play several times a week or sometimes every day. These regular gamblers are the gambling venues' best customers.

The research in this book explores gambling from a societal perspective where the community and the social environment are essential components to explain gambling and to understand pathways to excessive gambling. To understand adverse effects of gambling we need to understand the community and what is meant by the concept of community. By community we draw on Wellman's concept which (2001: 228) defines '… "community" as networks of interpersonal ties that provide sociability, support, information, a sense of belonging and social identity'. The definition captures the essence of community life in today's society where community life is a mediated affiliation of social belonging that keeps people, groups and organisations together through a spectrum of interactional possibilities from situations of direct human face-to-face interaction to indirect interaction through electronic communication. 'We find community in networks, not groups. … In networked societies boundaries are permeable, interactions are with diverse others, connections switch between multiple networks, and hierarchies can be flatter and recursive' (Wellman 2001: 227).

The research is situated within the community construct, a construct that has a spatial as well as a social connotation. The geographically defined community is especially difficult for individuals and groups to adjust to if they do not adhere to the same values as the dominant philosophy of the community. To be an outsider is difficult in any situation, but especially if the individual does not have other spatial or social networks to rely on, such as a family, work colleagues, ethnic group or live in a supportive community environment. The community ethos can be either inclusive or exclusive of residents who are seen as not embracing the accepted community and personal values (Dempsey 1990; White and Wyn 2004).

To belong to a community or a community network does not necessarily include the whole community, the whole household or the entire family setting. The community concept as related to issues and activities does not necessarily have a geographical or physical aspect, but rather it involves activities or networks that create an atmosphere of belonging, and where shared goals are the connections that keep people together. Essential factors in social networks are that people care about the same things and that they feel valued and important in that setting, this is what underpins their sense of belonging.

From this perspective, gambling analysis can focus on sociological and societal rather than individual psychological causes of gambling. This approach is applied in the following analyses where the focal point is young people and their initiation into recreational gambling activities, through local clubs' sporting activities and the subsequent adult pathways to excessive gambling. This continuation occurs in the social and physical milieux in which young people grow up and is especially prevalent in residential areas where alternative and affordable social recreational opportunities are limited. In such cases, the local sports, ethnic or professional club can become a social place, a 'second home' where people feel welcome and safe, irrespective of social status. This may be especially true for people whose personal circumstances are complex, who do not have a good relationship with their family, do not belong to a social network or perhaps are not interested in belonging to a social network. Where such characteristics exist, local clubs can compensate as social meeting places and create a community without social commitments.

1.2   Overview of the book

The book explores gambling in the local and global society, in its historical and contemporary context. It examines the history of gambling, the acceptance and early regulation of gambling and the expansion of gambling in a number of nation states. It analyses the interrelationships between government regulation, taxation, the gaming industry and the diversity of gambling forms, young people's introduction to gambling, experiences of gambling and adults' encounters with excessive gambling.

The presented national and international research is analysed from a societal perspective and the Australian research is grounded within the discipline of sociology. Thus the book explores gambling in the local community, it examines

Introduction 5

gambling as social and environmental constructs with the focus on societal factors which can encourage or restrict individual gambling. The societal perspective looks beyond the notion that an individual's problem can be explained through 'faults' in the character of the individual: 'faults' that are caused by personal or behavioural shortcomings, including a lack of self-control. Research that examines the phenomena from the perspective of the individual, frequently explains the 'problem' of excessive gambling as an outcome of the person's behaviour. This type of explanation is more commonly heard and therefore appears more acceptable because other players (including their social environment, access to gambling opportunities, government regulation and the gambling industry) are excluded as contributing to the 'problem', at least as long as the 'problem' does not become an embarrassment, too extensive or a public predicament for the jurisdiction.

By contrast the research which informs this book recognises the individual as the gambler, a person with a problem, but goes further by treating gambling as a social problem, that goes beyond the individual. This book therefore explores the social environment and the situation surrounding the gambler to gain a holistic understanding of pathways to excessive gambling. It follows the progress from the initial introduction of young people to gambling to the destruction of family relationships, work and financial despair.

Governments regulate the gambling industry in an attempt to mitigate its adverse effects. The book examines gambling regulation from a global perspective, with an overview of the gambling regulation in the jurisdictions of the United States, Canada, the United Kingdom and Australia. The extent of gambling in Australia is examined through research conducted into young people's introduction to and participation in gambling for money and through research about adults' pathways to excessive gambling. The Australian research is based on two research projects: one which explored young people's gambling experiences in rural and regional communities[1] and another that studied adults' gambling experiences and their pathways[2] to excessive gambling where professional counselling was required to manage the adverse effects of their gambling.[3,4] While the original research is based

---

1   A Comparative Study of Young People's Gambling Experiences.

2   The concept 'pathways' refers to the social context in which an individual make choices about life directions, influenced by personal behaviour, friends, family, social and environmental factors (cf. Blaszczynski and Nower 2002 regarding pathways models within problem and pathological gambling).

3   A Community Study of the Relationships between Unemployment and Gambling.

4   Selected segments of the research have been examined in the articles: Fabiansson, C. (2009) Why would anyone want to do gambling research? *Journal of the National Association for Gambling Studies*, 21, (1), 25–7; Fabiansson, C. (2008) Pathways to excessive gambling – Are young people's approach to gambling an indication of future gambling propensity? *Child Indicators Research*, 1, (2), 156–75; Fabiansson, C. (2006a) Recreational gambling – Young people's gambling participation in rural Australia. *Journal of Youth Studies*, 9, (3), 345–60; Fabiansson, C. (2006b) Pathways to excessive gambling within a social community construct. *Journal of the National Association for Gambling*

on Australian conditions, comparisons are made with national and international research as appropriate, thus analysing gambling from different jurisdictions' perspectives. As the analysis of gambling is from a societal perspective, it sets the presented research apart from the main body of gambling studies, which are undertaken within the psychology discipline with an individual focus.

The book is presented in seven chapters with a concluding chapter on the future of gambling research.

Chapter 1 introduces the gambling construct, what is meant by gambling, gambling's role in society and a brief history of gambling in Egypt, Middle East, China and Europe. Additionally, it discusses why gambling is a societal problem causing hardship for gamblers and their families.

Chapter 2 concentrates on a review of national and international gambling research. To present a comprehensive literature review of the whole field of gambling research and an inclusive representation of national and international gambling research is however, not feasible within a single monograph. The presented research is thus limited to national and international research relevant to the issues discussed, i.e. societal issues in relation to excessive gambling and issues related to young people's introduction and participation in gambling pursuits. This section is followed by an analysis of the 'leisure' concept, its expansion in contemporary society and how gambling has become an accepted social recreational activity. It also includes a discussion about the 'youth' construct; how the youth period is defined and young people's position in our contemporary society.

Chapter 3 sets gambling in a global context, it presents forms of gambling and details gambling expenditure in different jurisdictions. It examines international gambling research, gambling expenditure and gambling regulation. Gambling regulation and responsible gambling strategies have been implemented in most jurisdictions to limit the negative effects of excessive gambling, but have at the same time allowed the gambling industry to augment their activities within the regulatory framework. Regulation of gambling is examined in the United States of America, Canada, United Kingdom and Australia. Acceptance of gambling, how it is promoted in the media, how people are affected by excessive gambling and the implications of cultural differences are also discussed. Additionally, the chapter examines in detail, gambling regulation and electronic gaming machine expenditure in Australia and particularly in the state of New South Wales, in order to provide an in-depth understanding of the development of gambling, the scope of gambling and governments' taxation of the gambling sector.

Chapter 4 concentrates solely on gambling in Australia, the club culture and community clubs' contribution to local community life, especially the relationship between local clubs, sports activities, community social recreation and hospitality

---

Studies, 18, (2), 55–68; The research was funded by grants from the Queensland Government Treasury, Queensland Office of Gaming Regulation, Research and Community Engagement Division, New South Wales Government Responsible Gambling Fund and University of Western Sydney. The research was developed and undertaken as independent research.

and gambling activities. It explores the sports club environment with its mixture of sports activities, hospitality and entertainment, and gambling activities and how gambling is not only the key to the financial success of the club but is central to many club activities. This close relationship between financial concerns and recreational gambling pursuits is explored by considering local clubs' involvement in the Community Development Support Expenditure (CDSE) scheme. This is the official channel for local support where local governments identify projects and organisations in need of financial support. Clubs involved in the CDSE scheme gain tax credits for their financial commitment, thus creating an incentive to support local community projects. Furthermore, it examines ways in which clubs establish long-term relationships with local residents including introducing pre-school children to club-sponsored sports activities; this creates an enduring attachment that frequently remains throughout a person's life. The chapter also examines cultural acceptance of gambling and sports clubs' dominance in providing affordable social recreation and entertainment opportunities, especially in low socio-economic areas where alternative leisure activities are limited. Finally, the chapter examines the adult gambling profile, and electronic gaming machine gambling in Australia and in particular New South Wales.

Chapter 5 analyses the findings from the Australian youth research, it explores young people's gambling participation and their introduction to gambling within the family environment. It examines high school students' gambling experiences in two small rural and regional communities and sets gambling within the social recreational environment as a continuation of sports activities and as a part of their social and leisure activities pursued with family and friends. The risk-taking behaviour of young people is analysed in relation to gambling, how gambling changes from a social leisure activity to excessive gambling. Finally, it examines issues that trigger excessive gambling where the pursuit of winning becomes the gambler's only focus.

Chapter 6 presents case studies that elucidate people's pathways from recreational gambling to excessive gambling, from a person's early introduction to gambling and how the gambling developed into an activity that takes over the person's life and where counselling is ultimately sought. The research explores the circumstances surrounding the introduction to gambling, the importance of the first win, reactions to losing money, the gamblers socio-economic situation, and the circumstances that changed social recreational gambling into an activity with serious social, mental, legal and financial impacts and ramifications beyond the individual gambler.

Chapter 7 summarises the issues discussed and considers what conclusions can be drawn from the two research projects and from national and international gambling research. Finally, Chapter 8 explores the future of gambling research, its role in policy development and the implications of gambling on young people's well being.

The limitations of comparative and statistical research are well recognised. In all research where facts and statistical data are assembled from different sources, discrepancies will arise. This can be due to reporting irregularities, different classifications, different years of reporting and incomplete or non-verified official statistics; consequently many of the figures are necessarily estimates. Furthermore, federal and state governments do not always make public comprehensive statistical information or research reports about gambling – for a variety of reasons. There are further complications when making international comparisons.

The bulk of gambling research has hitherto concentrated on exploring individual factors in attempting to explain excessive gambling – even when the research has been broadened to include health issues and access to gambling opportunities. Furthermore, the main part of gambling research has been based on small samples, covering specific and limited issues relevant to a jurisdiction. There are only few national or international studies (cf. Parke, Rigbye, Parke, Wood, Sjenitzer, and Vaughan Williams 2007; Wood, Griffiths and Parke 2007), and even fewer studies analysing gambling from a sociological and societal perspective. Research based on limited samples makes comparative research more complicated because it restricts the possible generalisations and applicability of findings to other jurisdictions.

The text is comprehensively referenced for those who would like to research the issues in more detail. While every effort has been made to include current gambling data, up-to-date regulations and the latest responsible gambling strategies, it must be remembered that the area is under constant revision with adjustments based on new research data and information, amendments to accommodate new gambling products, and changes in policy direction. The references and websites included in the text should help the reader to seek the latest information.

The aim of the book is to create knowledge and stimulate debate about gambling when viewed from a societal perspective and to highlight gambling as a global phenomenon with ancient traditions. The book also emphasises that the individual is only one 'player', and that the society, the government, and the gambling industry are all participants in the creation of a leisure activity, which for most people is an occasional recreational pursuit without adverse consequences, but which for others leads to devastating outcomes.

The book is written for anyone who is interested in understanding gambling issues. In particular it provides new insights into the social culture of gambling, it's influence in individual's lives, it's broader community and societal effects, governments' response through policies and the economic and political power of the gambling industry.

1.3   What is gambling?

Gambling is a social recreational activity, it is an activity without noticeable social or financial drawbacks for the majority of occasional and even regular gamblers, but for a 'few' its consequences can be catastrophic. In societies where gambling is accepted and publicly promoted, gambling is classified as a social leisure activity, a recreational activity among other social leisure activities (Reith 1999; Bailey 1987). Gambling is not an activity limited within national borders, gambling has a global market where national borders are irrelevant – this has been achieved with exponentially increasing ease through access to the internet. All jurisdictions, to a degree, regulate gambling activities with the aim to enforce prudent business activities, safeguard people from negative effects of gambling and collect gaming revenue in the form of taxes and license fees. Gambling revenue is a highly significant economic factor for many governments and so gambling legislation attempts to balance the needs of individuals, the need to secure tax revenue and licensing fees, and the financial interests of a wealthy and influential gambling industry.

Today the term 'gambling' refers to the wagering of money or something of material value on an event with an uncertain outcome. The word 'gaming' comes from the Old English word 'gamen' – amusement, fun, and from Germanic origin 'gamenian' – play, amuse oneself. The word 'gambler' originates from 'gamel' – play games, or from the verb 'game' (United Kingdom Office of Public Sector Information 2005). The primary intent with gambling is to win additional money and/or material goods (UK Gambling Act 2005, Explanatory Notes). The UK Gaming Act 2005 defines gambling as betting, gaming and participating in lottery games (cf. Productivity Commission 1999). Traditionally gambling is done at designated places such as the horse track, casino, hotel, and club or betting offices. An extension of the personal direct contact between the gambler and the gambling event is remote gambling. Remote gambling refers to gambling where the participants are not face-to-face on the same premises, thus people are participating in gambling pursuits by means of 'remote communication'. These interactive communications are through the internet, telephone, television (interactive television and mobile telephony) or other forms of electronic technology to transmit the communication (United Kingdom Office of Public Sector Information 2005; The Allen Group 2009).

Gambling for money can be defined as: '... staking of money on the outcome of games or events involving chance or skill' (Slade and McConville 2003: 2). Gambling is based on an element of risk and the possibility to win, lose or status quo with the invested money or goods. In gambling the outcome is more related to chance than skills, even if some skills can be gained from knowledge about racehorses or poker playing for example. Nonetheless, skill rather than chance is the prerogative or virtue of the winner, while the loser might explain the loss as a spell of bad luck. Gambling is a social or cooperative activity where making a bet involves laying a wager against something, a person, activity or a machine (Smith and Wynne 2002: 17). Gaming and wagering pursuits are social recreational activities, assumed to be freely entered into, where a person is committing money or goods to make an investment with uncertain outcomes (Reith 1999; Bailey 1987).

Gambling is present in most cultures and societies, legally or illegally, government supported or not and current modern times are not much different from ancient and historical times (cf. Ashton 1968). In contemporary society, gambling pursuits are diverse, ranging from betting on horse and dog racing, poker and table gambling, gambling on electronic gaming machines, gambling on internet designed games, and sports betting (Productivity Commission 1999). Gambling with or without money is widespread within families and among friends, such as card and board games; these games may have an educational value in that they may require practice of arithmetic. However, anyone partaking in excessive gambling or gambling in excess of available funds is likely to experience social, financial, health and emotional problems for themselves, their family and friends, as well as for the community.

Contemporary gambling is an accepted social recreational activity that has a long tradition in many countries. Raffles to collect money for hospitals, schools or community projects by governments, community organisations, schools, and charities have been used in many societies and are still seen as a practical way to subsidize financial shortfalls for community projects. This is habitually not seen as gambling or creating excessive gambling problems, as the winning prizes are more likely to be donated goods or services of modest value, rather than large cash prizes, as in national and international lottery systems (cf. Table 1.1). It is only very recently that the involvement of children in school raffles has been questioned and even then, it is not the use of raffles as a means of collecting money for pivotal community projects, but the practice of having young children handling money.

Relative to village societies for example, where decision-making is a collective activity, contemporary Western societies have increasingly favoured competitive individualisation, necessitating a requirement for a high level of negotiating activity and skill on the part of the individual. Here individuals take responsibility for their personal and professional development and the requisite risks involved. Collective solutions and social structures have not vanished; they are however less valued or accessible. The demands on the individual to negotiate everyday life and to find solutions suitable for their specific circumstances are greatly increased (Beck 1992). From this perspective it is possible to see gambling and risk taking behaviours as acceptable parts of personal and professional life. For young people and people from disadvantaged circumstances, where lack of money, education or employment opportunities are impediments to success, gambling for money can be seen as the quickest or indeed the 'only' way to succeed. In a society that values wealth, this creates a perception that risks are a necessary or an acceptable way to legitimately compensate for adversity, and perhaps the simplest way to gain improvement. This perception contributes to a high tolerance for risk-taking behaviour, gambling on success, and the consequent creation of a society that accepts and/or favours risk takers (Beck 1999: 12). This focus on winning is also manifested in sports where the winner gets all the praise. A similar situation can be found in gambling for money, where people will talk about how much money they have won through gambling, but not how much they have lost to secure a win; the lost money can far exceed that gained.

It is intrinsic in human nature to strive for advantage and success. To achieve success and to be the best, to compete, to be a winner and to back a winner are inherent desires in most cultures; few, if any cultures, promote being second or last. Thus, risk-taking behaviour is present in most recreational pursuits; team

Introduction 11

and individual sports competitions demand strength and skill, but also include the need to take (at times audacious) chances. Children's early introduction to sports and recreational activities can be seen as a grooming pathway to embrace a risk-taking ethos as an accepted life strategy. Parents will actively support their children and the local sports club to gain success. Early in life, children internalise these values about the need to compete and to be a winner, mainly by observing parents' behaviour. Competitive behaviour at school or on the sporting field has become an accepted strategy of everyday life, where risk-taking behaviour can be condoned as long as no serious harm is inflicted. The perception that success and well being cannot be achieved without partaking in risk-taking behaviours creates a societal tolerance for such behaviours. This is especially significant for young people. If sports and school competitions are early introductions to competition and risk taking behaviour, the same can be said for gambling with money – as long as one is a winner, few will question the gambling.

Globalisation and technological developments have changed community structure, government, communication, education and employment structures, social and health services, delivery of financial services, recreational activities, social network systems and interactions between people. Structural changes in response to these overarching developments have filtered down through organisations and institutions to the community and the individual. Some changes are for the benefit of all community residents; others are only for a selected group (Castells 1997). Metropolitan, urban, and rural environments are continuously changing due to global demands and environmental strains – so too are the forms and places of gambling. Access to gambling opportunities has changed from being mainly confined to designated places for gambling such as the racetrack, to global internet gambling, which is accessible almost everywhere by anyone. Close proximity to a gambling venue or easy access to gambling through the internet, while of little concern to non-gamblers, is a serious problem for the excessive gambler with a gambling problem.

1.4 Gambling in a historical perspective

While the type of gambling – horse racing, sports, card and board games or casino games, might vary between different cultures, historical periods and societies – gambling is a world-wide recreational activity with some form of gambling present in most cultures and civilisations. Gambling has at times played a role in nations' history – as seen in the tale of the dispute between Norway and Sweden about the ownership of the Island of Hising in 1000 AD (Ekeland 1993). The dispute could not be resolved diplomatically, thus the Norwegian King and the Swedish King agreed to roll a pair of dice to settle the dispute. On their first rolls, both kings got double sixes; on their second rolls, the Swedish King came up with two sixes and the Norwegian King rolled six on the first dice. The second, however, is said

12 *Pathways to Excessive Gambling*

to have cracked and showed a seven. Norway received the territory, and the two kings reportedly departed on good terms (Dembski 2007: 134).

The origin of gambling is disputed as gambling did not start from a specific time period or country, but occurred in different parts of the world and at different times (Lesieur 1985).[5] Horse racing has a long tradition and it is assumed to have first been organised by the prehistoric nomadic tribesmen of Central Asia, who first domesticated the horse about 4500 BC (Parker 1998), then spreading to other Asian and Middle Eastern countries, well before horse racing came to Europe. In the Western world, horse racing is thought to have started after English knights returned from the Crusades with Arabian horses. It is believed that the first publicly organised horse race was run as early as the twelfth century in England (Parker 1998).[6]

Gambling is not only a secular activity but has also been described as profane. In Plutarch's ([1883] 1960) story of Isis and Osiris, Mercury plays 'tables' with the Moon. Mercury was in love with the goddess Rhea who represents the eternal flow of time and generations. Mercury wants Rhea released from the curse of the Sun. According to the story Mercury 'plays at tables' with the Moon and wins the seventieth part of each of her illuminations, this is said to make up the five extra days to make 365 days a year (Ashton 1968).

As is the case in the twenty-first century, the attitudes of the ancients towards gambling were diverse. This was true in Egypt and the Middle East and among the Chinese, Japanese, the Hindus, the Persians, and the Huns (France 1902; Ashton 1968). For instance, although gambling is unacceptable in Muslim societies, the Quran acknowledges that gambling exists, and that it is a game based on chance, which should be avoided: 'you who believe, intoxicants and gambling … and the games of chance … you shall avoid them, that you may succeed. The devil wants to provoke animosity and hatred among you through intoxicants and gambling, and to distract you from remembering God' (Khalifa 1989, Quran 5: 90–91).[7]

Participation in gambling, playing games of chance, betting in the hope of winning an advantage or to gain a preference has been and still is an activity that engages people as a form of leisure or even as part of commerce. Ashton (1968) gives examples of three games of skill played in Egypt, 'tau' (the Game of Robbers), the 'game of the bowl', and 'draughts'. Evidence of these games of skill have been recovered from Queen Hatasu (circa 1600 BC), a draughtboard and 20 pieces. Additionally, game boards and pieces have been found at the ancient Mesopotamian city of Ur. These finds, dated by Sir Leonard Woolley, date

---

5 A more detailed history of the gambling and extensive references can be found at the Ontario Problem Gambling Centre website: R. Wildman II: http://www.gamblingresearch. org/contentdetail.sz?cid= 2096&pageid=735.

6 The venue for the first race horse meeting in Britain was at Newmarket. Ascot was founded in 1711 by Queen Anne.

7 Quran: 832/57696, Intoxicants and Gambling Prohibited, http://www.submission. org/suras/sura5.html.

from approximately 3000 to 2500 BC (cf. Magnusson 1985). Ivory astragals or knucklebones, as mentioned above, are the earliest known form of dice games, circa 3000 BC, and were used to predict the future (Dickerson 1984).

In ancient Rome chariot racing was for the common people (an ancient community-based-activity), while more solitary games were customary among the noble classes. Young and old citizens played games such as 'nuts and mora' (Ashton 1968). Gambling implements have been found in excavations in Etruscan sites and Pompeii, for example the 'talus', 'astragals', 'tessere' dices and gaming tables. Ashton (1968) identified six variations of hazard games that involve different degrees of chance and skill, played by Praetorians. Archaeologists found in the ruins of ancient Rome 'gaming tables engraved or scratched on the marble or stone slabs'. It is believed that the Roman Emperors, Augustus, Caligula, and especially Nero and Claudius were avid gamblers (Sifakis 1990). A variation of the dice game, backgammon, was proposed to have been popular with Nero.

Before a currency system, the winner would get something of value that had an accepted and tradable value. Land, goods and services were used as payments before the introduction of a national currency system and gambling for money. Furthermore, gambling pursuits were also used as a way to solve competing preferences, settle disputes and successions and to divide up property. The ancient Jews used lottery to divide up land areas, and the Israelites were chosen for special dangerous missions though a lottery system (Sifakis 1990). For example, the drawing of lots to determine outcomes of property appears to have been practised amongst the Jews, the 'casting of lots', assumed to have been done with a dice. Thus gambling has a long tradition in commerce, but also for enjoyment as a leisure pursuit. Board and card games, dice competitions, and betting on sports competitions and horses were gambling pursuits before the introduction of mechanical and later electronic gaming machines.

Overall, the introduction to gambling was through the noble and the upper classes. It is assumed an Emperor introduced gambling to China already as early as about 2100 BC. Records found in Egypt give details of a man who was caught gambling, which was illegal at that time. The punishment was to be sent to work in the quarries, which was synonymous with hard labour. Even if the Quran prohibits gambling by Muslims, the Persians gambled and the Hun soldiers carried dice with them on their treks (David 1962).[8] There is a belief that the Egyptians, the Indians, the Chinese, and the Japanese were responsible for providing the skill element of gambling, while the ancient Jews and Arabs augmented the dimension of chance (Ashton 1968).

Card games are supposed to have come from the Chinese and possibly as early as the Tang dynasty (Imperial dynasty 618–907, Magnusson 1985). Card games came to Europe first in the fourteenth century and first to Italy. As in all gambling forms, card games have undergone changes, in shape, size, and texture of the cards. Modern cards, the pack of 52 cards is of French design. Playing cards

---

8   Cf. David, F. (1962) regarding the history of dice games.

were first used through the fortune-telling tarot cards, a secular diversion from the church's sovereign right and religious belief about a person's future destiny (Wykes 1964). The medieval tarot card game originated in Italy and had 78 cards, while Indian cards from the early 1500s included 98 'circular, hand-painted and lacquered cards' (Magnusson 1985: 362). British cards often had pictures of royalty and the cards also displayed moral, educational and political messages to the players.

In more recent times, it is documented that the American Indians were avid and skilful wagerers at the time of the Europeans' arrival (Allen 1952; Lowie 1975; Mason 2000). Consequently, gambling was prevalent at the time of the founding of the United States of America and early governments sanctioned gambling as a revenue method for public projects (Smith 1948).

Gambling in Europe can be traced back to ancient German tribes where games played an important part in gaining wealth. In Europe, gambling was a pursuit that first attracted the rich and wealthy. One of the first European modern casinos was built in Baden-Baden, Germany in the early nineteenth century as part of the already established health resort. It became internationally famous in the 1830s when gambling in France was forbidden. In France and England, gambling was perceived as a leisure activity for the wealthy groups of society, including a leisure pursuit for Henry IV of England and Louis XIV of France. Gambling was not exclusively a male activity and wealthy women did partake in nightlong gambling sessions (Kavanagh 1993; Barnhart 1992).

It was not until gambling spread and became common among the lower classes that regulation of gambling was introduced (Fleming 1978, cited in Shaffer 1989). Thus gambling was first seen as a danger to society when common people started to gamble. A description of gambling venues and gamblers in the early nineteenth century is perhaps not much different from how it could be described in the twenty-first century (France 1902, quotes Ashton's description ([1899] 1986):

> A table of this nature in full operation is a terrific sight; all the bad passions appertaining to the vicious propensities of mankind are portrayed in the countenances of the players. ... Many in their desperation strip themselves on the spot of their clothes, either to stake against money or to pledge to the keeper of the table for a trifle to renew their play, and many instances occur of men going home half naked, having lost their all (France 1902: 369–70).

The negative effects of gambling on people's well being were approached with attempts to regulate gambling through restricting access and opportunities to gamble. There is documentation, which shows that the rulers of Spain tried to abolish gambling as early as the fourteenth century and in Italy, attempts to abolish wagering started already in 1506 and continued to the end of the nineteenth century (France 1902).

Still today the negative effects of gambling are mainly managed through regulations and responsible gambling guidelines. Despite a long tradition of

Introduction

restricting gambling, it has not decreased, but rather increased and become more diversified in its forms and availability.

1.5   Why is gambling a problem?

The gambling philosophy, the quest to be rich and independent, is nurtured and promoted in commercial, wealth and risk creating societies. Gambling for the majority of regular and occasional gamblers creates no adverse effects, as the lost money is part of the entertainment budget. The diversity in gambling options and accessibility to gambling venues in the local community, gives people inclined to gamble, opportunities to gamble 24/7, locally and globally, in many jurisdictions. While the number of problem gamblers in the population is not large, gambling is a serious problem for a significant number of people because it also affects all the people who are socially, emotionally and financially dependent on the gambler (Gambling Research Australia 2008; Productivity Commission 1999, 2009).

Children's and young people's association with gambling begins with pre-school sports programs run by local community clubs. The clubs present diverse sports programs and facilities for all ages, thus establishing a continuing contact with families. The sports involvement extends to after sports events where families congregate to socialise at the local community sports club. The introduction of the club concept, and the roles of clubs as supporters of local community sports programs through organising and facilitating teams (from pre-school to nationally competitive), and their contribution to community projects and charities are well promoted. Thus local community clubs have developed an enduring goodwill – they are seen to have a community focus and the community's well being at heart. In many countries there is widespread fascination with sports activities, which is further emphasised by the benefits of young children's involvement in such activities, both as a social recreational pursuit and as part of a healthy life style ideology. In Australia, it is largely community clubs that are the main sports facilitators and for many local residents the main recreational meeting place. Clubs' role in excessive gambling relates to their high concentration of gaming machines, ease of access for the local community through long opening hours and even the design of the gambling venues themselves where it is difficult to keep track of time and money spent.

Clubs' activities and supporting community roles are largely underpinned by gambling revenue, gained from local and non-local gamblers, with a high proportion of the revenue coming from regular gamblers and excessive gamblers (Productivity Commission 1999, 2009). Sports clubs' widespread activities and involvement in the local community create an excellent and deliberate recruiting ground for families and entices young people to become future members; not necessarily future gamblers or problem gamblers.

However, it is not only through sports and the club environment young people are introduced to gambling. In the local community, children and young people also come in contact with gambling products through parents' everyday consumption, such as buying a weekly lottery tickets at the same time as grocery shopping, making a lottery ticket a weekly expense much like milk and bread.

Even if the majority of gamblers would not experience any adverse effects, there is a 'minority' group of gamblers who experiences severe problems because of their gambling pursuits. People's awareness of excessive gambling is often restricted to mass media reports, which highlights the pitfalls of excessive gambling only when a person has gambled vast sums of money at casinos or on horse tracks, while less mass media attention is given to people who play on electronic gaming machines (EGM) at local sports, ethnic or professional clubs. Gamblers who have a problem with gambling frequently finish the gambling session only when all the money has been lost. Gambling away all available money creates social, emotional, legal and financial difficulties for themselves and their families. This group of gamblers is much larger than the mass media portrayed problem gambler who gambles away millions once or twice in a lifetime.

The local community gamblers who have problems with gambling are likely to play for long times, reinvest their winnings and leave only when all the money has been gambled away. Long opening hours ensure a person will have plenty of time to gamble, there are no restrictions and no limits imposed. Gaming machines are considered one of the main factors contributing to excessive gambling and gambling related problems (Kweitel and Allen 1998; Productivity Commission 2009), because of the large number of people who gamble and the easy access to gaming machines in community venues. Furthermore, the design of the gambling venue and the design of the electronic gaming machine produce an environment of urgency through lights and noise, a perceived urge to play on, and the venue creates an atmosphere of insulation from time and place. Clubs are inclusive and have unrestricted or few exclusion rules for local and non-local residents (except an age limit for gambling areas and dress codes). Community clubs create an atmosphere of social belonging, a safe place for anyone and thus attractive for people who feel socially isolated, or culturally and financially excluded from the mainstream society. The socially attractive, secure and inclusive club environment, with its multitude of chances to gamble, increases gambling opportunities in Australian communities, an aspect that will be further explored in the following chapters, including an analysis of how gambling regulation is used to restrict adverse consequences of gambling.

Chapter 2

Gambling Research and Gambling as a Recreational Pursuit

2.1 Gambling research

The main body of research about gambling for money and problem gambling has focused on adults and individuals rather than on societal environments. Research undertaken within the psychology discipline has dominated, while more recent research has included social and environmental factors, access to gambling opportunities and problem gambling considered a health issue (cf. Welte 2008; Delfabbro and LeCouteur 2007; ACNeilson 2007; Rodda and Cowie 2005; Stinchfield, Govoni and Frisch 2005; Welte and Barns 2004; Independent Pricing and Regulatory Tribunal 2003).

To assess the negative effects of gambling, numerous jurisdictions have commissioned prevalence studies (cf. Productivity Commission 2009: 4 – The prevalence of problems with gambling). One aim of prevalence studies is to measure the negative effects of gambling and the number of problem gamblers within a jurisdiction or part of a jurisdiction. The studies have often been limited to adults and to specific areas such as prevalence studies covering a larger city or a state, rather than national or international studies.

Studies of gambling are mainly commissioned because of a specific problem or a situation rather than aiming to give a holistic understanding of people's gambling pattern, experiences and gambling frequency. To compare gambling prevalence over jurisdictions has its inherent problems as the level of access to gambling opportunities, type of gambling and regulation of gambling activities differs (cf. Focal Research 2008; Ipsos Reid Public Affairs and Gemini Research 2008; Queensland Government Treasury 2007; Canadian Partnership for Responsible Gaming 2007; Delfabbro and LeCouteur 2006; Wiebe, Mun and Kauffman 2006; The South Australian Centre for Economic Studies 2005, 2003; Volberg, Nysse-Carris and Gerstein 2006; Volberg 2003, 2002; Roy Morgan Research 2005; Ladouceur, Jacques, Chevalier, Sevigny and Hamel 2005; Smith and Wynne 2002).

The most common screens used to assess the level of gambling in studies of gambling prevalence are the South Oaks Gambling Screen (SOGS) (Lesieur and Blume 1987), the Canadian Problem Gambling Index (CPGI) (Ferris and Wynne 2001), and the screen more commonly used in the USA, the Diagnostic Criteria for Pathological Gambling (DSM-IV, Diagnostic and Statistical Manual of Mental Disorders) (American Psychiatric Association 1994). Along with the main screens used to assess gambling prevalence, several variations of the screens are also used to include national circumstances in gathering information about gambling predominance.

Screens have also been developed to assess gambling prevalence among young people. Examples include the South Oaks Gambling Screen-Revised for Adolescents (SOGS-RA) (Winters, Stinchfield and Fulkerson 1993; Winters, Stinchfield and Kim 1995), the Diagnostic Statistical Manual-IV-Adapted for Juveniles and the Diagnostic Statistical Manual-IV-Multiple Response-Adapted for Juveniles (DSM-IV-MR-J) (Fisher 2000) and the Gamblers Anonymous Twenty Questions (GA 20 Questions).

However, the various screens, when tested on the same sample, have shown different estimates of problem or pathological gambling. Derevensky and Gupta (2000) researched the gambling behaviour of 980 junior college students. They were given the screens SOGS-RA, DSM-IVJ and the Gamblers Anonymous Twenty Questions (GA 20 Questions) with the instruments presented in random order during normal class time. They found that the DSM-IV-J screen gave the most conservative measure of problem or pathological gambling. It identified 3.4 per cent of the college students as problem or pathological gamblers. The corresponding percentage for SOGS-RA was 5.3 per cent and for the GA 20 Questions screen it was 6 per cent. A further difference between the screens was that the SOGS-RA screen presented the largest number of male problem or pathological gamblers, 11 per cent, while GA 20 showed the largest number of females, 3.5 per cent, as problem or pathological gamblers. Derevensky and Gupta (2000: 231) concluded that:

> Each instrument is reported to have its advantages and disadvantages, with considerable overlap between measures. Similar to adult instruments (e.g. SOGS, DSM-IV, NODS), the notion of deception (lying), stealing money to support gambling, preoccupation, and chasing losses are common amongst instruments used for adolescents.

A similar conclusion was drawn from an Australian assessment of the screens by the South Australian Centre for Economic Studies (2003: i). They concluded that 'the use of different instruments and differences in criteria and thresholds leads to quite different prevalence rates even when administered to the same sample' (cf. Wiebe, Cox and Mehmel 2000; Skokauskas, Burba and Freedman 2009; Olason, Sigurdardottir and Smari 2006). Furthermore Jacques and Ladouceur (2003) stressed the importance of using the screens in their intended way, such as for the DSM-IV-J screen, where the scoring should be based on the nine criteria, not the 12 questions, as the latter would distort the scores and the results.

Another concern is that participants may not understand the questions and thus are unable to give well-informed and accurate answers. Ladouceur, Bouchard, Rheaume, Jacques et al. (2000) examined the level of understanding that 9 to 12-year-old children (580 students in grades 4, 5 and 6) had of the items in the SOGS-RA screen. They found that on average, children did not understand 26.7 per cent of the items. In a second study of 587 high school students (grades 9, 10 and 11) completing the SOGS-RA screen only 30.8 per cent of the students understood all the items correctly. However, after the participants had the items explained and clearly understood the items, the percentage of problem or probable pathological gambling was 41.8 per cent less than the initial percentage. Ladouceur et al. (2000) conclude that if the participants do not fully understand the items in the screen, false positives might follow, thus giving inaccurate problem or pathological gambling estimates. Equally, this does not preclude the possibility of false negatives (lower levels of gambling) also becoming a factor in the reliability of the screens.

The reliability of the screens for adults and the level of respondents' understanding of the questions have also been questioned by Blaszczynski, Ladouceur, Goulet and Savard (2006). In Australia the gaming industry's sales (player expenditure or losses) amount to approximately A$18 billion (Productivity Commission 2009). This corresponds to 3 per cent of total household expenditure (cf. Chapter 4.4, Table 4.8). However, it is not a simple matter to ascertain an accurate figure because of variations in reporting periods, definitions of what constitutes gambling, and reliability of the data (cf. Chapter 3). A parallel can be drawn between gambling expenditure and individual spending on gambling products. Blaszczynski et al. (2006) questioned the reliability of the estimates of how much people spend on gambling and how people participating in prevalence studies come to their estimated gambling expenditure. The Productivity Commission (2009) estimated a spending of between A$7,000 and A$8,000 per annum by a regular gaming machine gambler. However, Blaszczynski et al. (2006) concluded that nearly a third (30 per cent) of the participants did not follow the instructions given for the questions and that any estimation of gambled expenditure in prevalence studies needed to be treated cautiously because the methods used were ambiguous and the variations in how the participants calculated their gambling expenditure varied.

Orford (2003: 53) points out that the complexity of gambling makes it difficult to gain enough understanding through a single percentage figure: '... no single existing screening questionnaire adequately reflects the multi-dimensional nature of problem gambling'. Thus, the focus and analysis of gambling research needs to go beyond the simple figures. Policy-makers and the media generally focus their attention on the single number – the overall rate of gambling problems in the general population when the results of new gambling prevalence studies are published:

> Comparisons are made with prevalence rates in other jurisdictions and questions are asked about the number of problem gamblers that this overall rate represents ... While these are important reasons for conducting prevalence research, there is much more to learn by looking beneath and beyond the overall prevalence rate (Volberg 2004: 3–4).

The definitions of gambling and what special characteristic actions have to be classified as gambling varies, nevertheless, gambling for money has been defined as:

> Staking money on uncertain events driven by chance (Productivity Commission 1999: x);

> ... gambling, the act of staking money or some other item of value on the outcome of an event determined by chance (Blaszczynski, Walker, Sagris and Dickerson 1999: 4);

> ... wagering money or other belongings on chance activities or events with random or uncertain outcomes (National Research Council 1999: 16);

> ... the exchange of property (usually money but sometimes other property including slaves, ears and fingers) on the outcome of an event largely, if not solely, determined by chance (Allcock 2000: 253);

> ... staking of money on the outcome of games or events involving chance or skill (Slade and McConville 2003: 2).

The definitions of gambling all state the involvement of money and the uncertainty of the outcome. According to Smith and Wynne (2002: 17) four assumptions can be derived from the definitions of gambling. There is: the element of risk; the possibility to win, lose or status quo; a social or co-operative activity where gambling involves gambling against something, a person, activity or machine; and that gambling is a deliberate activity that the person is taking part in on a voluntary basis.

Gaming and wagering are deemed social recreational pursuits that require an investment, which has uncertain financial returns. It is proposed that authentic gambling should rely more on chance than skill, 'with the pure form demanding no skill whatsoever' (Slade and McConville 2003: 11), such as pushing a button on an electronic gaming machine.

As previously emphasised, the main focus in gambling research has been on the assessment and definition of problem and pathological gambling utilising the CPGI and SOGS screens especially in Canadian and Australian prevalence studies. There has been less research about gambling activities that cause harm to the non-problem gambler (Shawn, Currie, Miller, Hodgins and Wang 2009). Even for a gambler that is not identified as a problem gambler or a pathological gambler, the person's gambling can nevertheless cause harm to the gambler, his or her family and friends.

Definitions of 'problem gambling' include elements of lack of control over the gambling behaviour which causes a range of adverse personal, economic and social consequences (Productivity Commission 1999, 2009: 4), or as defined in the Australian national definition of problem gambling: 'Problem gambling is characterized by difficulties in limiting money and/or time spent on gambling which leads to adverse consequences for the gambler, others, or for the community' (Neal, Delfabbro and O'Neil 2005: i).

To describe the harmful effects of gambling beyond a person's safe levels, the concept of 'excessive gambling' is used throughout the text. Excessive gambling describes the situation where the gambler or people in the gambler's environment are harmed, whether or not the gambler can be classified as a responsible gambler, a non-problem gambler, a problem gambler or a pathological gambler. The threshold for harm varies depending on the gambler's social and economic situation, thus 'excessive gambling' relates to gambling that causes hardship to the gambler and the people who depend on the gambler, socially, mentally and/or economically. The level of hurt caused by excessive gambling differs between people and people's personal, social and financial circumstances.

Any gambling activity is part of risk taking behaviour where skills and chance are intermixed, and independent of the gaming form, the aim is to improve the investment. There can be a level of skill involved or it can be purely based on chance (Cassidy 2002; Mann 2003). Gambling enhanced by a level of knowledge is poker, horse betting and sports betting. To understand the principles of playing poker and remember what cards are played can improve the possibility of winning. The same can be said about horse and greyhound racing where knowledge about the horses and the dogs in the race can improve the chances of betting on a winning horse or dog. This is also to an extent true in sports betting where knowledge about the teams fitness level and previous results increase the chances of betting on the winning team, nonetheless, there is always a level of chance involved in gambling. The gained knowledge and skills might be unreliable or dated; the team can be unexpectedly successful that day or play surprisingly poorly and make simple mistakes (Binde 2005; Browne 1989). The skills in gaining prior knowledge will then not improve the outcome, as the chance will play an important role in influencing the end result.

Gausset and Jansbøl (2009), tried to show in a Danish study that the choice of gambling is related to personality. In their research using university students in Denmark, they found that business students preferred games that involved a level of skill, while social science students were more inclined to choose games based on chance. Gausset and Jansbøl (2009: 14) concluded: 'the different type of gambling correlates with the value that people attach to risk and money, as well as to social relations and private enterprise'. The difference between skills and chance in gambling might be arbitrary but the perception of having the skills to predict winnings can be an important gambling incentive.

Gaming machines, lottery products, bingo and roulette are randomising apparatus where acquired skills or practice will not change the outcome (Fantino, Navarro and O'Daly 2005; Reith 1999). Even if the gambler who gambles on electronic gaming machines is convinced of his or her ability to influence the randomised system, by pushing the button slowly or quickly, gambling for long sessions on one particular gaming machine, or only play on a specific machine at a specific gambling venue. These special playing techniques will not change the principles of the randomised system. Irrespective of the gambling techniques the chance to win is based on a random calculation system producing random wins, without being influenced by the gambler's personalised techniques or skills.

Despite the uncertain financial returns from gambling, gambling for money is a global activity; it is legal in many countries and in Australia approximately eight out of 10 adult Australians gamble annually. Four out of 10 of the gamblers, gamble regularly and of the regular gamblers nearly one in five gamble periodically at unsustainable levels (Productivity Commission 1999). These percentages were slightly adjusted in the 2009 Productivity Commission report with three out of four gambling annually. Approximately 15 per cent of Australian adults gamble regularly (excluding people who only gamble on Lotto and 'scratchies'), 5 per cent gamble weekly or more often on gaming machines, and of these, about 15 per cent gamble at moderate levels and 15 per cent at problem risk levels (Productivity Commission 2009: 4.1).

Gambling opportunities can be restricted to special gambling venues built around the hospitality industry such as casinos and resort complexes, but gambling facilities can also be readily available in local community settings at clubs and hotels. In local community settings gambling is more likely to be developed around team sports, professional interest groups or ethnic community groups than merely around hospitality. Local community sports clubs service the community by managing sports activities for pre-school children, youths and adults up to the elite level, but they also provide a level of hospitality and recreational activities. Clubs' gambling activities provide recreational pursuits for residents and generate revenue for the clubs' support of community sports and social activities. In Australia, gambling revenue is partly used to support and manage community sports activities, to give financial and in-kind assistance to charitable organisations, as well as to contribute to social and health projects in the community.

2.2   Youth gambling research

Initial gambling research and reporting of gambling activities excluded minors, as it was not apparent that young people engaged in gambling activities before they were legally allowed to participate. The Productivity Commission's enquiries concerning Australian Gambling Industries concluded that:

> All of the major state and national surveys have excluded under-age gamblers from their scope. However, there is abundant overseas, and some Australian evidence, that problem gambling also affects people aged under 18 ... Australian studies and international research, suggests that youth problem gambling is at rates somewhat higher than in adult populations (Productivity Commission 1999: 235).

Scholarly research about gambling and the negative aspects of excessive gambling have thus mainly focused on adult problem gamblers and adult related issues. It has only been during the last 20 years that youth gambling has been acknowledged as a problem and that young people develop problems with gambling well before their legal age of gambling with money.

The increased interest in youth gambling and the research that has been undertaken to explore young people's gambling propensity has led to a better understanding of risk factors, gambling trajectories and problems associated with youth gambling (Messerlian and Derevensky 2005). The research about young people's gambling has followed the adults gambling research strategy with a focus on addiction and psychological explanations rather than on environmental and societal factors.

Youth gambling research has undoubtedly shown evidence that the signs of problem gambling already exist among underage young gamblers (Derevensky and Gupta 2001; cf. Chapter 5). Even if young people's gambling activities are on par with adults' gambling, youth research indicates that young people's problem gambling rates are somewhat higher than for the adult population (Jacobs 2000; Productivity Commission 1999: 235). However, Derevensky and Gupta (2006) discuss in the article, 'Measuring Gambling Problems Among Adolescents: Current Status and Future Directions', methodological issues in measuring young people's prevalence of gambling and gambling related problems, as most instruments to measure youths' gambling prevalence are based on adaptations of adult gambling screens (cf. Winters, Stinchfield and Fulkerson 1993; Winters, Stinchfield and Kim 1995; Fisher 2000; cf. Chapter 2.1). In all prevalence studies, especially with the telephone-based surveys, the reliability of the responses needs to be considered before drawing any conclusions (Derevensky and Gupta 2000; Ladouceur et al. 2000; Orford 2003; Volberg 2004; Blaszczynski et al. 2006).

Youth gambling research shows that young people who gamble excessively experience social and financial problems before the end of their teenage years. Wynne, Smith and Jacobs (1996: 11) found that young people who had developed problems with excessive gambling, reported that they were introduced to gambling at an early age. Additionally, Wynne et al. (1996) reported that children as young as 10 years old had their first gambling experience in the company of a parent, family member or a friend.

The findings of Wynne et al. (1996) were supported in Fabiansson's (cf. 2006a; Chapter 5) research about young people's introduction to gambling in rural and regional communities. The research showed that youths were introduced to gambling within the family environment with the family playing board games and card games together. This would normally not be seen as gambling, but the same principles apply, to gain an advantage and to win. The introduction to gambling within the family environment progressed with buying of lottery tickets as part of the weekly shopping routine. The research also showed that gambling for money extended to family outings at the local community sports club. If the club has gambling rights it is likely that the cost of the dinner is subsidised by gambling revenue and thus very affordable to family groups. This enhances the possibilities for families to have dinner at the local club. The parents would pay for their children to play Keno games while they socialise with other parents. The research highlighted the interlinking of family activities and gambling activities where gambling becomes a natural part of the family's everyday life, from board and card games at home to buying a lottery ticket and having dinner at the local club where the social gambling is done in a family friendly and secure club environment (cf. Chapter 5).

The Survey of Clients of Counselling Agencies (Productivity Commission 1999) found that low starting age was a factor in developing excessive gambling problems. It found that 24 per cent of gamblers attending counselling for gambling and related problems reported that they had started gambling on a regular basis before the age of 18 years. Five per cent indicated that they had developed problems already before they were 18 years of age. Furthermore, research has found that there is a distinct difference in gambling propensity between males and females, with more males consistently gambling earlier in life than females and accordingly developing problems earlier than females (Productivity Commission 1999: 244; Griffiths 1998).

Griffiths (1998) found that UK parents often acted as proxies for their children when purchasing gambling products, e.g. buying lottery tickets and administering the financial transaction in wagering. Informal gambling, which is outside the control of any gambling supplier and regulator, is also a feature of youth gambling. Moore and Ohtsuka (1997) found that Australian minors tended to participate in gambling forms that are hard to detect, such as bingo, pool, cards or similar games for money, rather than wagering, table games or gaming machines in gambling venues. However, Fabiansson (2006a) found in an Australian study that underage young people's gambling practices were diverse and not restricted to 'hard to detect' gambling activities, but included most forms of gambling available. Youths played all kinds of gambling games at clubs and casinos. This may be explained by the frequently occurring attribute in young people of adventurousness, a willingness to challenge any age-restricted system, such as trying to access gambling activities in casinos. Fabiansson's (cf. Chapter 5) research of high school students showed that they were very familiar with gambling opportunities from lottery products, club gambling and casino table gambling. At a large metropolitan casino in Australia the number of underage gamblers caught trying to access the casino's gambling products increased during school holidays and Christmas (Fabiansson and Healey 2004). Thus, the conclusion of Moore and Ohtsuka (1997) that only 'hard to detect' games were played by underage youth was not supported in the Fabiansson research as it found that young people were accessing gambling venues and played on electronic gaming machines and table games at casinos before they turned 18 years of age, however, they were more likely to chose games at casino venues that they could quickly leave when security staff approached.

Stinchfield and Winters (1998) undertook an extensive literature review of young people's gambling experiences. They concluded that, as with most human behaviour, age restrictions are arbitrary. Young people's experiences of gambling included a range of different gambling activities. Most young people have participated in some form of gambling for money and many of them had gambled on games that were age restricted to adults. Furthermore, they concluded that male youths were more inclined to gamble than females, and that the gambling frequency increased with age (cf. Chapter 5). Additionally, the literature review of gambling research showed differences in gambling preferences due to ethnicity, culture and religious belonging. In a more recent study Jackson, Patton, Thomas et al. (2000: 13) found that gambling behaviour was not directly influenced by ethnic background, rural or urban residency, or socio-economic status, but young people from lower socio-economic environments, who were less academically inclined and had experience of risk taking behaviour such as drug and alcohol taking had a wider experience of gambling than young people who did not have these characteristics or experiences.

Additionally, Stinchfield and Winters (1998) highlighted in their research that young people start to gamble at an earlier age than anticipated, and they emphasised the existence of a relationship between parents' gambling patterns and their children's gambling behaviour, comparable to findings by other researchers (Wynne et al. 1996; Stinchfield 2000: 154; cf. Chapters 5 and 6).

The easy manner in which young people are introduced to gambling is underpinned by the fact that gambling is treated as a social recreational pursuit and made possible by societal acceptance and availability of gambling opportunities, such as betting shops, selling of lottery tickets in news agencies, and gambling facilities in local community sports, interest and professional clubs and in hotels. Research indicates that the period from recreational gambling to excessive gambling can be much shorter for young people than for adults, especially for young people who start gambling at an early age (Derevensky and Gupta 1996, 1999).

Research concerning gamblers' reasons for gambling have stressed the profit motive (Spanier 1987) or that some people are more inclined to gamble than others (Cameron and Myers 1966; Lowenfeld 1979; Kusyszyn and Rutter 1985; Slowo 1998), but also gambling for enjoyment, excitement and social recreation (Gupta and Derevensky 1998a; Neighbors, Lostutter, Cronce and Larimer 2002). Adult gamblers who had developed problems with excessive gambling also reported that the gambling could help them to cope with depression and loneliness (Fabiansson 2008; cf. Chapter 6). A study of college students in the US who gambled (N=184) showed that the majority gambled to win money, for fun, excitement, for social reasons or to have something to do, where winning money (42.7 per cent) and enjoyment or fun (23.0 per cent) were most often given as the primary motivation for partaking in gambling pursuits. In third place was gambling for social recreational reasons (11.2 per cent) (Neighbors et al. 2002: 367).

The individual gambling research perspective has enhanced our understanding of the causes of gambling and gambling related problems. Nonetheless, our understanding of gambling can be further improved if a person's actions are examined from a holistic societal perspective, where the individual's social circumstances and the social environment are considered together, this allows us to understand the rationale behind a person's actions. Actions that at first seem irrational can, if the whole situation of the person's circumstances is understood, be both logical and rational. For instance, a person's gambling behaviour can be influenced both by personal experience, life cycle, and environmental factors such as easy access to gambling opportunities and/or the design of the gaming machine that creates an illusion of a high chance of winning and thus encourages excessive spending (Horbay 2004; Parke, Griffiths and Irwing 2004).

While it is acknowledged within the gaming industry and governments regulatory bodies that problem gambling exists, the preferred approach is still to treat gambling problems as an individual issue, despite research that indicates that opportunities to gamble and the design of the gambling venues have a role to play in excessive gambling (Delfabbro 2008; Gambling Research Australia 2008; Lester 1994). The individual explanation perspective seems difficult to change despite, for instance, the general public health and prevention approach emphasised by Korn and Shaffer (1999) in the late 1990s gained support from researchers and health professionals (Shawn, Currie, Miller, Hodgins and Wang 2009; Nova Scotia Department of Health Promotion and Protection 2008; Martins, Storr, Ialongo and Chilcoat 2007), but less so by regulatory authorities (cf. Independent Pricing and Regulatory Tribunal 2005).

Gillespie, Derevensky and Gupta (2007: 51) ask the question: What is attracting young people to gambling activities and why do some develop problems when others do not? One assumption is that high-risk behaviour is determined by the interplay between psychosocial instigators (risk factors) and controls (protective factors). The risk and protective factors interact within a person's whole spectrum of personal and social environments and when the controls of risk factors are weakened, the person is more likely to participate in risk taking activities (Jessor 1998). Risk factors include activities such as unsafe consumption of alcohol and drugs, unprotected sexual activities, driving cars and motorcycles at unsafe speeds and under the influence of drugs and alcohol, riding on the roof of trains and criminal activities (cf. Derevensky and Gupta 2004a; Gupta and Derevensky 1998b; Hardoon, Derevensky and Gupta 2002; Langhinrichsen-Rohling, Rohde, Seeley and Rohling 2004; Stinchfield 2000, 2004). However, the interplay between risk factors and control factors cannot explain comprehensively why some young people gamble excessively and others not. It is not only the interplay between risk and protective factors that influence a person's behaviour, but also environmental influences such as peer pressure, acceptance or disapproval of the behaviour, and the possibility of undertaking the risk-taking behaviour with easy access to opportunities such as gambling (Johnston 2003).

In youth gambling Wynne et al. (1996) highlighted the importance of accessibility, availability and acceptance of the behaviour as features that influence young people's inclination to gamble at excessive levels. Furthermore, the general attitudes to gambling, as well as public policy and regulatory legislation cultivate an environment where gambling activities are generally socially accepted, and encouraged through public advertising (Nower and Blaszczynski 2004; Felsher, Derevensky and Gupta 2004a; Gupta and Derevensky 1997; Winters, Stinchfield and Kim 1995). The overall belief among young people and many adults is that gambling is a social recreational activity with few negative effects (Winters, Arthur, Leitten and Botzet 2004).

Gambling is a growing industry even in times of economic downturn when the dream of a win is perhaps nurtured more desperately (Binde 2006). Access to gambling opportunities has increased since the 1990s with the establishment of venues presenting diverse gambling options with extended opening hours in many jurisdictions (Delfabbro 2008; Productivity Commission 2009).

The widely available gambling opportunities in casino, hotel and club environments are promoted as social recreational pursuits through wide ranging publicity in mass and ether media. This is especially true for promoting the possibility to win large amounts of money, while the very low probability to actually win on lottery products or electronic gaming machines are seldom accentuated to the audience (Binde 2007; Monaghan, Derevensky and Sklar 2008).

From this perspective it is not surprising that research has found that underage gambling is widespread. Research from Canada, United States of America, the United Kingdom, Norway, and Australia show that between 63 and 82 per cent of young people aged between 12 and 17 years of age gamble annually. Between 4 and 7 per cent show signs of serious gambling problems and a further 10 to 15 per cent of them gamble at levels which are unsustainable (Delfabbro and Thrupp 2003; Derevensky and Gupta 2004a; Johansson and Götestam 2003; National Research Council 1999).

A Swedish study of urban youths' gambling activities, aged between 14 and 18 years, showed that 90 per cent of the youths (N=845) had gambled for money at least once and 84 per cent had gambled for money during the last twelve months (Spelinstitutet 2000). The percentage was higher in an earlier 1997–98 national prevalence study (N=7,139, including 336 youths aged 15–17 years), which showed that 95 per cent of the respondents had gambled for money at least once, not restricted to the last twelve months. The twelve months timeframe is commonly used in prevalence studies to measure gambling activities and this non-restricted time period can be one explanation to the higher percentage in the Swedish study than for comparable studies in the USA, New Zealand and Australia (Rönnberg, Volberg, Abbott, Moore, Andrén, Munck et al. 1999).

It is acknowledged that youth gambling occurs in most jurisdictions and the legislation that should prohibit young people from gambling is not enough to prevent them from doing so. Griffiths and Wood (2001) stressed that gambling advertisements introduce children and young people to different forms of gambling and contain the connotation that gambling is a fun, easy to participate in and an acceptable social recreational activity (Derevensky, Sklar, Gupta, Messerlian, Laroche and Mansour 2007).

The glamorizing and promotion of gambling can be attractive for young people who see the opportunity to win large amounts of money, without understanding the limited chances of actually winning. However, research is still inadequate to fully understand the effect gambling advertisements have on young people. Advertisement guidelines are frequently voluntary, emphasising that gambling products should be promoted in a responsible way (cf. American Gaming Association 2009). The supervision and regulation of gambling advertising is complicated because of the involvement of diverse jurisdictions, with federal and state authorities having responsibilities over different forms of gambling. In Australia, lotteries, club and casino gambling are state responsibilities and do not fall under federal jurisdiction. The situation is similar in the US for lottery gambling. Under Canadian law, only the government (and its licensed agents), charities, and the horse racing industry are legally entitled to offer gambling to the public (Criminal Code of Canada 2009). However, Griffiths (2005) has acknowledged that Loto-Québec has been praised for sound and responsible codes of practice and similarly the UK National Lottery Commission.

Gambling and sports activities are interconnected in that gambling revenue supports and is often the main guarantor of young people's sports practice and competitions. Despite legislation that has been successful in restricting advertising and sponsorship by tobacco companies of sports events, this has not been implemented for alcohol and gambling sponsorships (Curliss 2007; Maher, Wilson, Signal and Thomson 2006). An added influence of advertising is the endorsement of products by a well-known person. Thus, celebrity endorsement of products can influence young people's sports, education, and career choices as well as their perception of themselves (Bush, Martin and Bush 2004).

The spread of internet gambling has further made access to gambling a global phenomenon and an activity that can be undertaken anywhere where internet connections are established (Griffiths and Barnes 2008). Interactive gambling, through phone, the internet, and digital television allow the delivery of gambling services into the homes of consumers (The Allen Consulting Group 2009). These new technologies pose fresh challenges for government regulators in relation to harm minimisation policies and tax revenue schemes. Harm minimisation is of special concern regarding youth gambling, particularly the possibility of getting 'carried away' and gambling for more money than intended. Independent of restrictions, there will always be a group of technologically smart young people who will be able to gamble on the internet for money without parental consent or knowledge. A high level of access to gambling opportunities is not unique to the internet, some children look older than their biological age and can more easily gain admission to casinos, betting shops, clubs and hotels to gamble.

An Australian Council of Social Service study into 'Young People, Gambling and the Internet' (1997), found that 14–16-years-old young people regularly placed bets at the races, and that minors occasionally or even regularly played gaming machines in clubs. If anything, the statistics on youth gambling suggest that current levels of entry to physical gambling venues are likely to be much higher than documented and that young people's future access to online gambling can enhance their gambling propensity. Since gambling is publicly promoted, minors can easily be influenced to gamble through advertising in mass media or simply by exposure during family outings at the local club.

Gambling opportunities are increasing and new forms provide easy access. Internet gambling is the newest gambling form with national and international web-based gambling sites. Remote internet gambling sites have minimal investment costs compared with casino venues and sports clubs. They also make it possible for the gambler to gamble from nearly anywhere in the world, thus the internet provides unlimited opportunities for gambling in private – accessing global gambling markets from home or work (United Kingdom Gambling Commission 2009). The UK Gambling Commission 2009 survey found that 9.7 per cent of a sample of 8,000 had gambled remotely using a computer, mobile phone or interactive/digital TV the previous month; an increase from 7.2 per cent in 2006 and from 8.8 per cent in 2008.

Since internet sites can be based anywhere in the world and be accessed globally, regulation at the individual jurisdictional level will have limited impact. To effectively regulate global internet-based gambling sites, common regulation standards need to be adopted and enforced by all jurisdictions. Alternatively, internet gambling providers must accept self regulation and implement responsible gambling principles. The latter could include principles such as warning people about risks, show how much they have gambled for and lost, and their accumulated debts as well as information about local help services (cf. Broda, LaPlante, Nelson, LaBrie, Bosworth and Shaffer 2008; Ladouceur, Sylvain and Gosselin 2007; Monaghan 2009; Nelson, LaPlante, Peller, Schumann, LaBrie and Shaffer 2008). Gambling problems and pathological gambling through the use of the internet have not yet reached the critical level that accords with countries feeling obliged to make binding regulations that restrict gambling or prohibit gambling products.

Research into web-based gambling is still in its infancy but there is growing evidence which shows internet gambling can increase costs to society, especially in relation to credit card payments for gambling. It is more difficult to keep track of spending when using a credit card and losses incurred through credit card use are not immediately felt, as the information about the account balance is often not known until the monthly statement is viewed. Additionally, it is suggested that higher numbers of people gambling above the level of their available funds will likely increase the level of criminal behaviour in order to cover large debts; bankruptcies may increase and more people could experience problems with excessive gambling (Focal Research 2008; Griffiths and Barnes 2008; Volberg, Nysse-Carris and Gerstein 2006). Furthermore, there are indicators that suggest that people who would normally not visit a club or a casino to gamble, due to age restrictions or personal or cultural reasons, would gamble on the internet if it was available to them (Wood and Griffiths 2005; Wood, Griffiths and Parke 2007).

A larger internet gambling study conducted by the Global Online Gambler Survey (eCOGRA – eCommerce and Online Gaming Regulation and Assurance; Parke, Rigbye, Parke, Wood, Sjenitzer and Vaughan Williams 2007) included a sample of 10,865 people world-wide who acknowledged that they had gambled at internet casino and/or poker sites during the previous three months. Attraction to a website depended on its trustworthiness, how easy it was to navigate around the site, clear instructions about financial transactions (Nielsen, Molich, Snyder and Farrell 2000) and professional design (Belanger, Hiller and Smith 2002; Kim and Stoel 2004). In regard to responsible gambling practices the gamblers using the online gambling sites supported self-imposed spending and time limits, self-exclusion, regular updates about their financial situation, and self-assessment tests that helped them assess their spending and gambling situation. The preference was also to play with the larger well-known sites because it was assumed that they would allow less cheating among the gamblers using the site. Professional players, who prefer higher stakes tables, might annoy or provoke less experienced players in an attempt to force them to leave the site or switch to a lower stakes table. Such negative behaviours would be difficult to monitor or control (Wood and Griffiths 2008).

The Global Online Gambler Survey in 2007 found that casual Swedish online poker players preferred the overall experience of gambling, while professional players were motivated by the possibility to win money. Gender issues were also acknowledged with some female players 'switching' to male identities to feel less discriminated against by male players (Wood and Griffiths 2008; Wood, Griffith and Parke 2007; Parke et al. 2007).

Gambling opportunities have increased not only through the growth of internet gambling sites but also through new facilities in the local community and in metropolitan casino venues. The gambling industry is a growing business and for cash poor governments gambling revenue is welcomed. The question has been raised as to whether public opinion supports the increase in gambling venues and other opportunities for gambling that governments endorse. Many jurisdictions have, in the last decade, supported gambling operators' requests for extended opening hours. The 2007 British Gambling Prevalence Survey of 8,880 people 16 years of age and older, included questions about people's attitudes to gambling. The research showed that most people held negative views about gambling, believing that it is dangerous, does more harm than good to families, local communities and the society as a whole. The notable exception to these generally held views came from the heaviest gambler group, they did not hold a negative perception of gambling. This is perhaps not an unexpected response. However, to have a negative perception about gambling is not the same as supporting prohibition of gambling. There was clear support for not restricting people's freedom and a belief that people should have a right to do what they want with their resources (Orford, Griffiths Wardle, Sproston and Erens 2009: 39). Discrepancies between public opinion and governments' assumptions about acceptance of gambling have been highlighted in other studies as well (Centre for Gambling Research 2004; Wood and Griffiths 2004).

It seems the relationship between gambling and organised crime is an accepted view and frequently portrayed as being the case in numerous films, where it may be represented in either a positive or a negative light (Turner, Fritz and Zangeneh 2007; Ferentzy and Turner 2009), but Campbell and Marshal (2007) note that it is difficult to find objective and reliable data on the link between gambling and crime in the real world. Smith, Wynne, and Hartnagel (2003: 8) highlight four categories of criminal offences directly and indirectly related to gambling (concerning the Canadian jurisdiction, but also relevant to most other jurisdictions):

(1) illegal gambling – gambling activity that is counter to Criminal Code of Canada statutes, such as bookmaking, keeping a common gaming house, and cheating at play; (2) criminogenic problem gambling – such as forgery, embezzlement, and fraud, typically committed by problem gamblers to support a gambling addiction; (3) gambling venue – crimes that occur in and around gambling locations, such as loan sharking, money laundering, passing counterfeit currency, theft, assault, prostitution and vandalism; and (4) family abuse – victimization of family members caused by another family member's gambling involvement, (e.g. domestic violence, child neglect, suicide, and home invasion).

In addition to Smith et al. (2003), Campbell and Marshal (2007) also included increases in crimes specific to the expansion of casino venues; crime committed in the venue, such as money laundering; crime committed against the casino or other players, such as cheating; and corruption, but did not include family abuse. Turner, Preston, Saunders, Mcavoy and Jain (2009: 165) have, through researching prisoners crimes (N=254), established a link between people with excessive gambling problems and the financing of their gambling through crimes like, breaking and entering and theft. They were also able to establish that gambling was part of their criminal life style. Thus, these people were seen to be caught in a circle of crime and gambling. The situation is different for social gamblers where the gambling expenditure is part of the total social recreational expenditure and limited to their own available funds.

2.3 Introduction to leisure

The word 'leisure' comes from the Latin word 'licere', which means 'to be permitted' or 'to be free' and from the Old French word 'leisir', 'be allowed'. The concept of leisure can be found in literature in the early fourteenth century.

Gambling, especially recreational gambling is classified as a leisure pursuit and it is noteworthy here to understand the development of our current notion of leisure and the growth in the leisure industry. In the twenty-first century the leisure phenomenon is well established with work-prescribed leisure or annual leave and the consumption of recreational activities supported by an extensive leisure industry. The contemporary concept of leisure is thought to have emerged in the late nineteenth century in England with the Industrial Revolution (cf. Bailey 1987). Leisure time or time free from paid work did exist before the industrial revolution; it was associated with cultural and religious traditions rather than work obligations. Throughout history, life has often been hard for the common people with little time for leisure, except religious festivals, sports and hunting tournaments, dice and some board games i.e. chess, mah-jong and go[1] (Fairbairn

---

1 Legends trace the origin of the game to Chinese emperor Yao (2337–2258 BC), who had his counsellor Shun design it for his son, Danzhu, who was assumed to be unruly to teach him discipline, concentration and balance.

1995) that were played and were appreciated interruptions from long days of hard work. The Romans used the Coliseum for entertainment where the public could watch chariot races, competitions between people and between people and animals. The Greeks had amphitheatres where plays, drama and comedy were shown for the people, and the Greeks created the Olympic Games. References to organised or spontaneous music, singing and dancing can be found in literature throughout ancient history, these are also mentioned in the Bible.

The leisure construct is, in historical terms, new. Prior to there being a regulated employment market, leisure, with the exception of religious holy days, was seen as less dignified than paid work (Stebbins 2001; Rojek 1985, 2000). It was only people in the paid workforce who could benefit from time-off to pursue leisure activities, thus excluding the majority of women and young people who worked outside the paid-work employment market (Clarke and Critcher 1985; Wearing 1998: 24–5). Goodin, Rice, Bittman and Saunders (2005) emphasise that 'leisure' is only one component of 'free time'; time categorised as paid work time, unpaid household time, personal care time and free time – socialising, culture, hobbies, other recreation, and watching television. 'Leisure ... means some subjectively gratifying activity' (Andorka 1987: 151). Even if leisure is sought after, people who have 'too much free time' may not find it subjectively gratifying (Campbell, Converse and Rodgers 1976: 356–7; Robinson 1977; cf. Gershuny 2000: 202–11; cf. Chapter 6). Too much leisure time can be synonymous with being underemployed or unemployed.

With the introduction of trade unions and more work efficient production methods in industrialised enterprises, the number of hours worked per day gradually decreased and employers began to give workers part or all of Saturday free. This was in addition to the already observed Sabbath days. Throughout history each society has had specific days for worship. In the Christian traditions it has been Sunday, while Jewish and Islamic religions have Friday or Saturday as a non-working day. In more recent times, the prohibition with regard to engaging in work or conducting business on a Sunday has been relaxed, with many shops and leisure facilities now trading on Sundays.

Consequent to this increase in time spent outside work, the creation of a mass market for leisure pursuits is relatively recent both in the diverse range of opportunities and as an employment market. The meanings and experiences of work and leisure differ according to which level of society the individual belongs (cf. Veblen [1899] 1994), however, as with most new trends, leisure as a specific designated time and activity was first enjoyed by the upper and middle classes, who could more easily afford to participate in organised leisure pursuits such as individual sports, travel, sailing, and acquiring a vacation home, while low investment team sports were more often taken up by the working-class such as football (soccer).

Leisure can be classified as everything from structured, serious and competitive team and individual sports activities to having a casual stroll around the block, sleeping in or reading the newspaper. However, there is a difference in the status attributed to different classifications of leisure – where serious and structured leisure activities are generally given a higher status than casual and unstructured activities (Stebbins 2001). 'Although Stebbins claims to use these terms in non-evaluative ways it is self-evident that the term 'serious' carries with it strong moralistic connotations' (Rojek 2000: 17–18). Structured organised and serious leisure are often contrasted with unorganised, occasional and casual leisure, where casual leisure is defined as an immediately, intrinsically rewarding, relatively short-lived pleasurable activity that requires little or no special training to enjoy (Stebbins 1997: 18). In the twenty-first century regular morning or evening walks is one of the most common unstructured leisure activities in which people partake, an activity that is promoted as part of a healthy life style, for example in 2007–08, 47.5 per cent of the Australian population, 15 years of age and older walked for exercise (Australian Bureau of Statistics 2009).

2.4 The youth construct

The notion of a period in one's life called 'youth' has existed for a long time. In the last three or four centuries however, it became thought of as a discrete period, and in affluent societies where increasing levels of access to education grew, young people remained outside the workforce for longer and longer periods. These societies thus sheltered young people from adult life through the value placed on education over work – made possible of course by the society's ability to support its youth population. For economists, business organisations, social demographers, urban planners and policy makers, young people are seen as an important group in society – they are now regarded as a social and economic entity.

This transformation has facilitated the development of a youth period that is discrete and distinguished from adulthood where special systems for rewards and trends can be developed (Jones 2009; Berger 1972; Coleman 1974):

> Unemployment, the extension of education, and the decline of the family-based form began to create a social class of people who were neither children nor adults. As such, these people enjoyed a lengthy period of semi autonomy. This stage typically began after early childhood and stretched through the transition to adulthood, a stage that frequently endured into the third decade of life (Furstenberg 2000: 897).

It was during the 1950s that young people were first considered a social category instead of a biological category. The creation of a social youth entity paved the way for the formation of special trends and cultural manifestations specifically for young people. The phenomenon of distinctive youth cultures was first openly promoted in the United States of America (i.e. rock music and Elvis Presley). England and the rest of the world followed the youth inspired music and fashion culture. This was not a new music or fashion trend as it was already established among working-class youth, but it spread to the middle-class and they created the momentum for it to mushroom around the world (cf. Jones 2009). Middle-class youths were also more financially secure than their working-class counterparts and were thus a driving force for consumerism. A distinctive youth culture was capitalised upon by commercial interests and today young people are seen as imperative consumers.

The universality of news and entertainment and internet technology has dramatically shortened the distance between countries. The instantaneous nature of communication ensures the ability to be up to date with new trends and ideas all over the world and to reach people independently of place and time. This has created a seamless communication society for young people.

The focus on the teenage years as a problematic period of life was noted early in the twentieth century by researchers such as Hall (1904) and the problematic perspective of the youth period is still a focus in contemporary society (Furstenberg 2000). The focus on the attributes of young people and their problematic transition to adulthood has been the product of social institutions that insulate young people from adult responsibilities and opportunities. Surprisingly, this is often done as a preparation for future adult responsibilities. Commonly the youth period is promoted as a time period when young people can be adventurous by exploring new things, travel and delay education and work commitments, but at the same time, young people are criticised for being selfish, reckless, having destructive personalities, and being socially irresponsible (Farkas, Johnson, Duffett and Bers 1997). What is less frequently discussed is the reality that most young people manage to reach adulthood relatively unscathed; they are willing to accept and move into adult roles and to take on extensive responsibilities. Modest attention is given to young people's educational achievements, innovative approach to new technology and willingness to communicate and create global social networks.

The United Nations (UN: www.un.org), define 'youth', as those persons between the ages of 15 and 24 years and the World Health Organisation (WHO: www.who.int) proposes three overlapping subcategories with the 'adolescent period' classified as ranging between the ages 10 and 19 years, the 'youth period' between the ages 15 and 24 years, and the 'young people period' between 10 and 24 years.[2] However, youth, young people and the youth period are foremost social constructs defined by historical periods, social and national circumstances and cultural ideologies (cf. Jones 2009; Arnett 2004, 2006; Furlong and Cartmel 2007). Arnett (2006: 119) emphasises that, 'Any word that is intended to be applied to people in the entire age range from 10 or 12 until at least 25 cannot possibly

---

2 Young people 14 years of age and younger are categorised as 'children', however, in some instances the category 'children' includes young people up to the age of 18 years, to emphasise their need for protection.

work, because the typical 10, 12, 15 or 17-year-old is simply too different from the typical 25-year-old'. Consequently, for research and statistical purposes, biological age classifications are useful. In the text the concepts youth and young people are applied to people who are largely between the ages 14 and 25 years and regarding research findings the biological ages of the young people are given.

2.5 Youths' leisure environment

In societies with a prolonged education system and delayed entry to the paid workforce young people have excess free time to fill with activities. This free time has created opportunities for organised and unorganised sports and recreational activities. Sports and recreational activities for young people can be found in both urban and rural areas with a diverse variety of organised team and individual sports activities. Many communities have built sports facilities and swimming pools, they organise art and drama classes, and have built bike tracks and nature walks.

In Australia, organised sports activities from pre-school through to elite levels, are closely associated with community sports clubs. Gambling revenue has made it possible for community sports clubs to support a variety of junior sports and grade level sports of the different teams through local talent, but also by buying in players from other clubs.

The Australian sports and leisure culture is traditionally portrayed as being physical, with team sports and outdoor activities. The 2001 Survey of Involvement in Sport and Physical Activity (Australian Bureau of Statistics 2001: 3) showed that 27 per cent of the Australian population aged 15 years and older were involved in organised sports and physical activities (4.1 million) with the majority being active players or participants in at least one organised sports activity or physical activity (23 per cent). Approximately 1.4 million (9.5 per cent) were involved in non-playing roles (e.g. coaches, instructors or teachers, umpires, committee members, or administrators). Of the 4.1 million people involved in organised sports and physical activity, 5.9 per cent of all people (21.6 per cent of people involved in organised sports and physical activities) were both players and involved in at least one non-playing role. This leaves 73 per cent of the population, 15 years and older outside organised sports and physical activities. However, sports and physical activities do not need to be undertaken within an organised club structure, thus physical recreational activities are undertaken by a larger proportion of the Australian population than the organised sports and physical activity figures indicate. As noted above, the National Health Survey 2007–08 found that 47.5 per cent of adults (15 years and older) walked for exercise, 44.3 per cent of the men and 50.6 of the females mainly outside of a club or otherwise organised activity (Australian Bureau of Statistics 2009).

People born in Australia have a higher player participation rate in organised sports and physical activities (26.8 per cent) compared with people born in other English speaking countries (22.0 per cent). The lowest participation rate was recorded for people born in non-English speaking countries (10.3 per cent). In total participation rate including both players and non-players, the Australian born participation rate was 30.9 per cent, foreign born from English speaking countries 26.0 per cent and from other countries 11.8 per cent (Australian Bureau of Statistics 2001: 6, 10). The figures indicate that Australian born people have a higher participation rate in organised sports and physical activities both as active players and in support roles. Furthermore, people within the labour force (27.2 per cent) were more likely than unemployed people (19.1 per cent) and people outside the labour force (17.5 per cent) to be active as players in organised sports and physical activities (Australian Bureau of Statistics 2001: 5). A contributing factor in Australians' involvement in sports, outdoor leisure and recreational activities is the mild weather conditions, which makes it possible to participate in outdoor sports and leisure activities the whole year round.

Community clubs and organisations have often humble beginnings with local people coming together because of a sports interest, a concern for young people's welfare and their need of leisure activities. Frequently the parents have themselves been involved in sports or have a keen interest in sports activities. They might want their children to be part of sports or recreational activities that they themselves have had good memories of or perhaps they want to give their children the opportunities they missed. The parents often start their involvement with their young children in a non-competitive fun-based activity, which can grow into serious competition on local, state, national, and international arenas. The involvement is reasonable and manageable from the beginning and can easily be included into the daily home and work life, but as the organisation and competition levels increase the work responsibilities are growing exceptionally, demanding new and advanced business and management skills (Fabiansson 2005). Here the established local clubs have an important function to professionally take on the collective responsibility to manage organised sports activities from individual parents. Thus, modern community sports clubs have gained a broad sports focus in engaging local residents from pre-school age to elite levels (Fabiansson 2007). Nonetheless, the resources and level of volunteering by parents influence the level of diversity and quality of leisure activities for children and young people. Lack of resources, number of participants, and instructors decide the frequency of leisure activities such as art and drama, theatre, dance and music groups, more so in rural than in urban areas. In rural and regional areas it is difficult to secure funding to run small groups and to find qualified instructors.

As sports and leisure hubs, community clubs provide social meeting places for residents, community organisations and they organise sports activities for children and young people. In the evening they arrange music and other entertainment that is affordable for a wide range of local residents. Even if young people under 18 years of age cannot attend the drinking and gaming areas they can attend the dining area and the age appropriate entertainment. The general admission areas should be screened off from the gambling section; however, not all gaming areas are enclosed thus young people can walk past or through them, and maybe have a quick play on an electronic gaming machine.

Clubs have created safe social networking places for all people including people who lack language proficiency, and feel marginalised socially, culturally, and mentally in society. There is no entrance fee involved in visiting the local community club, except for people living within a five kilometre radius of the club, a yearly membership fee of approximately A\$10–A\$15 applies, thus a club visit is especially attractive for low income residents, families with children, and for people outside the workforce. The food and beverages are reasonably priced and, even if the person does not gamble, it is a welcoming, social meeting place for friends. The club concept is attractive because of its affordability, providing a secure and friendly atmosphere, and long opening hours. The Australian clubs system is special in the sense that it is locally based; the membership fee is low. The local community club is open for everyone, a welcoming and safe place where entertainment, food and beverages are competitively priced (cf. Chapter 4). However, none of this would be possible, to the same extent at least, if gambling revenue did not underpin and subsidise all other services and activities.

2.6 Gambling as a recreational activity

Gambling as a recreational or leisure activity now goes far beyond betting on horse races, it extends to casino gambling, gambling on electronic gaming machines, the internet, and general sports betting. The whole gamut of gambling opportunities is now present in most jurisdictions and widely available to adults both in their local community and globally. Independent of the acceptance of gambling for money, people participate in gambling behaviours in their everyday lives. People strive to create a secure social and economic environment for themselves and their families. Competition for resources and opportunities creates a situation where there are necessarily winners and losers – the winners are rewarded and the losers are left behind. The drive to compete and win is an intrinsic trait in humans, we strive to be winners and to back winners and this feature remains present in most cultures. Children understand early in life the necessity for competition, the need to compete for a leading position in the playground, at school, in play and in sports activities. The rules of competition are learnt from observation – including reactions from parents, peers and others. It is no surprise therefore that competition to be a winner is also manifest in gambling for money. The quest to be successful is a characteristic of most human endeavours.

For gamblers, this competitive urge may make them try to beat the gaming machines, win at the casino tables and in card games, or to predict the winner in sports events, believing any winning to be based on skills and knowledge rather than luck. Systems designed to enhance the chances of winning have fascinated people for centuries (Reith 1999). Approximately 75 per cent of the Australian adult population participate in some form of gambling each year (Productivity

Commission 2009) but for some people, who do not seek alternative recreational opportunities; it may be their only recreational outlet. This is of particular concern for young people and vulnerable people. Those who gamble in excess of available funds will experience social, financial, health and emotional problems themselves but these gambling related problems will also extend to their family and friends and to the community.

Australian community-based sports and leisure clubs, the main providers of community centred sports and recreational activities, like all commercial enterprises strive to secure future customers. Clubs may do this by diversifying their activities to include the whole family. They provide sports for active children and young people, gyms and health clubs for interested family members, and make entertainment activities age appropriate for children, youths and adults. Clubs with extensive gambling facilities located in areas where other affordable entertainment alternatives are limited, can afford to subsidise sports and health club activities, live entertainment, food and beverages to attract people.

The difference between social leisure gambling and excessive gambling can be arbitrary and depend on the person's personal situation. It is easy to overextend oneself in a gambling situation due to the encouraging gambling environment. Regular gamblers would have experienced situations where they have gambled above their limit. However, the important difference is whether it happens rarely, sometimes or regularly. Excessive gambling inflicts different levels of damage on people depending on their social and financial circumstances. Gambling regulation and gambling support services aim to minimise the adverse effect of excessive gambling. Support services are called on to address the effects of gambling problems rather than the cause to excessive gambling. Involvements of community organisations will aid the recovery of individuals who seek their help to overcome gambling problems, but the source of the problem needs to be understood, be it personal or societal-related causes, for a person to gain sustainable help and acquire skills to manage his or her future gambling.

The entertainment value of gambling is lost when it becomes prolonged and excessive. Excessive gambling does not result in financial or social problems and homelessness immediately, often it is a gradual process that progresses from social gambling to gambling in excess of available funds, but can ultimately lead to loss of home and family, employment and friends. The sheer complexity of gambling related problems intertwined with other problems makes any solution complicated to achieve (Fabiansson 2003).

The balance between social gambling as a leisure activity and other leisure activities coexists comfortably for most people. The convenient and trouble-free access to community-based social entertainment and gambling opportunities are promoted as a bonus for the residential area. Nevertheless, people with gambling problems can have difficulty in handling such easy access and inviting venues.

Compared with many other countries, Australia, and in particular New South Wales, have a high density of electronic gaming machines in relation to the population (Taylor Nelson Sofres 2006, 2008; cf. Chapter 3). Electronic gaming machines are exceedingly profitable for the gambling commerce and their stakeholders, i.e. for the gambling operators, governments in relation to their taxation of gambling revenue, affiliated businesses and residents who find employment within the sports, gambling and hospitality sector. Even if some of the gambling profits are channelled back into the community, either by the clubs themselves or by the state government's community development and support expenditure scheme (cf. Chapter 4), the social costs of gambling are substantial for the individual excessive gambler, the family and for the community (Chhabra, Lutz and Gonnerman 2005; Mangham, Carney, Burnett and Williams 2005; Collins and Lapsley 2003).

An additional issue is that a visit to a local club or a hotel is not time restricted in the same sense seeing a movie, going to a race meeting or a football match, where the recreational activity is limited to a specific time slot. Gambling venues have extensive opening hours.[3] One argument being to service the people who work night, evening or morning shifts, an inclusive approach to cater for all people, but there is a difference between serving food and beverage 24/7 and allowing gambling for extended times (cf. Tuffin and Parr 2008).

This chapter explored research about young people's gambling and related research about adult gambling. It examined the leisure concept and how gambling is seen as part of the social leisure environment. It also analysed the importance of the social entity of young people and youths as current and future consumers of sports activities and social recreational pursuits. In the next chapter the scope of global gambling is analysed along with the attempts there has been to regulate it and the attempts to impose safe gambling strategies to protect individuals.

---

3   In NSW gambling is closed down between three and six hours during a 24-hour period on Saturday–Sunday and Public holidays (cf. NSW Department of Liquor Gaming and Racing: http://www.olgr.nsw.gov.au/gaming_home.asp, for current regulation).

Chapter 3

Global Gambling and Regulation of Gambling

3.1 Global gambling

3.1.1 Lottery gambling

Gambling is a global phenomenon with a contradictory reputation. Individual gambling and especially excessive gambling has a rather unsympathetic reputation, while public lottery schemes have a more favourable standing servicing the good of the society. In modern history, lottery schemes have been used, and are still used to secure money to fund public projects, such as public hospitals, specialist health equipment, schools and community projects and are thus seen as contributing to the wellbeing of people and the community. The lottery scheme has been used in many countries as a way to secure money for public projects, and for instance building facilities for Olympic Games.

Around the world, lottery games can be found in approximately 200 jurisdictions, where they provide both entertainment for people and are used to collect funds for diverse public good purposes, but they also raise tax revenue for governments (Table 3.1).

Table 3.1   World lottery sales by region in 2004–2007

Region	Per cent of world sales*
Europe	50.2
North America	28.7
Asia, Middle East	16.8
Australasia	1.9
Central and South America, the Caribbean	1.8
Africa	0.6
Total	100.0

Note: * The region's proportional share of world lottery sales did not alter between 2004 and 2007.

Source: Based on data found at *La Fleur's Magazine*, May 2005; Australasian Gaming Council 2008: 211.

42 *Pathways to Excessive Gambling*

In 2004, Europe had half of the worldwide lottery sales (50.2 per cent), corresponding to approximately US$94 billion worth of sales. Europe was followed by North America, which reported sales of US$53.7 billion (28.7 per cent) of total world lottery sales. Asia and the Middle East reported the third highest percentage with 16.8 per cent of world lottery sales (North Asia 10.4 per cent, South Asia 6.1 per cent, India and Central Asia 0.3 per cent), US$31.4. The difference to the next group is less than the variation between Europe and North America (21.5 percentage points), but still a considerable gap (14.9 percentage points) with Australasia (1.9 per cent), Central and South America and the Caribbean (1.8 per cent) and Africa (0.6 per cent), all having a much lower percentage of the world wide sale of lottery products. This is a growing trend with world lottery sales increasing by 17 per cent between 2003 and 2004, the highest increase occurring in Europe with a 24 per cent increase since 2003. Additionally, a strong growth in lottery sales can be noted in Asia and the Middle East with a 17 per cent increase and in Africa an increase of 14 per cent was recorded between 2003 and 2004. However, a decrease in lottery sales was recorded in Central and South America and the Caribbean, the decrease was 7 per cent between 2003 and 2004 (*La Fleur's Magazine*, May 2005; Australian Gaming Council 2007; Australasian Gaming Council 2008: 211).

Since 1995, the overall worldwide value of lottery sales has increased significantly, from US$113.3 billion in 1995 to US$202.6 billion in 2006, an increase of 78 per cent. Between the years 2004 and 2007, the different region's proportional share of world lottery sales did not alter (*La Fleur Magazine* 2007), but world lottery sales increased between the years 2004 and 2006 with US$15.5 billion, an 8 per cent increase. However, looking at individual years, sales in 2005 decreased by US$4.7 billion while in 2006, sales increased by US$20.2 billion, an 11 per cent increase. The increase in world lottery sales between 2005 and 2006 was larger than for any previous period since 1995 (Australian Gaming Council 2007: 222; Australasian Gaming Council 2008: 211). Despite increased gambling opportunities and competition from newer gambling types, such as gaming machine gambling and internet gambling, buying a weekly lottery ticket is still an exceedingly popular form of gambling for countless people around the world. Lottery products are easily available in local communities and to buy a lottery ticket requires few skills, to select the required numbers or to have an auto pick. The popularity of lottery schemes is further enhanced with the amount of money that can currently be won by selecting the right numbers (cf. Table 1.1) and the media coverage surrounding each draw.

Individual countries with the highest sales in lottery in 2006 were the USA with US$58.3 billion, followed by Italy US$18.2 billion and Spain with US$14.9 billion, France with US$11.9 billion, Germany with US$11.4 billion, China (including Hong Kong) with US$11.1 billion – all countries above the 10 billion US dollar mark in sales. In the next group of high lottery sale countries were Japan with US$9.6 billion, the United Kingdom with US$9.1 billion, Canada with US$8.7 billion, and Greece with US$6.3 billion. These 10 countries together accounted for 78.7 per cent of all lottery sales in the world; US$159.5 billion out of a total US$202.6

Global Gambling and Regulation of Gambling 43

billion annual lottery sales (McQueen 2008; Australasian Gaming Council 2008: 212). When combined with horse racing and gaming machine gambling, global lottery sales make up an exceedingly valuable gambling industry.

3.1.2 Horse racing

Gambling on horse racing has a very long history and has occurred all over the world. It is thought to have its origins among the prehistoric nomadic tribes in Central Asia and spreading to Middle Eastern, Asian and Western countries (Parker 1998). In 2006 the United States of America ran the most horse races – 51,987 races were held with the prize money totalling US$891 million (Table 3.2). Although Australia held the second highest number of horse races (19,963), Australia was only third highest in terms of prize money with a total value of US$276.8 million. The second highest amount in total prize money was Japan with US$683.3 million, but only the third highest (17,939) in total number of races run (Australasian Gaming Council 2008: 221–2).

In 2006, 156,372 horse races were held in these countries with prize money totalling US$3,040.4 million (Table 3.2). The difference in prize money is noticeable between the US and Japan, but especially between the US, Japan and Australia. Regarding betting turnover, Japan had the highest betting turnover (US$25,461.8 million), followed by Great Britain (US$19,383 million) and the USA (US$14,051.3 million). France was in fourth place (US$10,394.3 million), followed by Australia (US$8,755.5 million) and Hong Kong (US$7,773 million). These countries were the only countries with a betting turnover in 2006 of US$7,500 million or more. The total betting turnover in 2006 was US$105,149 million (Australasian Gaming Council 2008: 221–2).

Korea, Turkey and Brazil showed the highest percentage growth in horse racing between the years 2004 and 2005. The number of races held in these countries increased with 12.5 per cent, 4.6 per cent and 3.9 per cent, respectively. Between 2005 and 2007, the increase in horse racing continued in Korea (1,238 to 1,697 races) and Turkey (3,165 to 3,526 races) while the number of races decreased in Brazil (5,105 to 4,455 races). The largest decline in horse race numbers was recorded in the United Arab Emirates, Macau and Japan. Their reduction in number of races held between 2004 and 2005 was 12.2 per cent, 9.6 per cent and 9.6 per cent, respectively. However, between 2005 and 2007, the number of races again increased in the United Arab Emirates (288 to 305 races), while the decrease continued for Macau (960 to 737 races) and Japan (18,213 to 17,608 races). The decrease in the number of horse races held was smaller in Australia with only a 1.2 per cent reduction this period (Australian Racing Board 2006, 2008).

Two of the three countries with the highest number of horse races in 2005, showed decreases in the number of races in 2007. In the US the number of races decreased with 953 (52,257 to 51,304 races), in Japan with 605, as noted above, and in Australia with 423 races (19,968 to 19,545 races). A slightly different trend was noted for some other countries when comparing the number of horse races

Table 3.2 International comparison of the number of horse races held and horse racing prize money in 2006

Country	No. of races (flat and jump)	Prize money* (US$m)	Betting turnover (US$m)	Country	No. of races (flat and jump)	Prize money (US$m)	Betting turnover (US$m)
USA	51,987	891	14,051.3	Turkey	3,237	72.8	981
Australia	19,963	276.8	8,755.5	New Zealand	2,987	27	819.8
Japan	17,939	683.3	25,461.8	India	2,854	12	306.8
Great Britain	8,841	192	19,383	Ireland	2,268	69	4,521.8
France	6,761	192.8	10,394.3	Germany	1,787	18.8	192.8
Argentina	6,737	30	144	Korea	1,670	126.8	5,139
Chile	6,136	20.3	199.5	Malaysia/ Singapore	1,401	40.5	1,413
Italy	5,842	85.5	3,632.3	Macau	785	26.3	346.5
Canada	5,281	107.3	1,411.5	Hong Kong	726	83.3	7,773
Brazil	4,742	14.3	122.3	United Arab Emirates	305	33.8	-
South Africa	3,883	34.5	-	Mauritius	240	2.3	99.8
Total					156,372	3,040.4	105,149

Note: * Recalculated from Australian dollar to US dollar, exchange rate 1 June 2006, 1A$ = 0.75 US$.

Source: Based on data found at Australian Racing Fact Book 2007; Australasian Gaming Council 2008: 221–3, Australian dollar.

held in 2005 and in 2007 with increases for Great Britain with 289 (8,588 to 8,877), Ireland with 156 (2,241 to 2,397) and France with 143 (6,687 to 6,830) races (Australian Racing Fact Book 2008, 2007, 2006; Australian Gaming Council 2007: 230; cf. Australasian Gaming Council 2008: 221).

3.1.3 Gaming machine gambling

In the twentieth and twenty-first centuries casinos have become common in many countries around the world and they offer a wide variety of games like blackjack, craps, roulette and baccarat, poker, gaming machines and other gambling games. Casino venues are found in Africa, Canada, the United States, Oceania, Central and South America and the Caribbean, Europe, Asia and the Middle East; all these places have designated casino venues. In 2008, the commercial casino industry in the United States comprised 445 casinos in twelve states (Nevada 266, Colorado 40, South Dakota 35 [limited-stakes gaming], Mississippi 29, Iowa 14, Louisiana 14, Missouri 12, Indiana 11, New Jersey 11, Illinois 9, Michigan 3, Pennsylvania 1) (American Gaming Association 2009). In Canada, there are two types of casinos; (1) commercial or destination casinos, which offer a wide range of activities and amenities compared to other casino-type facilities and (2) charity casinos which are associated with charitable organisations and where the revenue is directed towards charity projects (Canada West Foundation 2005). In 2007–08, the casino industry in Canada included 66 casinos in seven provinces (Alberta 23, British Columbia 17, Ontario 10, Saskatchewan 7, Manitoba 4, Nova Scotia 2, Quebec 3) (Canadian Partnership for Responsible Gaming 2008). Australia has 13 casinos all offering a diversity of table games and gaming machine gambling. However, gaming machine gambling is more associated with community club and hotel gambling in Australia than casino gambling.

Overall, there are three main groups of gaming machines, including electronic gaming machines. A gaming machine can be defined as:

> Any machine that is used for gaming purposes (whether mechanical or electronic) and offers the user a potential return on a single 'game' that is greater than the amount risked on that game (Taylor Nelson Sofres 2004: 2).

The following gaming machine types are included under the gaming machine definition: the Australian electronic gaming machines (EGMs), the US slots gaming machines, and other electronic gaming machines such as the Canadian slots machines, and Video Lottery Terminals (VLTs). Electronic gaming machines are also, for example, present in France, the United Kingdom, New Zealand and South Africa. The second group, are known as amusement machines with prize style winnings (AWP) machines where the maximum spending per game is low and the speed of play is slower than for modern electronic gaming machines. These amusement gaming machines also belong to the gaming machine category. Examples are UK AWP and jackpot/club machines, German and Spanish AWPs and Japanese pachislo

46 *Pathways to Excessive Gambling*

machines. The third group of gaming machines are pachinko and UK crane grab machines. Pachinko and pachislo gaming machines are common in Japan with the former commonly referred to as a ball bearing game and the latter a token-in/token-out game. These machines have low speed, the stakes are minor, and the prizes are for example often toys or candy for crane grabs, and biscuits, cigarettes and magazines for pachinko – although the prizes from pachinko machines can be exchanged for cash (Taylor Nelson Sofres 2004: 2–3).

Internationally the main areas for gaming machines are within the Asia Pacific region, which has the highest percentage of all gaming machines with 64.7 per cent, followed by Europe (23.4 per cent) and North America (10.3 per cent). A smaller percentage of machines are found in South America (1.4 per cent) and Africa (0.4 per cent) (Taylor Nelson Sofres 2006). In 2006, Australia had 2.4 per cent of the overall number of world gaming machines, calculated on all types of gaming machines. This percentage is down from 2.6 per cent in 2004, but Australia is ranked seventh in the world with 6.2 per cent of casino styled gaming machines (electronic gaming machines) (Taylor Nelson Sofres 2004, 2006). The estimated number of gaming machines in the world in 2006 was 7,981,099; of them 4.9 million were pachinko/pachislo machines (61.4 per cent), 2.98 million slot-casino style machines (37.4 per cent) and more than 97,000 video lottery terminals (VLT) (1.2 per cent) (Taylor Nelson Sofres 2006).

Of the top 10 countries with casino style gaming machines,[1] the United States and Italy have the highest number of casino style gaming machines, three times and twice (respectively) the number in the United Kingdom, Russia and Spain (collectively) (Table 3.3). Simple statistics in the number of machines can be misleading, it is important to understand the number of gaming machines present in any country relative to its population size. This gives a more meaningful understanding of the availability of machines and gambling opportunities. It should be borne in mind also, that while the ratio of number of machines to population size is an important measure, population-size statistics cover whole populations, even underage residents, thus giving a lower ratio than if it was only related to the adult population 18 years of age and above (or the legal age for gambling in respective country).[2] However, it is well known that underage people gamble, thus the true ratio of the number of people to the number of machines is likely to be somewhere between the whole population and only the adult population (cf. Productivity Commission 1999; Griffith 1998; Gupta and Derevensky 1998a).

Australia's population is comparatively small in contrast to the US and the UK. Among the 10 countries with the highest number of casino style gaming machines, Australia has the seventh highest number of machines but significantly, the lowest number of people per gaming machine (Table 3.3). Australia has 111 people per electronic gaming machine. This figure is calculated on the total population of

---

1　Casino style gaming machines are classified here as electronic gaming machines.

2　The statistics are presented by AGMMA, the Australian Gaming Machine Manufacturer's Association (AGMMA) (Taylor Nelson Sofres 2004, 2006).

Global Gambling and Regulation of Gambling 47

Table 3.3   Countries with the highest number of (electronic) gaming machines – casino-style machines 2006

Country	People per machine	Number of casino-style machines*
Australia	111	186,468
Italy	144	410,000
Spain	175	253,534
Czech Republic	196	52,185
United Kingdom	223	269,616
Canada	377	43,444
United States	404	692,306
Germany	407	202,600
Russia	502	255,494
Ukraine	578	80,000

Note: * Whilst European countries such as Italy, Spain, United Kingdom and Germany have particularly high counts of machines, many of these machines are what would be considered to be 'street style' gaming machines – gaming machines which include Amusement games with payouts and limited payment machines designed more for 'amusement' and entertainment rather than for the purpose of gaming (Taylor Nelson Sofres 2006: 7).

Source: Based on data found at Taylor Nelson Sofres 2006.

20,701,488 (30 June 2006, Australian Bureau of Statistics 2006c). It means that it is easier for people in Australia to access a gaming machine than it is for people in any of the other 10 countries with the highest number of gaming machines. Australia is followed by Italy with 144 people and Spain with 175 people per gaming machine.

If we only include people who are eligible to gamble, when calculating the number of electronic gaming machines, that is only adults from the age of 18 years (the legal adult age in Australia) and up to 84 years of age, when gambling pursuits have been shown to decline (Mok and Hraba 1991), there would be 83 adult Australians per electronic gaming machine on 30 June 2006 (15,477,960; 30 June 2006, 18–84 years of age, Australian Bureau of Statistics Census 2006). In his research into the effectiveness of the reduction in gambling machines in South Australia (cf. Chapter 3.3), Delfabbro (2008) observed that the number of machines seemed more than sufficient and few people needed to wait for a machine in the gambling venues he researched.

Other countries with low ratios between people and gaming machines in 2006 were Monaco (16), Aruba (29), Netherlands Antilles (36), St Kitts and Nevis (86), Gibraltar (90), Antigua and Barbuda (93), and Macau (106). All these countries are geographically small or islands with small permanent populations. These jurisdictions' main national commerce is founded on revenue from the hospitality and the entertainment focused tourist industries, thus the gambling and hospitality

48 *Pathways to Excessive Gambling*

industries are directed toward tourists and not derived from the permanent residents' gambling pursuits. Japan (26 people per machine) is an exception in that it also has a low ratio between people and machines, but the Japanese gaming machines are mainly the pachislo type, which are restricted to give goods of minor monetary value, thus not sophisticated casino type electronic gaming machines as in modern gambling venues.

Two years ago, the gaming machine situation was slightly different. In 2004, it was estimated that Australia had 198,751 electronic gaming machines, then the sixth highest amount in the world, according to the Australian Gaming Machine Manufacturer's Association (AGMMA) (Taylor Nelson Sofres 2004). In 2004, the Australian ratio was 99 people per machine. The Australian ratio was lower than the New Zealand 2004 ratio of 174 people per machine (197 in 2006), United Kingdom with 236, Canada with 393, and United States with 426 people per electronic gaming machine (cf. Table3.3; Taylor Nelson Sofres 2004). In Canada, the UK and the USA the ratio between people and machines decreased (less people per machine), while the ratio between people and machines increased in Australia and New Zealand. The machines have of course become more technologically advanced and more sophisticated, thus giving more opportunities to play simultaneous lines of games and give a higher turnover.

In summary, the number of verified worldwide gaming machines was 7,678,528 in December 2007/January 2008 (Table 3.4). The number of gaming machines has decreased since 2006 by 302,571 machines. The main decrease was in Europe (Italy, the United Kingdom, Norway and Portugal) followed by South America.

The reasons for the decreases in number of machines varied, for example, introduction of new laws or legality of gambling (Portugal and Italy), change in

Table 3.4   Total installed base of gaming machines by region in 2004, 2006 and 2008 by numbers and per cent

Region	Number of machines 2004	Percentage of total 2004	Number of machines 2006	Percentage of total 2006	Number of machines 2008*	Percentage of total 2008
Asia Pacific	5,068,037	66.5	5,164,121	64.7	5,143,493	67.0
North America	770,358	10.1	825,991	10.3	908,587	11.8
South America	73,162	1.0	108,889	1.4	61,255	0.8
Europe	1,683,254	22.1	1,848,595	23.2	1,536,250	20.0
Africa	25,447	0.3	33,503	0.4	28,943	0.4
Total	7,620,258	100.0	7,981,099	100.0	7,678,528	100.0

Note: * the actual total is larger than the above figure given the existence of unregistered and illegal machines; the figures exclude machines in China.

Source: Based on data found at Taylor Nelson Sofres 2008: 8.

Global Gambling and Regulation of Gambling 49

monopoly (Norway) and change in definition of what is classified as gambling (England) (Taylor Nelson Sofres 2008: 8). The last four years only small variations have occurred with minor increases for Asia Pacific and North America, after the decrease in 2006. Africa had only a marginal increase in gaming machines.

Nonetheless, as already indicated, gaming machines in different countries are of diverse technical sophistication, thus creating difficulties to compare gaming opportunities between countries. Gambling on modern electronic gaming machines is universally considered to be the type of gambling that creates gambling problems for the largest group of people (Neal et al. 2005; Gambling Research Australia 2008; Productivity Commission 1999, 2009). This is especially pertinent for people on restricted incomes and those who have access to limited leisure opportunities in the local community (cf. Chapter 6).

3.2   Gambling expenditure

The gross revenue for all gambling in the United States in 2006 was US$90,931 million, a 7.7 per cent increase from US$83,660 million in 2005. The highest amount of gambling revenue came from casino gambling (US$34,113 million), Indian Reservations controlled gambling (US$25,076 million) and gross revenue from lotteries (US$24,631 million). In Canada, the gross gambling profit 2003–04 was C$14,575 million. Between 2004–05 and 2005–06 the net gambling revenue collected by Canadian governments increased in the five jurisdictions of Alberta, (19.9 per cent), British Columbia (12.9 per cent), Manitoba (1.4 per cent), Ontario (1.6 per cent) and Quebec (1.6 per cent). On the other hand net gambling revenue decreased in the jurisdictions Saskatchewan (10.8 per cent), Newfoundland and Labrador (10.4 per cent), Nova Scotia (4.8 per cent) and New Brunswick (4.4 per cent). A small decrease was noted for Prince Edward Island (2.7 per cent) giving an overall increase in Canada of 4.3 per cent in the years 2004–05 and 2005–06 (Canadian Partnership for Responsible Gambling 2007; Australasian Gaming Council 2008: 209).

In the United Kingdom, the total gambling expenditure (i.e. stakes minus winnings)[3] in 2005–06 was £9,807 million, a decrease from the previous financial year which recorded £9,826 million, but an increase overall from 2001–02, when the gambling expenditure amounted to £7,216 million, thus showing an increase of 36 per cent (Australian Gaming Council 2007: 220–21; Australian Gaming Council 2008: 208–10). Expressed on a calendar year basis the household gambling expenditure increased from £7,638 million in 2002 to £9,748 million in 2006 (United Kingdom Office of National Statistics 2007; Australasian Gaming Council 2008: 210).

---

3   Expenditure and Gross Profit are interchangeable terms that mean gross amount wagered minus the amount paid out or credited as prizes or dividends. Expenditure is the amount lost or spent by players or the gross profit of the gaming operator.

In New Zealand the total gambling expenditure for the financial year ending 30 June 2007 was NZ$2,020 million and for the following financial year 2008 it had increased to NZ$2,034 (New Zealand Government 2009). The spending on gambling (player loss) for the financial year 2006–07 was highest for non-casino gaming machines (NZ$950 million), a recorded 5 per cent increase from the pervious financial year, with the second highest spending on casino gambling (NZ$469 million). Casino gambling was the only gambling type that showed a decrease in gambling expenditure (4.7 per cent) in New Zealand. All other gambling types increased between 3 per cent and 5 per cent. New Zealand's overall increase in gambling expenditure between the years 2007 and 2008 was 2.2 per cent (Australasian Gaming Council 2008: 210).

In Australia the gambling turnover in 2005–06 amounted to A$148,567 million, which was an increase from the previous financial year's turnover of A$142,779. The highest recorded turnover was for gaming machines with A$107,924 million in 2005–06, up from A$102,741 million in the previous period (2004–05). Wagering and casino gambling amounted to A$17,705 million and A$17,637 million in 2005–06, respectively. The turnover on lottery products was A$4,006, up from A$3,895 million, and on other gambling it amounted to A$1,295, up from A$1,238 million (minor gambling, interactive gambling and keno). Discounting winnings, a total of A$17,575 million was spent on gambling in 2005–06 with the highest spending on gaming machine gambling with A$10,381 million (Office of Economic and Statistical Research 2007; Australian Gambling Statistics 2004–05, 2005–06). Gambling tax revenue was A$4,694 million in 2005–06, an increase from A$4,452 million in 2004–05. The largest tax revenue share in 2005–06 was in NSW with A$1,522 million up from A$1,428 million in the previous financial year, 2004–05. The corresponding figures for Victoria was A$1,460 million up from A$1,369 million in gambling tax revenue (Extrapolated from Office of Economic and Statistical Research 2006, 2007; Australian Gaming Council 2007: 39; Australasian Gaming Council 2008: 39).

Within each country, there are a variety of different gambling types, gambling traditions and calculation systems and thus the expenditure and taxation revenue can be difficult to compare, e.g. Japan's high number of pachinko and pachislo gaming machines with prizes of low value goods cannot be compared with the modern high speed electronic gaming machines in turnover of money (Taylor Nelson Sofres 2008). What is evident however, from the sheer size of gambling expenditure and governments' tax revenue from gambling pursuits, is that the gaming industry is an economically and politically influential lobby group at all levels of government. This situation has made it possible for the gambling industry to have an influence on gambling policy and the regulation of the industry; this was noted by the Independent Pricing and Regulatory Tribunal (2008) in their review of the registered clubs industry in New South Wales and in the Productivity Commission draft report in 2009.

Gambling counsellors, support organisations and voluntary agencies are addressing the negative consequences of excessive gambling. While this is no doubt an important service, the irony is that such support organisations are often funded by tax revenue derived from the gambling industry. The responsible gambling strategies do not eliminate the causes of excessive gambling, but they aim to keep the adverse consequences of gambling at a reasonable level without changing the basic construct of gambling.

3.3 Gambling regulation

Except in its early days, gambling has been regulated in most jurisdictions. The requirements and level of regulation differ between jurisdictions and in different time periods. In general however, to organise any form of gambling, the organisers need government permission, often through a licensing procedure where the character of the person seeking the licence is assessed[4] as well as the suitability of the proposed gambling type. A licence to organise a gambling event is required both in regard to commercial as well as charity gambling, including a lottery, wagering on horse and dog racing or sports events. To establish designated gambling venues, such as casinos and sports clubs with gambling facilities, licensing is also required. The introduction of regulation is often an afterthought or a delayed procedure after the establishment of the gambling type and event, e.g. horse racing became regulated when the interest and betting spread outside the noble classes to non-horse owners and the public with the introduction of the 'pari-mutuel' betting and 'totalizator' systems.[5]

Currently, delayed regulation is especially the case for web based gambling, which has been difficult to regulate. The web based technology has moved fast with new and innovative gambling options before the regulatory authorities have managed to assess its implications concerning prudent business practices and client protection. The main aim of issuing gaming licences to approved individuals and organisations which are deemed suitable, is to gain insight into the intended gambling activities and the gambling organisation and to make sure that the organisers are following prudent business rules and fulfil legal requirements. Another key reason behind the issuing of licences is for taxation purposes. Most governments regulate gambling activities that include a transaction of money and taxation of gambling revenue has become an important income source for governments.

---

4 The presented gambling regulations are examples of some jurisdictions' gambling acts, but as regulations and amendments are changing continuously, it is recommended to revisit each jurisdiction to gain the most recent gambling regulation.

5 'Parimutuel betting': For most races, horses, dogs, camels, and some games jai alai, a pari-mutuel wagering system is used. The system was introduced in 1865 following the invention of the 'totalizator' by Frenchman Pierre Oller. The 'totalizator' is a calculating machine which records the amount bet on each competitor prior to the start of the contest (The Columbia Encyclopaedia, Sixth Edition. 2008. Retrieved 14 July 2009, from http://www.encyclopedia.com/doc/1E1-parimutu.html).

Depending on the type of gambling and its permanency, there are different requirements for staging a gambling activity. Even for a one-off gambling event such as a raffle to cover a shortfall in funding in the building and running of a hospital, or to collect money for school or community projects, a licence is needed. To arrange a raffle has long been an essential strategy in circumstances where there is a lack of public funding for community projects. Not-for-profit and charitable organisations have organised raffles to secure financial support for community projects and services. The gambling here is seen as supporting a good cause because the proceeds of the lottery go back into the local community. Raffles organised by not-for-profit and charitable organisations are hardly an activity that would lead to excessive gambling or gambling related adversity. Nevertheless, regardless of the type and purpose of the gambling, organisers of gaming and gambling events, including a one-off community raffles, need a licence to stage the event in most jurisdictions.

The emphasis on regulation in the twenty-first century has enhanced protection for vulnerable individuals and especially for young adults and children. The gambling industry has been required to take more responsibility for their business activities. Despite all the legislative effort, it is still easy for a person to over commit and to gamble away all their own money and money borrowed from others.

Gambling in the United Kingdom is regulated by the Gambling Commission within the Department for Culture, Media and Sports (DCMS). In 2005, a new gambling regulation was introduced, the Gambling Act 2005, which came into force on 1 September 2007 (UK Gambling Commission 2005). This Act updated the already existing gambling laws to include new gambling forms such as internet and online gambling. Additionally, the new gambling law included more protection for children, young people and vulnerable adults.

Furthermore, the new 2005 UK Gambling Act made it possible for the first time to establish resort style casinos, much like the United States Las Vegas type casinos. The aim was to introduce these 'super casinos' in a staggered process where cities could bid for the right to host such casinos. Manchester was the first to gain the licence in early 2007 but the gambling policy changed with the change in Prime Minister from Tony Blair to Gordon Brown. A hold was placed on 'super casinos' and a reassessment of gambling policy and the 2005 Gambling Act is being undertaken.

The United Kingdom has a long history with sports gambling, including betting on horse and greyhound racing, and football (soccer) games. The 1960 Gambling Act legalised off-course bookmakers, which made it easier to make bets without visiting the racetrack. Sports gambling has further been made easier through web based gambling. The legal age for sports betting in the UK and Ireland is 16 years of age and while a person 16 years of age is not allowed to buy lottery tickets or scratch cards in a registered public lottery (National Lottery), they can legally buy lottery tickets in privately organised lotteries. The UK National Lottery has over the years raised billions of pounds for good causes, distributed through grants. The changing technology and social environment of gambling preferences have made regular updating of gambling regulations a necessity. While, the 1934 UK Gambling Act legalised minor lottery,[6] amendments were introduced in 1956, 1976 and in 2007 (UK Gambling Commission 2005).

In England and Wales, a person under 16 years of age can visit amusement arcades and pubs, but cannot play on fruit machines (slot machines) giving a £10 or more cash payout. There is no lower age limit for playing on fruit machines with a maximum cash of £5 or token prize of up to £8. These machines (amusement with prizes – category D machines) are placed in arcades, in family entertainment centres (including seaside arcades, bowling alleys, motorway services and theme parks) and non-gambling premises such as cafes, fish and chip shops, take-away shops and taxicab offices (United Kingdom Parliamentary Business 2009). The same regulation is enforced for Northern Ireland, with no lower age limit for playing on fruit machines with a maximum cash of £5 or token prize of up to £8 in amusement arcades and similar premises. Fruit machines are easily accessible by young people and children; however, these fruit machines are intended to be phased out by the 31 July 2009 (UK Gambling Commission 2005).

In the United Kingdom, the Licence Conditions and Codes of Practice regulation stipulates that to gain an operating gambling licence the patron needs to fulfil three requirements. First, the person needs to be found 'fit and proper' – is the applicant suitable to take on a role in the industry? Secondly, the applicant needs to have adequate financial resources to run the gambling business and thirdly, the applicant needs to be appropriately knowledgeable and professionally competent to run a gambling establishment. The tests are aimed at directors and other persons holding positions of authority or influence over the gambling business. These new requirements are meant to improve the accountability of people running gambling activities and the licence will be issued only after rigorous investigation. Once the licence has been issued, there is ongoing monitoring of the gambling activities (UK Gambling Commission 2005).

The UK 2005 Gaming Act aimed to bring Britain into the twenty-first century in gambling regulation with the Act being fully implemented in September 2007. However, the changes included in the UK 2005 Gaming Act have been criticised for not going far enough. It has been criticised by people working within the support counselling services that handle the consequences of excessive gambling (Orford 2005) and has had 'a stormy reaction from an unusually broad political spectrum' (Room 2005: 1226), because the Act does not go far enough in relation to youth gambling. One of the intentions of the Act was to protect children and young people from accessing gambling venues and playing on fruit machines, however, in the United Kingdom it is still legal for young people to gamble on category D fruit machines – electronic gaming machines with low stakes and low prizes, a form of gambling, which is prohibited in most countries for underage people (Parke and Griffiths 2006). The criticism also highlighted that the opportunities to

---

6 A person buys a ticket and can win one or two prizes, e.g. raffle lottery, it excludes for instance, instant lottery and sweepstakes.

gamble had never been higher in the UK, while treatment places and support for counselling have not increased at the same rate (Moodie 2008).

Moodie and Reith (2009) assessed the implementation of the 2005 Gambling Act in Britain and gambling operators' compliance with the responsible gambling strategies imposed by the Act as conditions of the gambling licence, such as signage in the gambling area. They found in their observational study that:

> ... eighteen months prior to the implementation of the Act, only 4.1 per cent of the 1351 electronic machines located in Glasgow City Centre displayed signs promoting responsible gambling and signposting the national Gamcare helpline. One month after the introduction of the Act, which stipulated that all machines must display such signage, this was only evident on 65 per cent of machines (Moodie and Reith 2009: 5).

Their study highlighted two concerns: (1) 'most sectors of the gambling industry are not embracing the new social responsibility codes (or indeed even adhering to them)'; and (2) 'if licensing conditions are not made explicit, as is the case in Britain, the gambling industry can dictate what is meant by 'responsible' and so define what measures are sufficient to meet this criteria' (Moodie and Reith 2009: 5). This underlines the importance of upholding responsible gambling regulations through regular assessments of gambling venues and to make adherence to the gambling regulations a condition of the gambling licence.

If in the United Kingdom, the Gambling Commission is the central authority in implementing the regulation and licensing of gambling, there are decentralised systems in other countries. In the USA, Canada and Australia gambling regulation and the authority issuing gambling licences are the responsibilities of the individual states or their agents. Notwithstanding some variations between the countries, the basic requirements to gain a gaming licence are very similar. According to the United States federal law, gambling is legal in the USA and the individual states regulate the gambling licences:

> The Gambling Devices Act of 1962, 15 U.S.C. §§ 1171–1178, requires registration by any person or entity engaged in the business of manufacturing, repairing, reconditioning, buying, selling, leasing, using, or making available for use by others any gambling device before any such device enters interstate or foreign commerce (United States Department of Justice 2009).

As early as 1931, gambling was made legal in Nevada and perhaps the best recognised gambling city in the USA, is Las Vegas. Legalisation of gambling followed in other states with Atlantic City in New Jersey in 1976, and Tunica in Mississippi in 1990. These cities have built large casinos and holiday resorts to attract professional and recreational gamblers. In 1987, the US Supreme Court issued a decision, which made it legal for Native American tribes to have their own casinos. The Native American tribes are considered sovereign states and thus are regulated by federal laws and not by state laws (Flatt 1998). In the USA, almost all states have legalised gambling in the form of a state-run lottery schemes.

The Canadian gambling history is closely associated with the Canadian Criminal Code. In 1892, it proclaimed a complete ban on most forms of gambling activities. The only exception was horse racing (Canada West Foundation 1999). In 1969, the Criminal Code was amended to allow, under a licence arrangement, authorised provincial governments to manage and conduct lottery schemes and authorised charitable groups to arrange lotteries. Nevertheless, the ultimate control still rested with the federal government. The Canadian federal government arranged a national lottery in the 1970s to fund the 1976 Montreal Olympics (Campbell and Smith 1998).

A major amendment to the Canadian Criminal Code was undertaken in 1985. The provincial governments were given permission to control and regulate computer and video game devices, video lottery terminals and slot machines. This also included control over charitable groups arranging lotteries, thus giving provincial and territorial governments complete control over gambling commerce (Canada West Foundation 2001), where in most other nation states with similar governance systems, the federal government still keeps some part of the regulatory power (Stevens and Beristain 2004).

Australia's approach to regulating gambling is comparable with the main principles of the regulations in the USA and Canada. The different states and territories are the main regulators of gambling. The federal government's authority is mainly limited to international gambling, online gambling, and to organised national and international gambling related crimes. Each state and territory has their own office regulating gambling licences. In New South Wales it is the NSW Office of Liquor, Gaming and Racing within the Department of the Arts, Sport and Recreation. The NSW Office of Liquor, Gaming and Racing regulates the liquor, gaming, racing and charity events in the state. In Victoria it is the Commission for Gambling and Regulation, in Queensland the Office of Gambling Regulation, in South Australia the Office of the Liquor and Gambling Commissioner, in Western Australia the Department of Racing, Gaming and Liquor, in Tasmania the Gaming Commission, in the Australian Capital Territory (ACT) it is the Gambling and Racing Commission, and in the Northern Territory it is the Licensing Commission. In Australia, gambling regulation is tied to liquor licensing as gambling is closely associated with the hospitality industry in casinos, community and sports clubs, where the serving of affordable food and alcohol are enticing factors for people to patronise these establishments (NSW gambling regulation is presented in more detail in section 3.3.1).

Even if the internet gambling market is small in relation to lottery, electronic gaming machine gambling and to the total amount of gambling, it has unlimited potential in terms of gambling opportunities and diversity (UK Gambling Commission 2009), geographical distribution and customer base with low monetary investment – compared to establishing and running a casino or a sports club complex. The expansion and refinement of internet technology has made gambling possible without visiting gambling venues. It has made it possible to gamble from home with anyone in the world about anything people find to gamble on. There are no geographical barriers, thus gambling has a global market (Wood and Griffiths 2008; Wood, Griffiths and Parke 2007; Parke et al. 2007).

As with most laws and regulations the control of gambling is, as emphasised before, more of a post event procedure than a case of advanced planning, thus an activity needs to exist and be identified as a new activity and classified before it can be regulated (UK Gambling Commission 2009). The major difference between internet gambling and traditional gambling is in its disregard for geographical boundaries. The internet gambling website may be anywhere in the world and the gambler can access the gambling site from his or her home. Traditional gambling requires the gambler to physically visit the racetrack, a casino, club or a betting office. Gambling in private and gambling that is difficult to trace or follow will always be more difficult to regulate than gambling in public and in person. Internet gambling sites attract people from many different jurisdictions, and regulations in one jurisdiction will not automatically relate to another jurisdiction. This also complicates the situation for governments in recouping tax revenue.

The internet gambling market presents convenient and nearly unlimited possibilities to gambling 24/7 at diverse global gambling markets. It will for computer literate people, independent of age and gender, give access to a smorgasbord of gambling opportunities from the home computer. Even if gambling providers accept self-regulation and give individuals opportunities to set self-imposed restrictions or the gambling operators accept the government's regulations for the jurisdiction of the internet site, the sheer complexity of different and perhaps conflicting regulations from the diverse jurisdictions where the internet site can be accessed, makes it nearly impossible to regulate, implement and monitor whether each jurisdictions' regulations are being complied with.

Online commercial gaming includes casino table games and gaming machine games delivered through the internet. Unlike most forms of gambling in Australia, online gaming is the regulatory responsibility of the Australian Government. The Australian Government passed the Interactive Gambling Act 2001 (IGA), making it illegal for Australian residents to gamble at domicile online gaming sites (sites with URL address in Australia) (Productivity Commission 2009). Australian interactive gaming websites (Northern Territory) are supposed to be available only to overseas gamblers (Australasian Gaming Council 2008: 4). Despite gambling regulation and legislation it is clearly quite difficult for governments to control the internet gambling market. The size and complexity of this task is better understood when consideration is made of the need governments have to protect their own interests: governments collect taxation on the revenue that gambling generates and this revenue is a significant income source for governments.

Personal preferences in relation to traditional gambling with attending the event or a betting office are perhaps a generational question with the younger gambler preferring internet gambling. The scope of internet gambling is difficult to assess without monitoring of the gambling traffic. There are opportunities to hide or distort the gambling traffic and the characteristics of the gambler. This also raises questions about civil rights and how the personal internet traffic should be monitored. It is apparent that the internet gambling market is complex to regulate and to protect vulnerable gamblers, especially less experienced young people (Wood and Griffiths 2008).

3.3.1 New South Wales gambling regulation

To highlight in more detail the complicated and fluid regulation system of gambling, New South Wales acts as a useful example in examining the regulation of electronic gaming machine gambling. New South Wales (NSW) *Gambling Legislation Amendment (Responsible Gambling) Act 1999 NSW* outlines the legislative requirements for gambling operators in NSW, and determines how responsible gaming activities should be managed (New South Wales Department of Gaming and Racing 1999). This Act was the first comprehensive legislation concerning the gaming industry in NSW. The Gaming Machines Act 2001 followed the 1999 Act and in 2004, the Independent Pricing and Regulatory Tribunal (IPART) undertook a major review of gambling regulation in New South Wales. The NSW Government accepted and implemented some of the recommendations, while other recommendations were initially accepted but later amended. After an internal review in 2007 (NSW Office of Liquor, Gaming and Racing 2007a) the government made further amendments of the gambling regulations. The amendments were introduced and presented in the Gaming Machines Amendment Act 2008 and the Gaming Machines Amendment Regulation 2009[7] (The NSW Office of Liquor, Gaming and Racing 2009a). These amendments and implemented changes, since the recommendations in the IPART review, regulate caps on gambling machines, trading of machines, and assessment of the impact of gambling on the local environment. The amendments were implemented on 31 January 2009.

The previous NSW state wide cap of 104,000 gaming machines was reduced to 99,000, which is the present number of machines in the state. The intention was that the reduction of gambling machines should continue naturally over time when gaming machine entitlements were given up. The existing venue caps on gaming machines should be kept at 30 electronic gaming machines for hotels and 450 for clubs. A new cap was introduced on multi-terminal gaming machines in clubs. The cap on multi-terminal gaming machines is set at a maximum of 15 per cent of the overall number of gaming machines for the venue (NSW Office of Liquor, Gaming and Racing 2007a, 2008).

Concerning forfeiture of electronic gaming machine entitlements, the 2007 internal review proposed to maintain the existing requirement for gaming machine transfers. The entitlement stipulates that one machine should be forfeited, for

---

7 Additional acts regulating gambling in NSW: Gaming Machine Tax Act 2001 No 72; Gaming Machines Act 2001 No 127; Gaming Machines Regulation 2002; Registered Clubs Act 1976 No 31; Registered Clubs Regulation 1996; Unlawful Gambling Act 1998 No 113 (http://www.legislation.nsw.gov.au/ maintop/search/inforce).

every three entitlements, thus one machine is to be removed from operation when the electronic gaming machines are sold from a club to another club or a hotel to another hotel. A further amendment was introduced in 2009, in the Gaming Machines Amendment Regulation 2009, which provides exemptions from the forfeiture requirements when entitlements are transferred between related club premises within one kilometre in metropolitan areas, or within 50 kilometres in country areas. Furthermore, under the new regulations, no forfeiture is required when gaming machine entitlements are transferred between related club premises within the same Local Government Area (LGA). Transfers between related clubs' premises outside the LGA are subject to a forfeiture rate of one entitlement for every two transfer blocks rather than the standard one in three forfeiture rate (NSW Office of Liquor, Gaming and Racing 2009a).

The previous strategy would lead to a gradual reduction in the number of machines, as with every trading of entitlements, there would have been further reductions in the overall number of gaming machines in NSW. The changes with the new amendment were clearly a concession to the gambling industry and their claimed hardship due to increased taxation and the smoking ban in gambling venues. The hardship condition was an additional consideration introduced by the NSW government with freezing club and hotel gaming machine numbers. Clubs and hotels can now obtain more gaming machines on hardship grounds. The hardship gaming machines may be converted (upon application) to gaming machine entitlements three years after the hardship clause was invoked, provided they have met the required conditions. The Casino, Liquor and Gaming Control Authority, is the assessor of the hardship grounds.

As a further change from previous gambling regulations, the Gaming Machines Act now allows venues with approved amusement devices (AADs) to convert them to gaming machine entitlements on a three to one basis, one gaming machine entitlement is issued for every three AADs surrendered. Country venues may convert AADs to electronic gaming machine entitlements on a two AAD to one electronic gaming machine basis. All venues will now have three years from the commencement of these amendments to exchange AADs for gaming machine entitlements (e.g. until 31 January 2012) (NSW Office of Liquor, Gaming and Racing 2009a).

The number of multi-terminal gaming machines (MTGMs), as a proportion of all gaming machines a club may install has, in the 2009 amendment to the Gambling Act, been limited to 15 per cent of the total gaming machine entitlements held. This authorisation limit only applies to new authorisations; a venue can update an authorisation for a current MTGM terminal and clubs that currently operate MTGMs over the 15 per cent cap have five years to reduce their excess MTGM holdings to comply with the 15 per cent cap (NSW Office of Liquor, Gaming and Racing 2009a).

Furthermore, the government has introduced a concessional forfeiture scheme on transferring gaming machines into newly built areas. This scheme aims to encourage and assist clubs to move into new development areas, to provide community facilities, and entertainment for newly established residential areas and local communities. New housing developments are habitually starved of services, transport and entertainment opportunities, thus the local club has a community function (NSW Office of Liquor, Gaming and Racing 2009a), unfortunately however, this is underpinned by gambling revenue.

In the Independent Pricing and Regulatory Tribunal (2004) review, a reduction of gaming machine entitlements would be enforced if the gaming machines were traded out of local government areas (LGA). Thus, related clubs, such as those created by the merging of clubs, would be exempt from forfeiture if the venues were in the same local government area. However, related clubs located in different LGAs would have their forfeiture requirement reduced from one in three to one in six entitlements. The aim of this measure was to increase the clubs sustainability and to protect community facilities such as bowling clubs. As can be ascertained from the 2009 amendments the government has made further concessions to clubs, hotels and gambling venues to keep and increase their gaming machine numbers (NSW Office of Liquor, Gaming and Racing 2007a, 2009a; Independent Pricing and Regulatory Tribunal 2004).

Delfabbro explored the effects of a reduction of electronic gaming machines in local communities in South Australia and concluded that: 'proximity of gambling opportunities to homes is what makes EGM gambling so attractive to many Australian residents, and that reducing the number of venues with gambling opportunities may remain a potentially useful strategy' (Delfabbro 2008: 20), however, to have an effect, the number of gambling venues and machines should be substantially reduced. Delfabbro's research in South Australia did not show changes in gambling expenditure, but as the reduction in machines was minor, venues adopted strategies to counter loss in profitability. Moreover, there seems to be an oversupply of gaming machines at some venues, thus those people who want to play can easily find an available machine.

In NSW organisational changes were recommended in the 2007 review with the existing Social Impact Assessment to be replaced by a Local Impact Assessment (LIA), under the Casino, Liquor and Gaming Control Authority. Local government areas would be divided into three classes based on the number of gaming machines, expenditure, population, and socio-economic data. The three bands: (1) LGAs with low numbers of gaming machines, low expenditure on gaming machines and high socio-economic rankings; (2) LGAs with moderate numbers of gaming machines, moderate expenditure on those machines and moderate socio-economic rankings; and (3) LGAs with high numbers of gaming machines, high expenditure on those machines and low socio-economic rankings (NSW Office of Liquor, Gaming and Racing 2009a).

Venues in band two and three that wanted to expand their number of machines through buying entitlements from another local government area would need to be assessed by the Local Impact Assessment Authority. Band three venues must undergo a rigorous local impact assessment (Class 2 LIA), while band two venues have to undergo either a Class 1 or Class 2 LIA, as determined by the authority. The utilisation of problem gambling services in local communities would be taken into account in the decision making process. Band one venues wanting to buy machines from a venue in a different LGA only have to undergo an LIA if they are seeking more than 20 additional machines and venues located in the same LGA, regardless of their band classification, will not have to undergo an LIA before trading poker machines, but forfeiture provisions would still apply (NSW Office of Liquor, Gaming and Racing 2009a).

A further amendment in the legislation strengthened the power of the licensee holders in allowing them to object to the transfer of entitlements from a leased hotel. Additionally, concerning rural venues, there is an avenue for a community to object to the removal of all electronic gaming machine entitlements from the last remaining hotel or club in their town to prevent the potential loss of the facility. A general perception is that a club or a hotel cannot be sustainable without having electronic gaming machines; however there are a few clubs and hotels in New South Wales that manage without gambling facilities.

Finally, a temporary freeze on new applications was imposed on clubs and hotels to increase their gaming machine threshold (the maximum number of gaming machines allowed to be kept on the premises) on new applications for additional multi-terminal gaming machines (MTGMs). The temporary freeze was imposed on clubs already above the 15 per cent cap or if the proposed increase would result in the club breaching the 15 per cent cap. Furthermore, a temporary freeze was introduced on new applications for the sale of hotels' electronic gaming machine entitlements by the proprietor, where consent had not been given by the licensee and others with a financial interest in the licence or business (NSW Office of Liquor, Gaming and Racing 2007a, 2009a).

Further to these reviews and amendments of the 2001 Gaming Machines Act, the commencement of the Gaming Machines Amendment Act 2008 and the Gaming Machines Amendment Regulation 2009 (31 January 2009) introduced a number of reforms that include further responsible gambling measures and simplifying the regulatory burden on businesses. The amendments followed on from the five-year statutory review of the Gaming Machines Act 2001, which was finalised in December 2007 (Department of the Arts, Sport and Recreation 2007). In summary, the changes introduced by the new laws include:

- Reducing the state-wide cap on gaming machines by 5,000 to 99,000,[8]
- A new Local Impact Assessment process to gauge the impact of additional gaming machines in certain local government areas;
- Banning credit card withdrawals from ATMs and EFTPOS facilities in gaming venues;
- New powers to direct venues to move or shield gaming machines that act as an advertisement to those outside the premises;

---

8 As noted above the previous cap was 140,000 machines but the existing machines were approximately 99,000, thus only an adjustment to the actual number of registered machines.

- Requiring jackpot prize monitors to be located only in restricted areas of a hotel or club, such as the bar area or gaming room;
- Removing the requirement to hold an advisor's licence;
- Placing a cap on Multi-Terminal Gaming Machines (MTGMs) in clubs; and
- A new mechanism to assist clubs wishing to establish in new development areas.[9]

Source: The NSW Office of Liquor, Gaming and Racing 2009a.

As can be gauged from the reviews and later amendments the earlier focus has changed somewhat from the consumer to the clubs, hotels and the gaming industry. The new regulations are more accommodating to the gambling industry than what the IPART (2004) review recommended. One interpretation of this is that the government has accepted the clubs' and hotels' assessment of hardship and that the freeze on the number of electronic gaming machines, taxation changes, and the smoking ban have caused the gambling businesses hardship, while it has been assumed that the negative aspects of gambling can be kept at a manageable level.

It is uncertain if any of these changes and reviews of the Gaming Machine Act 2001 and the most recent amendments in 2008 and 2009 will have any real influence on the prevention and escalation of gambling related problems, people's access to gambling venues and opportunities to gamble. Gambling research and counselling services have not documented a decline in clients needing support and counselling services (Fabiansson 2008), however, there is a void in longitudinal and reliable evaluations of the effects of regulation to limit excessive gambling (cf. The South Australian Centre for Economic Studies 2003: i; Productivity Commission 1999).

3.3.2 Legal age of gambling

One of the most universal restrictions on gambling participation is the age restriction. Commonly, there is one exception to the age restriction, and this concerns buying charitable and community raffle tickets. Children and young people are often engaged as sellers of raffle tickets, especially in relation to school and sports supported raffles. Raffle ticket campaigns are the only form of gambling where participation is legal for people under 18 years of age in most jurisdictions. Local fundraising is imperative and essential for many charitable organisations and community groups to sustain recreational activities and to survive financially. The beneficiaries are often local children and young people, who would otherwise be without extra funding for schools, sports activities and support services in the community.

---

9   For specific details of amendments refer to the Gaming Machines Amendment Act 2008 and the Gaming Machines Amendment Regulation 2009.

Even if there are common agreements, about the need for age limits on participating in gambling activities and there are age restrictions implemented worldwide, there is less agreement about at what age young people should be allowed to gamble. There are some variations in what is considered to be an adult, but in principle a person is classified as an adult, when they have adult responsibilities in handling money, are mature enough to understand consequences of their actions and are able to legally sign documents. In Australia, the age restriction for all types of gambling is set at 18, but the age limit can vary in other countries depending on the type of gambling and the individual state regulation.

In the USA each state has their own age limits, although for the majority of the states there is an 18 years age limit for buying lottery tickets (Nelson Rose 2000). However, since 2000 the trend has been for the states to increase the legal age of gambling, not to decrease it.[10] As of September 2008 the age restrictions for gambling are 21 years of age for the states Arizona, Colorado, Delaware, Georgia, Illinois, Indiana, Iowa, Kansas, Louisiana, Louisiana, Maryland, Detroit Casinos, Mississippi, Missouri, Nevada, New Hampshire, New Jersey, New Mexico, New York, North Carolina, North Dakota, Pennsylvania, Puerto Rico, South Carolina, South Dakota, Virginia, West Virginia, and Wisconsin (Virgin Islands). The age restrictions of 18 years of age for lottery type gambling and 21 years of age for casino type of gambling are imposed by the states California, Connecticut, Florida, Oklahoma, Oregon and Washington. Nineteen years of age is the gambling limit for Michigan and in the states of Hawaii and Utah gambling is not legally permitted.

In the United Kingdom lottery gambling is differentiated from other types of gambling pursuits. The minimum age for buying lottery tickets (National Lottery) is 18 years of age, except for privately organised lotteries. Young people in the UK can bet on horse races and sports events when they are 16 years of age, but need to be 18 years of age for entering adult gambling venues and play on gaming machines with more than £10 in prize money. However, playing on category D fruit machines with a maximum cash of £5 or token prize of up to £8 is still not age restricted (2005 UK Gambling Act, UK Gambling Commission 2005).

Even if jurisdictions have imposed age restrictions on most gambling forms it can be nearly impossible to fully enforce such restrictions. It can be difficult to judge a person's age by appearance only. To ask for proof of age can be seen as intrusive, especially for people who look younger than they are. Age restrictions are also difficult to implement with online gambling, which can be undertaken in private, without any possibility to control the identity and age of the gambler.

In countries where gambling is legal there are often no legal gender restrictions. Both men and women can take part in gambling activities. However, there can be social, cultural, religious and traditional limitations where gambling can be

---

10   For current information about gambling law and regulation consult the respective jurisdictions' gambling regulation, often accessible through their website.

seen as tarnishing the woman's reputation if she frequents public gambling places, irrespective of if she gambles herself or if she is part of a social group visiting the gambling venue (cf. Chapter 6). Within some faiths, for example the Muslim faith, gambling is not allowed for either men or women. However, this is not to say that gambling for money does not occur or exist in Muslim countries, but the gambling is not legally accepted. In these societies, women would not be allowed to gamble, even in the illegal gambling places, together with the men. In these circumstances, it is the society and the faith that sets the boundaries and regulates the gambling. However, the same people might not feel the same restrictions on gambling in other countries such as Canada, the USA, Australia and the UK, where gambling is seen as an acceptable leisure activity. People, who would not gamble in their home country, could very well gamble in societies with more open attitudes to gambling (cf. Chapter 6).

3.4 Responsible gambling

Responsible gambling guidelines refer to a safe approach to gambling where consumers are given the knowledge to make informed and educated decisions about their gambling pursuits. In addition, responsible gambling incorporates harm minimisation approaches designed to improve the health and well being of people affected by problem gambling, such as self-exclusion from the gambling venue. It is proposed that responsible gambling occurs in a regulated environment where the potential for harm associated with gambling is minimised and people make informed decisions about their participation in gambling activities. Responsible gambling is the outcome of collaborative and collective actions by all involved in the gambling event. The ownership of responsible gambling strategies is shared between jurisdictions as regulators of gambling activities, the gambling industry, individual gamblers and local communities. Responsible gambling strategies emphasise that the whole community, residents – gamblers and non-gamblers – businesses and governments, need to work together to achieve outcomes that are socially responsible for all residents and responsive to community concerns.

Gambling can be classified as causing problems when the safety and well being of gamblers, their family and friends are placed at risk, and when negative impacts extend to the broader community. Even if the gamblers, the gambling industry and the government have shared obligations for responsible gambling, it is ultimately the duty of the government's regulatory authority to implement the regulations and to supervise the industry's applications of the gambling regulations. The government, the industry and the gamblers have contradictory roles and purposes in regulating, supplying and enjoying gambling. There is a conflict in the double role of governments as the regulatory authority over gambling and the collector of gambling revenue. There is pressure from the supply side in that the gambling industry fiercely protects its business interests, lobbies governments and campaigns to minimise regulatory limitation on gambling commerce. Notwithstanding, governments attempt to set restrictions for individuals who would like to gamble, drink and smoke, but at the same time require protection from gambling away all their money.

This is to a certain extent a 'Catch 22' situation with contradictory aims. Governments aim to regulate gambling enough to avoid negative consequences of excessive gambling, but still allow enough gambling activities to be able to continue to collect high amounts of tax revenue from the gambling sector. The gambling sector aims to maximise their patronage and revenue, but to avoid public vilification of encouraging excessive gambling. The gambling industries' best customer is the regular gambler who gambles until all or nearly all his or her money is gone, including any winnings during the gambling session. The social recreational and occasional gamblers, who gamble for 20 dollars and leave when the money is gone or when they win, are the less profitable customers.

A principal strategy concerning the responsible gambling program is early intervention before problems become entrenched. This strategy involves identifying groups of people, especially young people, who are at risk and to target those groups through communication and outreach activities. It is anticipated that identifying problem gambling as a public health issue would encourage people with gambling problems to seek help (Korn and Shaffer 1999; Volberg 2004: 3–4).

As summarised in the 2003 report for the Commonwealth Department of Family and Community Services and Indigenous Affairs by the South Australian Centre for Economic Studies, *Measurement of Prevalence of Youth Problem Gambling in Australia: Report on Review of Literature*, the status of gambling research and the benefit of a holistic longitudinal perspective was noted:

> … a longitudinal study where gambling issues are integrated into broader health issues may in fact, be the preferred approach. It is clear that gambling preferences (and opportunities) change with age while high youth prevalence rates do not appear to translate into equally high rates for adults. Documenting changes in preferences would be part of any longitudinal study (The South Australian Centre for Economic Studies 2003: i).

Research shows that young people are introduced to gambling well before the legal age for participation (Gillespie, Derevensky and Gupta 2007; Griffiths 1998; cf. Chapter 5). Furthermore, research has documented the need for an appropriate balance in the provision of gambling support services, while at the same time accepting the entertainment value of gambling. The gaming industry provides affordable food, drinks and entertainment and employment for many people. Notwithstanding the positive aspects of recreational gambling and employment opportunities, the government, the industry, and community groups have acknowledged the high social costs of excessive gambling (Productivity Commission 1999, 2009). Unfortunately, the negative aspects of excessive gambling are mainly seen as an individual addictive problem not a society wide health problem, thus focusing on the individual, rather than on government regulations, access to gambling in local communities, or commercial gambling interests.

Gambling is present in many cultures and ethnic groups like Western, Middle Eastern and Asian cultures. Although not condoned within all faiths, there are always grey areas where the restrictions can be more or less accepted. Close-knit families might prefer to deal with any gambling related problems within the family, while in other cases, when the generosity of families and friends has been exhausted, community and charity support services become the last recourse. In cultures where the family unit is strong, such as in the Macedonian and Arabic speaking communities, the family unit might be the primary source of support when problems arise, thus problems are in the first circumstance dealt with within the families. Excessive gambling can also be kept a secret for the family because of the shame it would cause the person and the family, if the excessive gambling became generally known (The South Australian Centre for Economic Studies 2005: 37, 115). Research shows that gambling is prevalent in Western cultures, the Vietnamese and Chinese cultures, but it is also established in Middle Eastern cultures. Habitually in most cultures, gambling is talked about when people win but hidden when money is lost (interviews with representatives for the Arabic speaking, Macedonian and Vietnamese communities 2005; Wesley Mission 2006; Arab Council Australia 2006; Fabiansson 2007).

Responsible gambling measures are in place in most jurisdictions and they range from information about counselling services, to restriction on how much money, value of the notes or coins that can be inserted into the machine, and in some jurisdictions the possibility for a gambler to gain self-exclusion from a gambling venue. The international review of responsible gambling strategies and evaluation to their effectiveness undertaken by Abbott, Volberg, Bellringer and Reith (2004: 15), stressed the importance of a monitoring system involving (1) an integrated database of information on gambling participation, expenditures, problems and services, (2) a basic research effort generating data to inform policy analysis and service development, and (3) a process for dissemination of data and research to enhance timely new or reviewed responses to developments or information. Furthermore, it was acknowledged that there was a need to develop and to use credible measures of problem gambling to give a clear and conceptual account of problem gambling, and its different components. In addition, there is a need to demonstrate that the research and information are based on reliable, valid, applicable and practicable research underpinning policy and strategies. Useful strategies aim to move away from the notion often held by the gambling industry that pathological gambling is a rare mental disorder that is predominantly physically and/or psychologically determined (Abbott et al. 2004: 19). Additionally, the review stressed the importance of raising public awareness of the risks associated with excessive gambling, the need to expand counselling services for problem gamblers, strengthening of the regulatory requirements for gambling commerce, and implementation of public health harm reduction measures. These strategies were assumed to counteract adverse effects from increased availability of gambling venues in local communities and the increased diversity in types of gambling (Abbott et al. 2004: 17). These reviews of policy and responsible gambling strategies to get governments and the gambling industry on board to accept and implement proposed responsible gambling strategies are complicated even when the reviews are based on solid research.

The ideal outcome for implementing responsible gambling policies and codes of practice is to create an environment where individuals, communities, the gambling industry and governments gain a shared understanding of responsible gambling practices, so that all involved know their rights and responsibilities. Furthermore, that the gambling industry provides safe and supportive environments for the delivery of gambling products and services where customers can make informed decisions about their gambling practices. Finally, that harmful effects from gambling pursuits experienced by individuals and the broader community be minimised and that people adversely affected by gambling have access to timely and appropriate assistance and information (cf. Queensland Government Treasury 2004: 9).

Self-exclusion implies that a person can exclude themselves from a gambling venue, but it also means that the gambling operators need to have a system that makes it possible for the person to use the procedure and that it is adhered to. According to Hing and Mattinson (2005), Ladouceur, Sylvian and Gosselin (2007), and Nowatzki and Williams (2002) self-exclusion can, if properly employed, be an invaluable responsible gambling tool. To be a valid strategy it needs to be clearly signed at the venue and information leaflets need to be made easily available (Moode and Reich 2009).

Independently of the perspective taken, every participant involved in providing gambling services for money or the consumer of gambling activities, aim to gain a profit or enjoyment from the activity. Thus, the individual pursues a recreational event and hopefully wins, the venue and the gambling industry gain an income from supplying gambling opportunities, and the government acquires gambling revenue from taxation of the gambling profit. A small part of the government's collected revenue is returned to the community through grants to counselling and support services to combat problems arisen from excessive gambling. Gambling clubs can also receive tax deductions on revenue if they support community projects identified by the local government (cf. Chapter 4.2). However, the gamblers who lost their money will not have any recourse to recoup their lost money except further gambling.

The Australasian Gaming Machine Manufacturers Association's (AGMMA) responsible gambling fact sheet from 2009 gives an insight into how gaming machines operate. They describe the operation in the following way:

> All game results are determined by a Random Number Generator (RNG). This is a 'chance machine' that selects the symbols for each game. Technology controls all aspects of the game from coin or note insertion to determining the outcome of each spin (Australasian Gaming Machine Manufacturers Association 2009).

As the outcome of any game is difficult to predict the player should expect to lose their money, especially if they play for a longer time. 'Therefore you should EXPECT to lose money in the long run, as you cannot use any form of skill to beat the machine' (Australasian Gaming Machine Manufacturers Association fact sheet 2009, emphasis in original). This is an important message emphasised by AGMMA that the person playing on gaming machines always should expect to lose their money. Furthermore, AGMMA explains in their fact sheet that people should not gamble if they are not prepared to lose the money and they should keep track of their wins and losses to know how much money they have played with. The AGMMA responsible gambling fact sheet also warns the players about drinking alcoholic beverages when playing as it can cloud their judgments. These are very sensible suggestions, but at the same time AGMMA members develop the machines to attract people to gambling through a well developed enticing design of the machines.

Table 3.5 presents a random number generation system and the theoretical scenario of the gamblers likelihood to experience a win or a loss of money played on electronic gaming machines playing a single session on an average machine.

From the table it can be concluded that at best, less than a third of players can expect to get more than 100 per cent of their money back. It is likely that the player will lose the money and if the player loses all their money on the first game, it is a 100 per cent loss. To understand that the wins are randomly produced is especially

Table 3.5 AGMMA's win and lose table – the randomly calculated hypothetical percentage of return of total amount staked that players might experience

Total units staked in a single play session*	Proportion of players experiencing more than 100% return, %	Proportion of players experiencing between 80% and 100% return, %	Proportion of players experiencing between 60% and 80% return, %	Proportion of players experiencing less than 60% return, %
$2,000	31	33	28	8
$3,000	28	41	27	4
$4,000	26	48	24	2
$5,000	24	51	24	1
$6,000	21	56	22	1
$8,000	19	63	18	0
$10,000	16	67	17	0

Note: * Assumes all games played on a single line with one coin staked per game (sd 10: mean .90) (Bet: 1 unit, one line).

Source: Based on data found at Australasian Gaming Machine Manufacturers Association fact sheet 2009; http://www.agmma.com/pdf/responsible_gaming_machine_play.pdf.

important for excessive gamblers who are likely to end their gambling session only when all their money is gambled away, including any wins gained during the gambling session. A not uncommon perception among excessive gamblers is that it is possible to change or influence the machine to deliver a win. This is not the case, all machines are programmed to give wins randomly thus the win can come anytime during the gambling session or not at all.

3.4.1 New South Wales responsible gambling strategies

Again New South Wales' responsible gambling regulations are used as an example of how such a regulation can be developed and implemented. In New South Wales the regulatory requirements for registered clubs were presented in the *Registered Clubs Amendment (Responsible Gambling) Act 2000 NSW*.[11] This legislation was complemented by the Club Safe program, which was developed by the NSW club industry association, Clubs NSW. The program includes both voluntary and mandatory strategies in management of responsible gaming. The program emphasises 'an approach where the environment in which gambling is conducted minimises harm and meets community expectations' (Clubs NSW 2000).

The *Registered Clubs Responsible Conduct of Gambling Code of Practice: Best Practice Guidelines* (Clubs NSW 2000) was approved by the Minister of Gaming and Racing in 2000 (1 May 2000). The guidelines encourage clubs to:

- Provide gambling services and practices that conform to all applicable Acts and Regulations.
- Promote responsible gambling practices that conform to local community standards and expectations.
- Establish a patron complaint resolution process.
- Implement policies to encourage responsible practices in advertising and promotions relating to gambling and ensure compliance with relevant legislation.
- Develop a policy that ensures all legislative requirements relating to cheque cashing, payment of winnings and financial transactions are implemented and encourages patrons to develop responsible practices in the use of finances for gambling purposes.
- Introduce procedures for handling personal information relating to gambling patrons in a club to protect their rights of privacy.
- Establish a pleasant and safe gambling environment.
- Inform and train staff on legislative requirements, harm minimisation issues, the risks of not complying with legislative requirements or not adopting

---

11 NSW Office of Liquor, Gaming and Racing, Department of the Arts, Sport and Recreation are reviewing the act in 2007, they commissioned the report; Prevalence of Gambling and Problem Gambling in NSW – A Community Survey 2006, published in March 2007 (ACNielsen 2007).

and practising harm minimisation strategies and taking appropriate steps to promote patron and employee care.

- Encourage patrons to take responsibility for their gambling activity through an effective self-exclusion or other mechanisms.
- Inform patrons and staff of the club's responsible gambling policy and program, the nature of gambling products and the availability of support services for problem gamblers.
- Develop links between the club and relevant community organisations that will provide support and advice for problem gamblers and their families.

These guidelines are a combination of binding, government imposed regulations, and non-binding strategies that are upheld through training and education of the staff, signage, information in venues and on gaming machines, pamphlets available to gamblers about support groups, guidelines on how to participate in self-exclusion programs and delayed payment of large wins. ATMs and EFTPOS facilities are to be located outside the gambling area, but could still be within the gambling complex. However, even with the guidelines in place, their contribution to responsible gambling is ambiguous (Hing, Dickerson and Mackellar 2001).

The Productivity Commission (1999) emphasised the need for an evidence-based approach to responsible gambling and highlighted the difficulty in validating the effectiveness of responsible gambling strategies. In 2004 the Independent Pricing and Regulatory Tribunal of New South Wales presented its assessment of issues relevant to responsible gambling in NSW, *Gambling: Promoting a Culture of Responsibility* (Independent Pricing and Regulatory Tribunal 2005), which was followed by the NSW Government Government's response, *Towards a Culture of Responsibility in Gambling* (May 2005). The Tribunal's recommendations go beyond the individual gambler and emphasise the connection between excessive gambling and health issues, an approach made already in the late 1990s by Korn and Shaffer (1999). The Tribunal's main recommendations were:

1. The governance arrangements for responsible gambling policy should be revised. The minimum change is to make the Department of Gaming and Racing (DGR) responsible for policy development including:

    - The development of responsible gambling measures that would apply to gaming machines. In future, the DGR would develop amendments to legislation or regulatory instruments. The Liquor Administration Board (LAB) would then reflect these in the Technical Standards, where applicable.
    - The policy aspects of various existing programs including counselling, research, community education and awareness and community projects which are now undertaken by the Casino Community Benefit Fund (CCBF).

2. The Government should also consider the option of transferring the administration of existing CCBF funded programs (including counselling, research, community education and awareness and community projects) from the CCBF Trust to the DGR. The CCBF Trust would continue to make recommendations to the Minister on the allocation of funds to community bodies under this option.

3. DGR should develop better linkages with the relevant areas of the Department of Health in relation to policy development for the counselling program. Consideration should also be given to the following options in relation to the administration of the counselling program:

   - better linkages with the Department of Health should be developed by either the CCBF Trust or DGR, depending on who is allocated the role of administering the program, or

   - DGR should contract with the Department of Health to administer the counselling program. The Minister for Gaming and Racing would continue to approve the program's funding.

4. The DGR should ensure it has a strong performance management system in place for the responsible gambling programs.

5. The Government should review the revised governance arrangements after five years of operation (Independent Pricing and Regulatory Tribunal 2005: 1).

The New South Wales' government accepted the main parts of the wide-ranging Independent Pricing and Regulatory Tribunal recommendations at the time of the reporting and a number of the recommendations have already been implemented while others are in the process of being implemented (New South Wales Government 2005). However, some of the recommendations were later adjusted to accommodate hardship claims by the gambling industry (see Chapter 3.3.1 *New South Wales gambling regulation*). A later review by Independent Pricing and Regulatory Tribunal concluded that:

> IPART notes that clubs do attract some favourable treatment from the NSW Government (for example, lower rates of taxation on gaming machine profits compared to hotels and higher numbers of gaming machines permitted per venue). The case for government support of the clubs industry rests principally upon the social benefits they provide and the assumption that these outweigh any costs they impose on their local communities (Independent Pricing and Regulatory Tribunal 2008: 1).

The Independent Pricing and Regulatory Tribunal's assessment of the relationship between the government and the community clubs was demonstrated in relation to the proposed increased gambling revenue taxation in 2003 and the introduction of the smoking ban in 2007. The club industry and its members were vocal protesters to the increase in taxation and introduction of a smoking ban. The clubs managed to water down the taxation and delay the introduction of the smoking ban. It can therefore be assumed that Club NSW is an active lobby group and political force in the development of government gambling policy and regulation. The gaming industry's contribution to the economy with tax revenue and employment of community residents are important factors for the NSW government and reflected in the frequent proposed amendments to gambling policy, gambling regulation and responsible gambling guidelines. The social benefits are often clearly identified while the negative aspects of excessive gambling are less clearly articulated, partly influenced by NSW government's lack of transparency in making available comprehensive gambling data, thus restricting longitudinal scholarly research of gambling.

3.5 Promotion of gambling

In the twenty-first century, globalisation, individualism, and the emphasis on material goods – the urge to have it 'today' with or without the financial means – make gambling an attractive way to access money. The dream of becoming a 'millionaire' is present in many consumption societies. The illusory nature of the carefree lifestyle offered by gambling advertising is perceived by some to be a viable route out of poverty, isolation, unemployment, and financial despair.

The publicity and promotion of gambling is enhanced by its legality and the public acceptance of gambling as a recreational pursuit. Gambling advertisements are found in mass and ether media and in local shopping centres. It is not only the agents for gambling commerce that advertise gambling products, state governments, who are the ultimate owners of the gambling products such as lottery games, also advertise their products (e.g. Australia – NSW Lottery, Sweden – Spelinstitutet, UK – National Lottery). The influence of gambling advertisements however remains unclear according to Griffiths (2005).

The popularity and public acceptance of gambling might work to convince some people into thinking that gambling is an easy way to create a financially secure future. Chasing 'the big win' that will turn everything around is part of many people's dreams – an ultimately elusive dream nevertheless. Inherent in many cultures is an emphasis on being rich, having an easy lifestyle, having access to financial resources and being able to effortlessly provide for family and relatives. However, hoping for the big win has a much more common downside. Excessive gambling contributes to family breakdown, loss of employment (Fabiansson 2007) and can ultimately lead to homelessness (Fabiansson 2003). The principle of the gambling system is that more people lose money through gambling than win money (cf. Chapter 3.4, Table 3.5, about the probability of winning on gaming machines). The prospect of taking a shortcut to prosperity through gambling is a delusion that is present among many people but perhaps more so among young people and people from disadvantaged backgrounds. Young people who feel that they have missed out on education and work prospects might be enticed into gambling. Their ability to amass the equivalent of a large gaming machine or lottery win through a lifetime of work is minute. The trap of excessive gambling is nevertheless not illusory, but a reality for a significant number of people, especially for young people starting gambling well before their legal age (Derevensky and Gupta 2004a). The following interview highlights the reality of a life where gambling has taken over:

> I have had gambling problems for the last nine years betting on horses. My gambling has caused me to appear before the courts on no less than four occasions. I have been homeless many times and my life has become unmanageable. When I am gambling, I do not think of the consequences, I don't care about anything else. I have readily blown my rent and food money to have one more chance to win. It doesn't worry me. My second wife has left with the two children, both under three years of age. Even so, all I can dream of is the big win which will turn my life around for the better (Blaszczynski 1998: 18).

Advertising is a part of any business' strategy to entice customers and gambling venues are no exception. Gambling venues are designed to be welcoming with friendly staff serving affordable beverages and food, a secure place for every customer to gamble and socialise as well as an attractive place to visit. The design of gambling venues emphasises the perception of inclusiveness – a place where ethnicity and gender are not relevant, they are welcoming places where time becomes distorted. The lack of natural light through windows and of prominent wall clocks, gives patrons no real sense of time spent in the venue nor time spent gambling. The gambling and club industries have succeeded in making gambling venues attractive places to visit and the 'luxuriousness' of some of the larger venues creates an atmosphere where people can feel a sense of status and importance. This may be particularly the perception when a person takes their friends to a prominent club or casino (Victorian Casino and Gaming Authority 2001: 15).

To be seen at a high status club or casino enhances their image as a successful person (Tanasornnarong, Jackson and Thomas 2004). This is especially important in some cultures where gambling success may be afforded a superstitious meaning. The purpose of the visit to the casino or club is often primarily to partake in social recreational gambling, to be with friends and especially to be seen by others in order to create an image of success. The non-judgemental, warm and welcoming atmosphere created in casinos and local community clubs are features that are in stark contrast to the general circumstances of young men of Middle Eastern and Asian backgrounds living in Australian and other western societies, where they struggle to gain acceptance. For a student or an unemployed person with a considerable amount of 'free' time, avoiding the feeling of isolation, loneliness, boredom, or being a target

Global Gambling and Regulation of Gambling 73

for harassment, local community clubs and even city casinos can be seen as safe havens, where a person can seek both protection and status (Binde 2006).

The elusiveness of winning at gambling is well known. The shame of losing and the unwillingness to admit escalating gambling debts is a core problem. Shame is associated with losing face and respect among members of the community. Loneliness and social isolation feed gambling interests, and when gambling becomes excessive, it is a private matter kept within the family or even only to the person involved (Tanasornnarong et al. 2004). Unemployment, loneliness and lack of meaningful activities were emphasised as reasons for gambling within the Greater Western Sydney Arabic speaking communities (Arabic speaking gambling counsellor October 2006; Fabiansson 2007).

Expectations and responsibilities are part of any social network. This is perhaps especially relevant to community groups during cultural and family celebrations, where gambling is an integral part of the celebration, for example the Lunar Year – New Year celebrations. The gambling that takes place is perhaps not appropriate to the financial situation of the person, but where gambling is a social expectation, it is difficult for a person not to participate, as it would lead to loss of status in the community group (Fabiansson 2007).

3.6 People affected by gambling

According to the Productivity Commission (2009) 75 per cent of the Australian adult population gamble annually and 5 per cent of them gamble on gaming machines. Fifteen per cent of the people gambling on gaming machines are problem gamblers and responsible for approximately 40 per cent of gaming machine spending. Another 15 per cent of gaming machine players are moderate risks gamblers. The main group of gamblers do a variety of things, from buying a lottery ticket, betting on a horse race, gambling on casino tables and/or gambling using the internet. In 2006, the NSW Office of Liquor, Gaming and Racing, Department of the Arts, Sport and Recreation commissioned a survey presented in the report; *Prevalence of Gambling and Problem Gambling in NSW* (ACNielsen 2007). The survey found that in NSW, the most gambling prolific state in Australia, 69 per cent of the NSW adult population gambled at least once during the 12 months before the survey was conducted. This 2006 survey reported a decrease of approximately 11 percentage points in the number of gamblers compared with the 1999 Productivity Commission report (80.4 per cent) and six percentage points below the Productivity Commission assessment in 2009. These decreases, in the number of people gambling, occurred despite an increase in gambling opportunities and gambling revenue in the period since the Productivity Commission's research in the late 1990s.

It should be acknowledged that the NSW prevalence survey (ACNielsen 2007: 8) based their classification of gambling on the Canadian Problem Gambling Index (CPGI) (Ferris and Wynne 2002), while Productivity Commission (1999: xii–xiii, sections 6.2–6.3) relied on the South Oaks Gambling Screen (SOGS) (Lesieur and Blume 1987), thus some differences in results are the consequence of the use of these two different screens (cf. Chapter 2.1). Furthermore, the Productivity Commission used different (independent) sources of research for their report, while the NSW Office of Liquor, Gaming and Racing, Department of the Arts, Sport and Recreation commissioned the ACNielsen report. The findings are based on the participants' self-assessment of their own gambling and experience of problems during the preceding 12 months. It is well known that people with a gambling problem underestimate their own gambling and the severity of their problems, thus the reliability and response rate, (often between 30 and 40 per cent) is an issue for surveys using telephone interviews to cover sensitive issues (Productivity Commission 1999; Volberg 2004). The ACNielsen (2007: 150) survey gained only 15.4 per cent completed questionnaires (N= 5,026 responses, sample 32,676).

The NSW prevalence survey found that 0.8 per cent of the NSW adult population falls within the problem gambling group. A further 1.6 per cent is considered to be moderate risk gamblers and 2.1 per cent low risk gamblers, equating to 4.5 per cent of the population with some level of gambling risk (ACNielsen 2007: 9). The Productivity Commission (1999) assessment of pathological gamblers and at-risk gamblers Australia wide (1997–98) amounted to 2.1 per cent of the total population (292,737 people) and for New South Wales the corresponding percentage was 2.55 per cent (122,300 people). In 2006, the NSW prevalence percentage was the next highest after Victoria. NSW recorded a prevalence rate of 3.93 per cent (CPGI 3+), Victoria 4.19 per cent (2008) Queensland 3.09 per cent (2006) Northern Territory 2.77 per cent (2005) South Australia 2.36 per cent (2005), and Tasmania 1.96 per cent (2007). The average percentage across Australia was 3.05 per cent (Productivity Commission 2009: 4.27).

Additionally the NSW ACNielsen report states that 64.5 per cent of the adult population are non-problem gamblers and 31 per cent do not participate in any form of gambling. According to the NSW study, participation in gambling activities was highest for lottery products (56 per cent), followed by electronic gaming machines (31 per cent) and betting on horse and dog races (20 per cent). Around one in 10 of the NSW adult population participate in Keno (11 per cent) and sports betting (8 per cent) and 5 per cent or fewer participate in table casino games, private card games and internet casino games (ACNielsen 2007: 9).

The NSW ACNielsen report concluded that lottery products attract the highest participation rate; they are just as likely or more likely to be purchased by non-problem gamblers (85 per cent) as those identified as risk gamblers (77 per cent). Previous research has confirmed the role of electronic gaming machines in problem gambling. This was acknowledged in the NSW ACNielsen report, which found that 95 per cent of problem gamblers and 87 per cent of moderate risk gamblers were significantly more likely to use electronic gaming machines than the 69 per cent of non-problem gamblers (ACNielsen 2007: 9; Productivity Commission 2009; cf. Chapter 6). The ACNielsen Report concludes:

While the results indicate that gambling does not negatively impact on the majority of the NSW adult population, just under 5 per cent are at risk of gambling problems. For 0.8 per cent of the population, their level of risk falls in the problem gambling category (as defined by the [Canadian Problem Gambling Index] CPGI). However, it is important to recognise that all 'at risk' gamblers (moderate/problem) manifest gambling problems, not just the 'problem gambling' group. The CPGI categories are compatible with a public health approach which recognises that gambling problems can occur along a continuum of harm. It is therefore important to recognise all degrees of problems along the gambling continuum (ACNielsen 2007: 141).

Furthermore, in summary the NSW ACNielsen report (2007) states that gamblers positioned at the higher end of the gambling risk continuum tend to have higher gambling participation rates across most gambling activities (with the exception of lottery products). These gamblers participated in a greater number of activities, 60 per cent of those 'at risk' participated in four or more activities in the preceding 12 months compared with 34 per cent of the low risk group. The 'at risk' gamblers participated more frequently and gambled at least once a week. They played electronic gaming machines at least once a week with 71 per cent of those 'at risk' compared with 63 per cent of the low risk gamblers involved in this activity. They also played for longer durations, at least one hour. Sixty-one per cent of 'at risk' gamblers usually spent one or more hours playing electronic gaming machines on each occasion compared with 37 per cent of low risk gamblers. This pattern particularly applied to problem gamblers playing electronic gaming machines. Problem gamblers, who played electronic gaming machines, did so at least weekly, and 80 per cent of these gamblers spent one or more hours playing on each occasion (ACNielsen 2007: 9).

The percentage of people gambling to excess can be seen as being low however the Productivity Commission (1999: 7.34) estimated that another 7.3 people (in 2009 Productivity Commission estimated an average of 7.5), other than the gambler, are affected by adverse consequences of the gambling, including the family, friends, work colleagues and the wider community. If this scenario is used to estimate how many people are affected, a calculation based on the percentages of 0.8 high risk, 1.6 at moderate risk and 2.1 at low of risk problem gamblers, according to the NSW survey (ACNielsen 2007) would indicate that there are 38,947 high risk gamblers, 77,894 moderate risk gamblers and 102,235 low risk gamblers among people between 18 and 84 year olds living in NSW (N=4,868,344) (Australian Bureau of Statistics 2006c).[12] To apply the Productivity Commission's estimate of adversely affected people another 7.3 people would be adversely affected by excessive gambling, thus another 290,832 (high risk), 568,626 (moderate risk) or 746,315 (low risk) people in NSW would be negatively affected by gambling for

---

12   Calculated on people 18 to 84 year olds, 4,868,344, out of a total population of 6,549,177.

shorter or longer periods. Totalling the numbers, 219,076 gamblers and 1,599,258 people associated with the gamblers would be affected by a person gambling at levels assessed as ranging from high to low risk. If these estimates show the real consequences of gambling, and that gamblers in all risk groups, fluctuate between excessive, controlled and recreational gambling, then the total number of people belonging to the gambler's family, friends and community negatively affected by gambling (annually), could in fact exceed the above calculated number of people affected by gambling at any one time.

Adversity of this magnitude would normally be of concern for governments, commercial interests and social services. The gambling industry presents a dilemma because it creates employment opportunities, provides entertainment, supports local communities and provides governments with enormous tax revenues as well as contributing to the problem of excessive gambling – it would however be difficult to find another recreational activity with such negative impact on people.

Research shows that a person's gambling problems are often not the only issues the person is battling. The excessive gambler frequently displays compounded problems; emotional, mental, relationship and social issues (Blaszczynski and Nower 2002). Even if for the majority of people, gambling activities have an entertainment value; it can be different for people with multiple problems. Their gambling can be used as a safety valve to forget other difficulties. While inevitably their excessive gambling will lead to financial and other troubles, the gambling session creates a period of perceived relief. The reality that gambling pursuits do not solve problems but rather exacerbate compound problems, can be irrelevant for the excessive gambler, time spent gambling is time to cherish each day.

In conclusion, it is difficult for many excessive gamblers to acknowledge that they have a problem with gambling, to admit it to their family and to seek professional help. To seek professional gambling help is often the last recourse for excessive gamblers and it is often not done until family members or employers demand they attend counselling programs in order to save the family, relationships or employment (cf. Chapter 6). Thus the real impact of gambling on the individual, the family and the community is difficult to estimate.

3.7 Conclusion

This chapter explored the global gambling phenomenon and the associated gambling industry on the one hand and gambling regulation and responsible gambling guidelines on the other. Organised gambling in the form of popular lotteries can be found in at least 200 jurisdictions, many other gambling forms are equally widespread providing entertainment and excitement, but the chapter also pointed to the related problem of excessive gambling. It highlighted the double role of governments as regulators and receivers of revenue through taxation of gambling. Additionally, governments introduce, promote and rely on lottery systems as an accepted form of gambling to support public projects, such as hospitals, community services and schools, and sports facilities in relation to arranging big events like the Olympic Games.

Statistics summarised in the chapter show that many gambling forms are on the increase. Lottery sales have increased over the past few years in many parts of the world with a decrease seen only in Central and South America and the Caribbean. Horse racing, a traditional form of gambling, continues to be a popular form of gambling for many people, with a betting turnover of A$140,198 million in 2006. In 2007, it is an increasing pastime in Korea, Turkey and the United Arab Emirates, while a decline was seen in Macau, Brazil and Japan.

Lottery systems, is the gambling type enjoyed by a majority of people, while gambling on gaming machines is less popular but creates adverse effects to the largest group of people. There are extensive data about the number of gaming machines and types of gaming machines globally, but not of the expenditure for the respective countries or regions, as was presented in this chapter for lottery products and horse racing (cf. Australasian Gaming Council 2008; Taylor Nelson Sofres 2008, 2006, 2004).

The regulation of gambling products was introduced historically when the common people began to participate in gambling activities (cf. Chapter 1.4). One of the most universal restrictions on gambling participation is the age. However, research shows that young people are often introduced to gambling well before the legal age for participation. Although governments may have the best intentions when trying to regulate gambling, their efforts have not diminished the occurrence of excessive gambling and gambling problems are still very much part of the gambling industry. The balance between regulating the gambling industry, protecting the gambler and governments' gambling revenue appears difficult to attain. Looking at the sheer size of gambling expenditure and governments' tax revenue from gambling pursuits, it can be concluded that the gaming industry is an influential, economically strong and potentially powerful lobby group at all levels of government (cf. Independent Pricing and Regulatory Tribunal 2008). Their strong position has also allowed them to be influential in the creation of gambling policy and regulation of the industry (cf. Productivity Commission 2009).

The chapter also reviewed policies for responsible gambling and the introduction of codes of practice as ways of protecting vulnerable individuals from the effects of excessive gambling. The intention of these policies is to create an environment where individuals, communities, the gambling industry and governments gain a shared understanding of their rights and responsibilities in relation to responsible gambling practices. The gambling industry is encouraged to provide a safe and supportive environment for the delivery of gambling products and services; a setting where customers can make informed decisions about their gambling practices. The assumption is that through regulating and introducing harm minimising strategies, the detrimental effects of gambling experienced by individuals and the broader community can be contained and minimised and individuals adversely affected by gambling are given access to timely and appropriate assistance and information to manage their problems. Nonetheless, gambling is a commercial venture promoted as a recreational activity and gambling environments are conducive to continuous playing. It is therefore a difficult matter to create safe gambling practices without affecting the overall gambling revenue. A strategy that addresses both sets of incompatible needs appears to be currently unattainable.

Chapter 4 looks closely at gambling in Australia across the different states and territories, with particular attention paid to the scope of gambling in New South Wales.

Chapter 4
Gambling in Australia

4.1 Introduction

Australia's public and legal gambling history began in the early nineteenth century (Table 4.1) with horse racing and the first publicly organised race meeting was held in New South Wales in 1810. Races had been run previously but this was an officially sanctioned race followed by a ball, thus a social event. The Melbourne Cup, an internationally recognised race, was first organised in Victoria in 1861. The race is still run on the first Tuesday in November each year as part of the Victorian Spring Racing Carnival and it is a major social event in Australia. Lotteries were introduced in the early twentieth century. The Queensland Government was the first to establish a lottery scheme – the Golden Casket Lottery in 1920. Gaming machines were legalised through a licence arrangement in New South Wales clubs in the middle of the twentieth century, but they had been introduced to Australia in the 1920s. The first casino in Australia was opened in Tasmania, the Wrest Point Hotel Casino in 1973, followed by a casino in the Northern Territory in 1979 (MGM Grand Darwin, later Sky City Casino). The first online regulated and land based casino in Australia (Lasseters) began its operation from the Northern Territory (Alice Springs) in 1999.

In Australia, as in many other countries, the expansion of gambling has been extensive since the 1990s with the introduction of electronic gaming machines into hotels and casinos, having been introduced into Australian clubs in 1956. Gaming machines were not originally legal in hotels as they did not have the same community focus and type of community engagement as clubs. For clubs, gambling revenue was seen as essential for their continued existence while hotels relied more on serving beer and other alcohol. The gaming machines of the 1950s were very different from the twenty-first century electronic gaming machines. The old machines were slow, took low value coins and were operated by dragging a handle downwards. Modern electronic gaming machines are highly sophisticated computer programmed machines. They give the gambler the possibility of playing several lines of games simultaneously, take coins and notes, the speed of the game is high, and the encouraging gambling environment all contribute to 'making money disappear' very quickly, sometimes without the gambler realising it (Productivity Commission 2009). The modern technically advanced gaming machines can be programmed to give small wins to maintain excitement and keep the gambler hopeful of a larger win. Caps introduced on electronic gaming machines intended to restrict access to gambling has often had its benefit offset by machines that are

Table 4.1 History of gambling in Australia

Year	Gambling introduction
1809–10	First organised race meet in Australia (New South Wales)
1861	First Melbourne Cup run in Victoria
1879–80	Tote first introduced in Australia (South Australia)
1915–16	First automatic totalisator machine installed in Australia (Western Australia)
1920–21	Golden Casket lotteries established in Queensland as the first government-run lottery in Australia
1930–40	'SP' [starting price] bookies flourish in most Australian states
1942–45	Race meeting and lotteries restricted due to the Second World War
1955–56	Poker machines legalised in licensed clubs in New South Wales
1960–61	Victoria the first state to legalise TAB off-course betting
1965–66	South Australia the last state to introduce state-run lotteries following a referendum
1972–73	First casino in Australia opened in Tasmania; Minor gaming [raffles, bingo, lucky envelopes] introduced in South Australia
1973–74	Lotto introduced in South Australia; Minor gaming introduced in Tasmania
1974–75	Pools introduced in Victoria; TAB introduced in Tasmania
1975–76	Pools introduced in New South Wales, Queensland and Tasmania
1976–77	Lotteries, lotto and gaming machines introduced in the Australian Capital Territory
1977–78	Minor gaming introduced in Victoria; Off-course bookmakers phased out in Tasmania
1978–79	Instant lotteries introduced in South Australia; Lotto introduced in Western Australia and the Northern Territory; On-course/off-course bookmakers, lotteries, pools and minor gaming introduced in the Northern Territory
1979–80	Lotto introduced in New South Wales; Pools introduced in the Australian Capital Territory; On-course totalisator and instant lotteries introduced in the Northern Territory; First casino opened in the Northern Territory
1980–81	Pools introduced in South Australia; Lotteries re-introduced in Tasmania
1981–82	Lotto introduced in Queensland; Instant lotteries introduced in Victoria, Tasmania and the Australian Capital Territory
1982–83	Instant lotteries introduced in New South Wales and Western Australia
1984–85	Instant lotteries introduced in Queensland; Pools introduced in Western Australia
1985–86	First casino opened in Queensland, South Australia and Western Australia; TAB introduced in the Northern Territory
1988–89	Minor gaming introduced in Western Australia

Table 4.1   Continued

Year	Gambling introduction	Year	Gambling introduction	Year	Gambling introduction	Year	Gambling introduction
1989–90	Lotteries phased out in South Australia	1990–91	Gaming machines introduced in Victoria and the Northern Territory Off-course bookmakers phased out in the Northern Territory Minor gaming introduced in Queensland Minor gaming phased out in the Northern Territory	1991–92	Gaming machines introduced in Queensland Keno introduced in New South Wales and South Australia	1992–93	Lotteries phased out in Western Australia Casino opened in the Australian Capital Territory
1993–94	Keno introduced in Victoria	1994–95	Casino opened in Victoria Gaming machines introduced in South Australia Keno introduced in Tasmania Sports betting introduced in New South Wales, Victoria, South Australia, Western Australia, Tasmania and the Northern Territory	1995–96	Casino opened in New South Wales Minor gaming phased out in Victoria Sports betting introduced in Queensland and the Australian Capital Territory	1996–97	Gaming machines introduced in Tasmania
1997–98	Keno introduced in Queensland	1998–99	Interactive gambling introduced in the Northern Territory Productivity Commission releases landmark study of gambling in Australia	1999–00	Interactive gambling introduced in Queensland and Tasmania Australian Gaming Council formed	2005–06	Betting exchange licensed and begins operation in Tasmania

Source: Based on data found at Winter, G. (2002), *Gambling: An Australian Tradition on the Up!* Department of the Parliamentary Library, Research Paper no. 14 2001–2002, Statistics Group, 14 May 2002; Australian Institute for Gambling Research (1999) Australian Gambling Comparative History and Analysis, Report prepared for Victorian Casino and Gaming Authority, Melbourne, October 1999, University of Western Sydney; Australasian Gaming Council 2008: 225–6.

82 *Pathways to Excessive Gambling*

more sophisticated, thus the gambling capacity has increased rather than decreased (cf. Delfabbro 2008; Productivity Commission 2009).

Electronic gaming machines have become one of the easiest ways to lose money at clubs and hotels. Even if people can lose substantial amounts of money on horse racing and casino table games, the electronic gaming machines affect a larger group of people (Productivity Commission 2009), especially people from the lower middle and lower socio-economic classes, people who have less financial resources to sustain frequent gambling losses. Electronic gaming machine gambling is also accessible for longer time periods than most other recreational activities. In New South Wales, clubs only close for six hours per 24 hours, some only close for 3 hours per day (often during normal low patronage times), which makes it possible to gamble for 18 to 21 hours seven days a week at local community clubs (NSW Office of Liquor, Gaming and Racing 2009a). In local gambling venues such as community clubs and hotels, gaming machine gambling is an easily accessible gambling form – a visit to a local club needs few arrangements.

Gaming machines have grown in popularity both among suppliers and gamblers. In Australia they have become a defining feature of club culture. An overview of gambling in Australia shows that the turnover on gaming machines is almost six times higher than for wagering and casino gambling, thus the highest gambling turnover is derived from gaming machine gambling. Adult spending is also highest within this gambling form. While the participation rate is highest for lotteries, the expenditure on lottery products per adult is one sixth of the spending on gaming machine gambling. The taxation on gaming machines is 2.6 per cent of turnover, while the taxation on lottery products is 27.3 per cent of turnover, thus lottery products are the highest taxed gambling form in Australia (Table 4.2).[1]

In Australia, gaming machines gambling has the highest turnover of all gambling forms with $107,924 million (Table 4.2). This corresponds to an average adult spending of $663 annually on gaming machine gambling. The next highest average spending on gambling by adult gamblers is within casinos, including wagers on table games, gaming machines and keno systems, with $187 annually. The overall participation rate is highest for lottery products, where 60 per cent of adults participate followed by gaming machines with 39 per cent.

The following chapter will explore the significance of the low ratio between gaming machines and people in Australia, particularly in New South Wales (cf. Chapter 3, Table 3.3), a situation that makes access to gambling opportunities effortless. We will also look at the clubs' (predominantly sports clubs) role as providers of pre-school up to elite sports programs, their involvement in community support projects, and the clubs' role as the main facilitator of social entertainment, hospitality and gambling opportunities in residential areas with a mainly low socio-economic profile.

---

1   In Chapter 4 all monetary values are shown in Australian dollars.

Table 4.2 Gambling turnover, participation rate and number of businesses in Australia 2005–06 (Australian dollar)

Gambling form	Turnover $m[1]	Adults participation %[2]	Spend per adult $[1,3]	Total spend $m[1,3]	Businesses N[4]	Tax $m[1]
Wagering[5]	17,705	24[6]	148	2,323	4,652[7]	384
Gaming machines[8]	107,924	39	663	10,381	5,833[9]	2,849
Lotteries[10]	4,006	60	107	1,683	4,756[11]	1,093
Casinos[12]	17,637[13]	10[14]	187	2,930	13	361
Other[15]	1,295	na	16	258	na	7
Total	148,567	82	1,123	17,575	15,254[5]	4,694

Note: 1) Refers to 2005–06, Office of Economic and Statistical Research (2007), Australian Gambling Statistics 2005–06; 2) Refers to 1997–98, Productivity Commission (1999); 3) Due to rounding total may not equal sum of individual values; 4) Refers to number of businesses providing gambling services within venues. 5) Includes racing and sports betting; 6) Bet on horse or greyhound race in the previous 12 months; 7) Includes TAB facilities in retail outlets (standalone shops), clubs, pubs, taverns, hotels, casinos, on course and other; 8) Does not include gaming machines in clubs and hotels; 9) State/territory Gaming Authority annual reports; 10) Includes lottery, lotto, tattslotto and instant lottery and pools; 11) Industry interviews (as at January 2008); 12) Includes wagers on table games, gaming machines and keno systems; 13) Caution should be taken in interpreting casino turnover as this represents 'handle' (rather than true turnover); 14) Played table games at a casino; 15) Includes minor gaming, interactive gaming and keno.

Source: Based on data found at Australasian Gaming Council 2008: 1–2.

4.2 Local clubs' role in the community

Community clubs in Australia are often established to meet a particular community need. This may be to support a local community issue or cause, it may provide a meeting place for working people, or a place where local sports interested people can congregate and practice their sports activities; 'groups of people having a common interest who have bonded together to pursue or promote that interest' (Registered Clubs Association of NSW 1999: 5). In the early stages, committed people contribute in a voluntary capacity to the club and for the benefit of club members, and also for the broader community. The club structure is based on personal membership arrangements, all visitors within a five kilometre radius need to be club members to visit the club, while people living further away can visit without being members, but need to register as visitors. The clubs are organised around local social, cultural, ethnic, professional and sports interests and they aim to service local, cultural, sports, leisure and entertainment interests. The different clubs in Australia are mainly not-for-profit organisations (Registered Clubs Association of NSW 1994).

In 2004, approximately 88 per cent (1,375 clubs) of the clubs in New South Wales were registered members with Clubs NSW. The membership share increased to 90 per cent in 2007, while the number of clubs decreased to 1,359 (The Allen Consulting Group 2008: v). The most common type of clubs registered in NSW in 2007, were bowling clubs (34 per cent), Returned Services League of Australia (RSL) and ex-servicemen's clubs (21 per cent), golf clubs (18 per cent), sporting and recreational clubs (10 per cent), league/football/soccer (5 per cent), ethnic/religious (3 per cent), communities/workers clubs (2 per cent), and other clubs whose shared interests are described as graphic arts, social, business people, cultural, and music (6 per cent) (The Allen Consulting Group 2008: 8).

The membership base in NSW clubs in 2004 was approximately 4.8 million and in 2007, the membership base increased to 5.5 million members (The Allen Consulting Group 2004: 8, 2008: 9). In 2007, the smallest club, a rural bowling club reported 24 members and the largest club accounted for 76,597 members. On average clubs have approximately 6,000 members, although 73 per cent of the clubs reported fewer than 6,000 members. These figures underline the high number of small clubs often in rural and regional communities, area where the club is the only social recreational venue in the community, apart from the hotel (The Allen Consulting Group 2008: 9).

People can be members of more than one club at the same time and it is common that people are members of several clubs as the benefits outweigh the cost of the membership fee, about $10 to $15 annually. The NSW clubs with the highest number of members are Returned Services League/services clubs with 34 per cent of the total club membership, followed by the league/football sports clubs (16 per cent), the communities/workers clubs (14 per cent), the sporting and recreational clubs, and bowling clubs (each 13 per cent), ethnic/religious and golf clubs (each 4 per cent) and other clubs 2 per cent of the total club membership (The Allen Consulting Group 2008: 10).

A casino licence was granted to Sydney Harbour Casino in 1994. A temporary casino was opened in 1995 and from 1997 in its permanent Pyrmont location. With the licensing of the StarCity Casino in Sydney, gaming machine licences were extended to include hotels and the casino. NSW hotels were initially allowed to have a limited number of electronic gaming machines, up to 15 per hotel. This changed a year later with hotels allowed to have up to 30 gaming machines while the casino was allocated 1,500 gaming machines. The hotels had been allowed since 1984 to have a limited number of 'amusement devices' which is a form of gaming machine or slot machine, however slower and with lower values of money involved. Despite the opening of the market for electronic gaming machines to hotels and casinos the registered clubs in NSW have retained their dominance in electronic gaming machine gambling.

A club's income is based on revenue from gaming machines, other gambling activities such as TAB, and Keno, and to a lesser extent from food and bar services (Productivity Commission 2009). Membership fees and ancillary business activities make up the rest. Clubs total revenue in 2003 was approximately $4.6 billion, which was an increase since 1999 with 4.2 per cent per annum. The revenue was estimated to be $5.4 billion in 2007, a 16 per cent increase since 2003, or an annual growth of 4.1 per cent (The Allen Consulting Group 2008: 15). Thirty-eight per cent of the clubs with gaming facilities earn more than one million dollars each from gaming revenue (The Allen Consulting Group 2004: 32). In 2007, the gaming revenue component of the income had decreased by 5 per cent since 2003, but still the gaming revenue made up 63 per cent of the clubs total revenue. Membership, food and bar sales increased, especially for smaller clubs since 2003 (The Allen Consulting Group 2008: 15).

The social contribution to the local community by NSW clubs is estimated to be $1.8 billion per year, including clubs' cash support, in-kind support, and total taxation paid (The Allen Consulting Group 2004: 56).[2] In 2007, clubs in NSW supported local community projects with $89 million in cash grants and donations and approximately $20 million in in-kind support, in total $108 million. Since 2003, the community support has increased by about 5.5 per cent per year or approximately $5.5 million (The Allen Consulting Group 2008: 47).

The clubs organise a range of entertainment activities such as live entertainment, music and plays, but they also cater for the wider community with conferences and private function facilities. The clubs' non-gambling activities are subsidised by gambling revenue thus clubs are able to offer competitive hospitality rates and attractive deals for governments, community groups and private functions on an occasional or regular basis (Fabiansson 2007).

Larger clubs with electronic gaming machines are required to support local activities to gain tax concessions. Local committees define local needs based around the community's development support expenditure model (CDSE) and derived from funding priorities identified in the local government area:

> The Community Development and Support Expenditure (CDSE) Scheme is designed to ensure that larger registered clubs in NSW contribute to the provision of front-line services to their local communities; and to ensure that the disadvantaged in the community are better positioned to benefit from the substantial contributions made by those clubs.

> The Gaming Machine Tax Act 2001 outlines the legislative arrangements for the granting of a rebate of gaming machine tax levied on registered clubs. Under the Act, a tax rebate is made available to registered clubs of up to 1.5 per cent of their gaming machine profits over $1 million provided that the Casino, Liquor and Gaming Control Authority (the Authority) is satisfied that an equivalent amount has been applied to expenditure on

---

2 A change in calculation methodology makes it difficult to compare the 2007 expenditure figure of total contribution $1.1 billion with the 2003 figure of $1.8 billion as the new calculation does not include the total taxation paid by clubs in NSW and therefore can not be compared (The Allen Consulting Group 2008: 44).

community development and support. In the Act, a distinction is made between two classes of expenditure:

Category 1   expenditure on specific community welfare and social services, community development, community health services and employment assistance activities;
Category 2   expenditure on other community development and support services.

To qualify for the gaming machine tax rebate of 1.5 per cent, clubs must contribute at least 50 per cent of those funds to Category 1 purposes, with the remainder allocated to Category 2 purposes. Category 1 expenditure in excess of 50 per cent may be used to cover shortfalls in Category 2, but the reverse does not apply. (NSW Department of Gaming and Racing, Gaming 2004: 1; New South Wales Office of Liquor, Gaming and Racing 2009c: 4)

When electronic gaming machines were allowed into hotels and later into casinos in NSW, it changed the clubs' monopoly on gaming machines and they experienced a financial setback due to their reliance on gambling income to subsidise club activities. The second issue that gave rise to much anger among club operators was the proposed increase in 2003 in the tax on gambling revenue; however, in 2006 the clubs' operators together with their large membership base, after an intense campaign, managed to lobby the NSW government to reduce the '2003 gambling tax'. The ban on smoking in enclosed areas came into force in July 2007, but the definition of 'an enclosure' was amended to a 75 per cent or less enclosure for a smoking ban to be enforced at a club or at a hotel (New South Wales Government, Department of Health 2009). Governments are well aware of the large membership base, which makes clubs important lobby groups in all regulatory affairs, especially in what the clubs classify as 'adverse regulation' (Independent Pricing and Regulatory Tribunal 2008: 1).

Australia wide casinos contributed in 2004–05 with $29.5 million in levies to state governments' community benefit schemes, an increase of 6.8 per cent or $1.9 million from the 2002–03 period, when they contributed $27.7 million. Outside the levies, the casinos made voluntary contributions of $6.7 million. The highest amount went to sponsorship of cultural and sporting events ($3.4 million). In NSW, clubs contributed with $51.8 million through the CDSE scheme in 2004–05 and $71.5 million in 2007 (Clubs NSW supplied figures; Australian Gaming Council 2007: 43). The community support scheme, CDSE, and voluntary contributions are often used to highlight community clubs' benefit for community sports and cultural events. For any proposed restrictions, like the introduction of a ban on smoking, increase in taxation or expected downturn in profits, the community support program is always mentioned as something the clubs would need to restrict to maintain their financial viability. In reality the clubs only give a small percentage of their total net revenue to local activities and for any contribution under the community development and support expenditure scheme the clubs receive a tax deduction, a circumstance rarely highlighted in the debate about financial viability.

4.3 Adult gambler profile

To reiterate, it was estimated in the 1999 Productivity Commission review that annually approximately 80 per cent of adult Australians gamble for money, which is legal for people 18 years of age and older in Australia. In the 2009 Productivity Commission review this rate had fallen to 75 per cent. In 1999, two out of five gamblers gambled regularly and of the regular gamblers nearly one in five gambled periodically at an unsustainable level (Productivity Commission 1999, 2009). In the 2009 Productivity Commission review, the lottery and 'scratchies' gamblers, which are the majority of all gamblers, where excluded from the calculations as these forms of gambling are not seen as causing severe gambling problems. It was estimated in 2009 that 15 per cent of gamblers gambled regularly (gambled at least weekly or more on a gambling form other than lotteries and scratchies) and approximately 15 per cent of the regular gamblers were classified as problem gamblers with an additional 15 per cent as moderate risk gamblers, in total 30 per cent as problem or moderate risk gamblers of the regular gamblers gambling on gaming machines. Overall, they estimated that 5 per cent of adults play weekly or more often on gaming machines and of these – classified as problem gamblers (15 per cent) contribute to 40 per cent of total spending. In total it was estimated that 125,000 adults (0.75 per cent) in Australia were problem gamblers and a further 290,000 were moderate risk gamblers (1.7 per cent) (Productivity Commission 2009: xiv, xxi). For every excessive gambler it is anticipated that another 7.3 people close to the gambler, family, friends and work colleagues are affected by the gambling. In the Productivity Commission review in 2009 between five and 10 people (average 7.5) were estimated to be negatively affected by a close person's excessive gambling, thus a slight increase from the 1999 assessment of people negatively affected by gambling.

It is a fraught task to try to categorise the gambler, as the majority of Australians participate in gaming activities, if lottery products are included. Walker (1992), among others, has suggested sociological categories of gamblers. Walker suggests regular players, part-time players, professional and serious players, this places the gambling frequency in a social context. Gamblers can also be categorised as recreational or excessive gamblers in relation to their financial means. Irrespective of classification, it is imperative to be aware that a gambler is not static in his or her gambling pursuits, but moves easily between the different gambling stages – from controlled gambling to excessive gambling. Recreational gamblers, who gamble within their means can, due to personal or work related factors, change their gambling behaviour and pass through a number of gambling stages to ultimately gamble beyond their monetary circumstances. This might follow a course from gambling as a social leisure activity, among other recreational activities, to a level of gambling where it is their main leisure activity. The group of gamblers who gamble at excessive levels are a fluid group with some gamblers gambling periodically at unsustainable levels, while at other times controlling their gambling. Consequently, the number of people affected by the adverse effects of gambling is larger than the estimated percentages indicate (Productivity Commission 1999, 2009).

Research exploring the gender, age and socio-economic profile of gamblers and type of gambling is limited, but a few studies have shown that gambling is negatively related to age, thus older people gamble less than younger people (Kallick, Suites, Dielman and Hybels 1979; Li and Smith 1976). Mok and Hraba (1991) found a negative correlation between age and gambling as well as a relationship between age and type of gambling. All gambling types declined with increasing age of the gambler, except for bingo, which continued to be played by older gamblers (65 years and older) at a higher rate than for younger gamblers (Mok and Hraba 1991: 332). Feeney and Maki (1997) reached a similar conclusion in their research with age emerging as the most important demographic determinant of gambling behaviour. People aged between 18 and 34 years of age were two-thirds more likely to be gamblers than people over 70 years of age. Nonetheless, with the increased access to casinos and local gambling venues through clubs and hotels, access to gambling opportunities is increasing for all ages (Feeney and Maki 1997; Lester 1994; Shaffer, Hall and Vander Bilt 1997; Vander Bilt, Dodge, Pandav, Shaffer and Ganguli 2004; Zaranek and Chapleski 2005). When gambling is related to the age of gamblers and non-gamblers, the older gamblers increased their gambling with age, while older non-gambling people did not start to gamble, thus overall gambling decreases with age for all people, but not for the people who already gambled before retirement (Welte, Barnes, Wieczorek, Tidwell and Parker 2002; Stitt, Giacopassi and Nichols 2003). Increased gambling pursuits can be seen in the context of improved affluence, improved general health, mobility, and longevity and increased access to low cost gaming venues, as well as the enhanced legality and acceptance of gambling in many societies.

The Productivity Commission's (1999) enquiry into the gambling industry and the gambler are hitherto the most comprehensive Australian research in the area and recently updated and complemented by the Productivity Commission's draft report in 2009. The profile of Australians, gamblers and non-gamblers are described in Table 4.3, based on the 1999 assessment.

The regular gambler differs from the non-gambler especially in relation to gender, they are male more often than the non-gambler. There are fewer females as regular gamblers than non-gamblers (39.6 per cent and 55.0 per cent, respectively). The regular gambler is more likely to be a young person (18–34 years) or a mature person (50–64 years) than the non-gambler. The education level of the gambler is lower for the regular gambler than for the non-gambler, with minor differences in relation to employment and annual income where the regular gambler has a marginally higher income profile and full time employment than the non-gambler.

Gambling in Australia 89

Table 4.3   Social and demographic characteristics of all people, gamblers and non-gamblers 1999 in per cent

Characteristic	Category	All people	Non-gamblers	Non-regular gamblers	Regular gamblers*
Gender	Male	49.1	45.0	48.6	60.4
	Female	50.9	55.0	51.4	39.6
Age	18–24	13.3	11.2	13.2	17.8
	25–34	20.4	17.4	21.4	18.2
	35–49	30.1	30.0	31.0	24.0
	50–64	23.3	22.7	23.2	25.4
	65+	13.0	18.7	11.3	14.7
Marital status	Married	66.1	66.3	66.9	60.2
	Separated, divorced, widowed	9.8	11.1	9.0	13.2
	Single	23.8	21.9	23.9	26.7
Household type	Single person	8.6	10.8	7.7	11.5
	Couple with children	50.0	48.5	51.2	43.9
	Couple with no children	22.3	23.7	22.1	22.7
	Other, one parent family with children, group household	18.8	16.7	18.9	21.6
Education	Up to 4th year high school	28.6	24.6	28.1	39.3
	Finished high school	27.7	24.0	28.3	30.3
	TAFE/technical education	10.5	7.8	11.3	10.5
	CAE/University	33.2	43.7	32.3	19.8
Income ($'000)	<25	44.4	49.4	43.8	41.6
	25–35	18.6	16.1	18.9	20.4
	35–49	18.5	15.9	19.0	18.6
	50>	18.5	18.5	18.3	19.5
Work status	Working full-time	47.2	41.9	48.2	49.7
	Working part-time	15.9	15.3	16.4	13.4
	Home duties	10.0	9.2	10.7	6.4
	Student	5.6	6.6	5.4	5.1
	Retired, self supporting, pensioner	17.1	22.1	15.1	22.6
	Unemployed, looking for work, other	4.0	4.4	4.0	2.9

90   *Pathways to Excessive Gambling*

Table 4.3   Continued

Characteristic	Category	All people	Non-gamblers	Non-regular gamblers	Regular gamblers*
Main income source	Wages/salary	61.6	52.8	64.0	60.8
	Own business	14.6	18.2	14.2	10.7
	Unemployment benefit	2.2	2.0	2.4	1.9
	Aged/invalid pension, retirement benefit, sickness benefit, supporting parent benefit	14.7	18.4	13.1	20.0
	Other, private income	5.7	6.5	5.5	5.5
Location	Metropolitan	64.7	70.1	64.0	59.8
	Non-metropolitan	35.3	29.9	36.0	40.2
Country of birth	Australia	76.7	72.1	77.4	80.2
	Elsewhere	23.4	27.9	22.6	19.8
Aboriginal or Torres Strait Islander		1.5	1.0	1.5	2.5

Note: * Regular gamblers are those who participated in any single gambling activity (apart from lottery games or instant scratch tickets) at least once per week in the last 12 months, or whose overall participation in gambling activities (apart from lottery games or instant scratch tickets) was the equivalent of weekly (that is, at least 52 times per year). Non-regular gamblers includes those who participated in any single gambling activity less often than weekly in the last 12 months, but also includes those who only played lottery games and instant scratch tickets weekly. Non-gamblers are those who did not participate in any gambling activity (apart from raffles) in the last 12 months.

Source: Based on data found at Productivity Commission 1999: 3.18–19, National Gambling Survey, Section 3.4, Table 3.4.

A regular gambler is more likely to be a wage earner than the non-gambler. The gambler is also more likely to live outside a metropolitan area and to be born in Australia, than the non-gambler. However, the differences are sometimes marginal between all people, non-gamblers, non-regular gamblers and regular gamblers because gambling is such a ubiquitous activity in Australian society.

While gender is the main difference between the regular gambler and all other people, (more men gamble than females) and while the education level is lower for the regular gambler than for all other people, the differences are often minor. It is however fair to say that of education levels among non-gamblers, there is a higher percentage (43.7 per cent) with a university or college level education than the regular gambler (19.8 per cent) (Productivity Commission 1999: 3.18–19, Main findings, section 3.4, Table 3.4).

The Productivity Commission inquiry findings show similarities with the New Zealand Gaming Survey (1999), in the regular gambler (gambling at least once a week) being more likely to be male than female and having less formal educational qualifications. Those who gambled on electronic gaming machines outside casino venues in New Zealand were also more likely to be male, employed, lack a degree or higher qualification, and be below 35 years of age (Abbott 2001: 16–18).

Research concerning gamblers' reasons for gambling has stressed the profit motive (Spanier 1987) or that some people are more inclined to gamble (Cameron and Myers 1966; Lowenfeld 1979; Kusyszyn and Rutter 1985; Slowo 1998). A survey of gambling college students showed that the majority gambled to win money (42.7 per cent), for fun and excitement (23.0 per cent), for social reasons or to have something to do (11.2 per cent) (Neighbors, Lostutter, Cronce and Larimer 2002: 367). The same sentiments were emphasised in the New Zealand prevalence study where many gambled because they enjoyed doing so and gambling was a legitimate leisure pursuit. Some of the gamblers daydreamed about getting a big win, the gambling gave them pleasure and fun, or the gambling occasion was a social event with family or friends. Personally, they felt excited by gambling and they felt relaxed when gambling. Furthermore, gambling activities created a social conversation topic among family and friends. For some gamblers, especially those gambling excessively, the gambling activity helped them to cope with stressful situations and feelings of stress (Abbott 2001: 23). As has been mentioned previously, Blaszczynski and Nower (2002: 489–90) found that problem or pathological gambling were often not the only problem people present. People with gambling problems can also struggle with mental, social and personal issues and gambling pursuits can temporarily decrease anxiety and stress for people and different gambling types can affect males and females in different ways (Marks and Lesieur 1992; Getty, Watson and Frisch 2000).

4.4 Gambling prevalence in Australia

In Australia the electronic gaming machine (EGM) is more popularly called a poker machine or a 'pokie'. Gambling opportunities are abundant in Australian local communities in clubs and hotels and gambling for money is an enjoyment and considered popular entertainment for many people without it having adverse effects for the majority. Nevertheless, as in most social recreational activities there is a risk taking element and it is a fine line between acceptable, safe, risk taking and excessive behaviour where gambling pursuits range from a social recreational activity to an excessive gambling activity. To reiterate, in gambling activities, people can effortlessly fluctuate between being social recreational gamblers, controlled gamblers, and excessive gamblers. It is, for instance, easy on electronic gaming machines to play for more money than anticipated as the atmosphere, the construction of the machines, and the noise encourages quick responses to the machine's demand for more money. A major loss might also encourage continued playing to recoup the lost money. The scope of the negative impact of gambling in Australia is mainly highlighted through data about gaming machines as it affects

92   *Pathways to Excessive Gambling*

a broader group of people than people betting on horse racing and participating in casino table gambling (Neal et al. 2005; Productivity Commission 2009, 1999).

The number of gaming machines or casino style gaming machines in Australia fluctuated between 198,751 in 2004 (Taylor Nelson Sofres 2004), 199,930 in June 2005 (Australian Bureau of Statistics 2006b), and showed a decrease to 186,468 in 2006 (Taylor Nelson Sofres 2006). However, the Australian Gaming Council (2007: 8) reported the number of gaming machines as 199,986 for the financial year 2004–05 and the Australasian Gaming Council (2008: 8) gave the total number of gaming machines for clubs, hotels and casinos to be 199,271 in the financial year 2005–06, thus a somewhat higher figure than shown by the Taylor Nelson Sofres's reports (2004, 2006), especially for the year 2006 (2005–06).[3] The number of gaming machines in Australia was the seventh highest among the countries with the highest number of casino styled gaming machines and Australia had the lowest ratio of people per machine (cf. Chapter 3.1.3; Table 3.3). Even if the number of gaming machines has decreased in Australia, the same decrease was not reflected in the money gambled, as the gambling expenditure has not decreased correspondingly (Australasian Gaming Council 2008).

The number of gambling businesses in Australia varies between states and territories (Table 4.4). New South Wales (6,834) has more than double the number of gambling businesses than Queensland (3,239). These two states have 67.1 per cent of all the gambling businesses in Australia. Western Australia is the only state or territory, which does not allow electronic gaming machines in clubs and hotels. Electronic gaming machines are only allowed in casinos. Overall there are more hotel venues with gaming machines than clubs, but the clubs have a higher number of gaming machines per venue (Table 4.5). New South Wales has the highest number of gambling venues (1,784 hotels and 1,352 clubs) of all the states and territories. NSW is also the most population dense state (6.5 million) followed by Victoria (4.9 million) and Queensland (3.9 million) (Australian Bureau of Statistics Census 2006b), but still NSW has a higher proportion, more than double the number of gambling businesses and venues (3,137) with gaming machines than the other states and territories.

The electronic gaming machines are divided between casinos, clubs and hotels (Table 4.5). Overall, the minor decreases in gaming machines seen in the last few years, between 2004–05 and 2005–06, from 199,986 to 199,271, are mainly due to the introduction of caps (cf. Delfabbro 2008; cf. Taylor Nelson Sofres 2004, 2006). In all categories, New South Wales has the highest number of machines in Australia, followed by Queensland.

To understand the scope of gambling and to make it possible to compare between different states nationally and countries internationally the calculation

---

3   The discrepancies in figures can be related to calculation methods, calendar or financial year and source of information. Cf. Taylor Nelson Sofres (2006: 4), the Australian Gaming Council (2007) and the Australasian Gaming Council (2008) for more detailed information regarding the sources for the calculations.

Gambling in Australia 93

Table 4.4   Estimated number of gambling businesses in Australia by state/ territory, 2004–05 and number of venues with gaming machines in Australia by state/territory 2005–06

Location/venue	Number of gambling businesses 2004–05	Hotels 2005–06	Clubs 2005–06	Casino(s) 2005–06	Total 2005–06
New South Wales	6,834	1,784	1,352	1	3,137
Victoria	1,904	249	274	1	524
Queensland	3,239	770	573	4	1,347
South Australia	1,488	499	79	1	579
Western Australia	849	na	na	1	1
Tasmania	318	94	10	2	106
Australian Capital Territory	216	14	65	0	79
Northern Territory	160	38	32	2	72
Total	15,008	3,448	2,385	12	5,845

Source: Based on data found at Australian Casino Association 2005, Annual Report 2004– 05; industry interviews and State/territory Gambling Authority annual reports; Australian Gaming Council 2007:16; State/territory gaming authority annual reports 2005–06 and Australian Casino Association 2005; Australasian Gaming Council 2008: 9.

Table 4.5   Estimated number of gaming machines in Australia by venue type 2005–06

State/territory/location	Hotels	Clubs	Casino(s)	Total
New South Wales*	24,053	74,273	1,500	99,826
Victoria	13,657	13,490	2,500	29,647
Queensland	18,556	22,024	3,593	44,173
South Australia	11,003	1,595	850	13,448
Western Australia	n/a	n/a	1,500	1,500
Tasmania	2,217	183	1,277	3,677
Australian Capital Territory	84	5,066	0	5,150
Northern Territory	344	706	800	1,850
Total	69,914	117,337	12,020	199,271

Note: * Legislative changes to the hotel cap are currently proposed to bring it into line with the 99,000 state-wide cap. As of February 2005, profit organisations (i.e. hotels) have been allocated a reduction in gaming machine entitlements. Venues licensed for 28 or more machines receive eight less than the approved number, venues approved for between 21 and 27 machines receive 20 entitlements and venues licensed for less than 20 machines received entitlements equivalent to their approved number. An entitlement trading system

Source: Based on data found at State/territory Gaming Authority annual reports 2005–06; NSW Office of Liquor, Gaming and Racing 2006; and Australian Casino Association 2005; Australasian Gaming Council 2008: 8.

94 *Pathways to Excessive Gambling*

of the number of machines per 1,000 adults (18 years of age and above) and the number of adult persons per machine enhances our understanding of the ratio of machines in relation to the population (Table 4.6). As noted above, internationally Australia had the lowest ratio between people and machines with 111 people per machine or 83 adults (18–84 years of age) per machine in 2006.[4] Only marginal changes downwards emerged between 2004–05 and 2005–06 in the states and territories except for a small increase in Tasmania and the Northern Territory. The Australian Capital Territory (ACT) had a higher ratio per 1,000 adult residents and gaming machines in 2004–05 as well as in 2005–06 than New South Wales, both showing a small decrease (0.3 and 0.5, respectively). The state with the next highest ratio was Queensland (14.6 and 14.4 machines/1,000). The lowest figure was in Western Australia with only one machine per 1,000 adults.

In 2004–05, ACT (48.3) had the lowest number of people per gaming machine, followed by NSW (51.3). This trend continued for the year 2005–06 where ACT and NSW also had the lowest number of people per gaming machine (52.1). Except for Western Australia and Tasmania, the ratio between electronic gaming machines per adult residents increased, thus showing a decrease in the number of gaming

Table 4.6   Gaming machines per 1,000 adults and per adults in Australia by state/territory 2004–05 and 2005–06

State/territory	Gaming machines per 1,000 adults 2004–05	Gaming machines per 1,000 adults 2005–06	Gaming machines per adults[a] 2004–05	Gaming machines per adults 2005–06
New South Wales	19.5	19.0	51.3[b]	52.1[c]
Victoria	7.7	7.5	129.9	139.4
Queensland	14.6	14.4	68.5	72.7
South Australia	12.6	11.1	79.4	93.4
Western Australia	1.0	1.0	1000.0	984.8
Tasmania	9.7	9.9	109.0	98.4
Australian Capital Territory	20.7	20.4	48.3	na
Northern Territory	12.3	12.6	81.3	138.4
Australia	13.0	12.6	76.9	80.9

Note: a) Place of residence of people 18 years and older; b) (49.5/NSW+ACT); c) (NSW+ACT)

Source: Based on data found at Australian Gaming Council 2007: 9; State/territory Gaming Authority Annual Reports 2004–05; Australian Casino Association 2005; Australian Bureau of Statistics, Census 2006; Australasian Gaming Council 2008: 9; Taylor Nelson Sofres 2004: 12; 2006: 14.

---

4   Except for smaller countries with gambling focused hospitality industry, cf. Chapter 3.1 Global gambling.

machines in the states and the territories (cf. Taylor Nelson Sofres 2004: 12; 2006: 14; Australian Bureau of Statistics Census 2006b). In 2005, 58.4 per cent of the gaming machines were licensed to hospitality and sporting clubs, 35.6 per cent to hotels, pubs, taverns and bars. Six per cent of all the gaming machines were licensed to casino venues (Australian Bureau of Statistics 2006a: 6,12).

During the period 2004–05, the total gambling expenditure in Australia was $16.9 billion. The following period 2005–06 gambling expenditure had increased to $17.6 billion and in 2006–07 to approximately $18 billion, thus gambling continues to increase with gambling on gaming machines still being the largest component. Expenditure on gaming machines in 2004–05 was $10.1 billion and in 2005–06 it had increased to approximately $10.4 billion (Table 4.7). As a whole, gaming machine gambling in Australia makes up the highest share of gambling expenditure, 59.1 per cent in 2005–06 and 59.7 per cent in 2004–05. In New South Wales in 2003–2004, the gambling expenditure was $6.57 billion with gaming machines having 71.2 per cent of the total gambling market. New South Wales also had the largest state share of the Australian expenditure on gaming machines with 49.0 per cent followed by Victoria with 24.0 per cent and Queensland 15.7 per cent (Office of Economic and Statistical Research 2005).

The proportions between the different gambling forms show that in 2005–06 wagering accounted for 13.2 per cent of gambling expenditure ($2.3 billion), expenditure on lotteries, the most common gambling forms, and pools accounted for 9.6 per cent of overall spending ($1.7 billion). The casino gambling expenditure was $2.9 billion and accounting for 16.7 per cent of all gambling expenditure in Australia and 1.4 per cent was related to other gambling (Australasian Gaming Council 2008: 20). The more recently introduced caps on electronic gaming machines have not decreased the spending on gaming machines (cf. Productivity Commission 2009) and, as was noted before, the newer machines are more sophisticated and can take notes instead of coins and notes of higher denominations, which makes it possible to insert a higher amount of money in a given time period. It is possible with some gaming machines to lose up to $1,200 per hour and regular gamblers are estimated to play for approximately $7,000–$8,000 annually on gaming machines (Productivity Commission 2009: xxiv, xxviii).

From Table 4.7 it can be concluded that the average gambling expenditure per adult person (gambler and non-gambler) in Australia was in total $1,123 in the period 2005–06, an increase of $26 from $1,097 in the period 2004–05. The Northern Territory had the highest per adult capita gambling expenditure during the same period with $2,197 and $1,918, respectively, an increase of $279, but their gambling venues attract a large proportion of interstate and international gamblers and are thus not a reliable figure to get an actual measure of the Northern Territory residents' gambling expenditure (Australian Gaming Council 2007; Australasian Gaming Council 2008). New South Wales had the second highest average gambling expenditure per person 18 years of age and older with $1,357

Table 4.7   Summary: Aggregate and per capita gambling expenditure in Australia by state/territory 2005–06

State/territory	Wagering[b]		Lotteries[c]		Gaming machines[d]		Casino[e]		Other[f]		All[h]	
	$ m	$/adult	$ m	$/adult	$ m	$/adult	$m	$/adult	$m	$/adult	$m	$/adult
New South Wales	800	154	527	101	5,024	964	638	122	84	16	7,072	1,357
Victoria	663	170	389	100	2,472	635	1,027	264	6	2	4,559	1,170
Queensland	318	105	363	120	1,776	585	578	191	86	28	3,121	1,029
South Australia	109	90	99	83	751	624	125	104	24	19	1,109	922
Western Australia	244	158	241	157	0	0	344	223	21	14	850	552
Tasmania	28	77	29	79	109	295	100	270	20	55	287	776
Australian Capital Territory	27[g]	107	18	72	192	764	19	75	1	3	257	1,022
Northern Territory	133	916	16	110	57	391	99	678	15	102	319	2,197
Australia	2,323[h]	148	1,683[h]	107	10,381	663	2,930	187	258[h]	16	17,575	1,123

Note: a) Per capita figures relate to the population aged over 18 years.; b) Includes racing and sports betting; c) Includes lottery, lotto, tattslotto, instant lottery and pools; d) Excludes gaming machines at casinos; e) Includes wagers on table games, gaming machines and keno systems; f) Includes minor gaming, Keno and interactive gaming; g) Sports Betting data unavailable; h) May not add due to rounding.

Source: Based on data found at Australian Gambling Statistics 2006; Australasian Gaming Council 2008: 20, 22; Extrapolated from Office of Economic and Statistical Research (2007).

and $1,336, respectively, a small increase of $21, while a much larger increase[5] has occurred since 1993–94, of 52 per cent in New South Wales. Victoria recorded $1,170 average adult gambling expenditure per capita in 2005–06 an increase of $36 from $1,134 in 2004–05, the highest increase among the states and territories, except the Northern Territory. Above the national average were New South Wales (20 per cent) and Victoria (4 per cent) and below the average were Queensland and the Australian Capital Territory (approximately 10 per cent) while South Australia was 18 per cent below the Australia average. The Northern Territory average was much higher than the national average, but it is not representative of the average gambling expenditure by its residents, as noted above. The lowest average adult gambling expenditures per capita was in Tasmania ($776) and Western Australia ($552). Tasmania was the only state and territory where a decrease per capita gambling expenditure occurred, from $814 to $776, a $38 decrease between 2004–05 and 2005–06. In South Australia there was no change in the two years.

Adult gambling expenditure per capita on gaming machines was highest in New South Wales in 2005–06 with $965, up from $953, followed by Australian Capital Territory with $764, up from $746. The Australia-wide average was $663, up from $655 in 2004–05. All states and territories showed an increase in gambling expenditure on gaming machines except South Australia and Tasmania (Australian Gaming Council 2007; Australasian Gaming Council 2008):

> Not only does New South Wales have the highest density of EGMs in the world for any comparably sized jurisdiction, but poker machines in this State are also played to such an extent that they are the major cause of gambling-related problems (Walker, Matarese, Blaszczynski and Sharpe 2004: 1).

Another way to measure the influence of gambling is to relate the gambling expenditure to Household Disposable Income (HDI), the amount of income households have left over after they have paid their taxes, the amount of money left to spend on consumer goods and services (Table 4.8). The average proportion of gambling expenditure as a proportion of HDI in Australia in 2005–06 was 2.93 per cent. For Australia as a whole the average percentage had decreased slightly since 2000–01. The highest proportion of HDI gambling expenditure after the Northern Territory (5.11 per cent) was NSW with 3.44 per cent. Overall the variations between the measuring periods were minor. In 2005–06 all states and territories except Western Australia (0.01 percentage point) and Northern Territory (0.28 percentage points) decreased their HDI gambling expenditure. Western Australia had the lowest HDI expenditure with only 1.44 per cent.

The Australia wide proportion of HDI expenditure, which was spent on electronic gaming machines in 2005–06 was 1.73 per cent out of the total

---

5 The 'real' increase means adjusted for the effects of inflation. Per capita refers to people over the age of 18 years. This figure does not include sports betting with the totalizator in NSW.

98 *Pathways to Excessive Gambling*

Table 4.8   Proportion of HDI spent on all gambling forms in Australia by state/territory between 2000–01 and 2005–06 in per cent

State/territory	2000–01	2001–02	2002–03	2003–04	2004–05	2005–06
New South Wales	3.50	3.45	3.58	3.56	3.51	3.44
Victoria	3.58	3.63	3.41	3.18	3.06	3.01
Queensland	2.91	2.90	2.98	3.10	3.02	2.91
South Australia	2.46	2.51	2.70	2.76	2.76	2.63
Western Australia	1.58	1.50	1.40	1.39	1.43	1.44
Tasmania	2.69	2.87	2.81	2.74	2.62	2.36
Australian Capital Territory	2.05	2.07	2.01	1.95	1.78	1.73
Northern Territory	3.92	4.72	5.27	5.30	4.83	5.11
Australia	3.13	3.12	3.12	3.07	3.00	2.93

Source: Based on data found at Office of Economic and Statistical Research 2006, 2007; Australian Gaming Council 2007: 29; Australasian Gaming Council 2008: 28.

expenditure of 2.93 per cent on all gambling (excluded are EGMs at casinos). The corresponding percentage for New South Wales was 2.44 per cent spent on gaming machines and 3.44 per cent spent on all gambling (Table 4.8), thus the HDI gambling expenditure on gaming machines was the dominant gambling expenditure in New South Wales, with only 1 per cent spent on other gambling (Australasian Gaming Council 2008: 29).

Gambling revenue comes primarily from the states and territories taxation, licence fees and mandatory contributions such as the Community Development Support Expenditure Scheme in NSW (cf. Chapter 4.2). For state and territory governments, the tax revenue from gambling is a significant income source. In NSW gambling tax revenue largely funds (among other area) counselling and gambling support services.

The gambling taxes in Australia totalled $4.69 billion in 2005–06. The overall gambling tax revenue was highest in NSW in both 2004–05 and 2005–06 ($1,428 million and $1,522 million) followed by Victoria ($1,369 million and $1,460 million) (Table 4.9). However, calculated per adult the gambling tax revenue was highest in Victoria in 2004–05 with $357, but in 2005–06 the Northern Territory moved to having the highest gambling tax revenue per adult with $380 from being the third highest in 2004–05 with $321. Victoria moved to second place in 2005–06 with $375 per adult, followed by South Australia with $339.

Gambling tax revenue, as a proportion of total tax revenue, was largest in the Northern Territory in 2004–05 and in 2005–06 (15.6 per cent and 15.1 per cent) followed by South Australia (13.6 per cent and 13.4 per cent). While NSW has the most gambling opportunities, the percentage of tax income revenue was lower than for the other states and territories, 9.3 per cent in 2004–05 and 9.6 per cent in 2005–06, except for Australian Capital Territory (6.7 per cent and

Gambling in Australia 99

Table 4.9 Gambling taxation revenue, gambling tax as a proportion of total tax revenue and gambling expenditure as percentage of gambling tax revenue in Australia by state/territory 2004–05 and 2005–06

State/territory	Gambling tax ($m)		Gambling tax per adult ($)		Gambling tax* %		Gambling expenditure^ %	
	2004–05	2005–06	2004–05	2005–06	2004–05	2005–06	2004–05	2005–06
New South Wales	1,428	1,522	277	292	9.3	9.6	20.7	21.5
Victoria	1,369	1,460	357	375	13.1	13.4	31.5	32.0
Queensland	800	835	271	275	11.6	11.4	27.0	26.8
South Australia	408	408	343	339	13.6	13.4	37.1	36.8
Western Australia	267	283	177	184	3.1	2.8	34.0	33.3
Tasmania	78	75	214	203	11.8	11.2	26.3	26.1
Australian Capital Territory	56	55	225	218	6.7	6.0	22.6	21.4
Northern Territory	46	55	321	380	15.6	15.1	16.7	17.3

Note: * as a proportion of total tax revenue; ^ as percentage of gambling tax revenue.

Source: Based on data found at Australian Gaming Council 2007: 39, 41; Australasian Gaming Council 2008: 39, 41; Extrapolated from Office of Economic and Statistical Research 2006, 2007.

6.0 per cent, respectively) and Western Australia (3.1 per cent and 2.8 per cent, respectively).

The gambling expenditure as a percentage of gambling tax revenue showed that South Australia had the highest percentage in 2004–05 as well as in 2005–06 with 37.1 per cent and 36.8 per cent, respectively, followed by Western Australia with 34.0 per cent and 33.3 per cent, respectively. A small increase between 2004–05 and 2005–06 was shown for Victoria (31.5 per cent and 32.0 per cent). New South Wales had the lowest gambling expenditure as a percentage of gambling tax revenue of all states and territories, except the Northern Territory. NSW had 20.7 per cent in 2004–05 with a small increase to 21.5 in 2005–06. The Northern Territory increased the percentage of tax revenue from 16.7 per cent in 2004–05 to 17.3 per cent in 2005–06 (Table 4.9). The national average was 26.3 per cent in 2004–05 and increased to 26.7 per cent in 2005–06.

In New South Wales the gaming machine tax rates are calculated on metered profit and are collected quarterly with different taxation scales according to annual revenue. In 2007 (1 September) the annual taxation structure of tax payable by registered clubs was amended so that clubs that do not exceed

$1 million in annual gaming machine profits do not pay any tax while clubs with an annual gaming machine profit between $1 million and $1.8 million are taxed at 29.5 per cent. Clubs earning over $1.8 million annually pay no tax on the first $200,000 metered profit, 10 per cent on $200,000 to $1 million, 19.5 per cent between $1 million and $5 million, 24.5 per cent between $5 million and $10 million, and 27.5 per cent for gambling revenue between $10 and $20 million and for metered profit above $20 million a 29.4 per cent tax is applied. In addition to these tax scales, an amount equal to 1.5 per cent of gaming machine profits over $1 million is payable at the end of the tax year if clubs do not contribute 1.5 per cent of their gaming machine profits to eligible community projects, under the Community Development and Support Expenditure (CDSE) scheme during the year (cf. Chapter 4.2; NSW Office of Liquor, Gaming and Racing 2009d).[6] In New South Wales the club tax rates will stay at the 2007 (1 September) level until 2012 (31 August) and the goods and services tax (GST) rebate payments will continue to be provided to all clubs on the first $200,000 of gaming profits from 2004–05 (Australasian Gaming Council 2008: 44). These tax scales are lower than the proposed taxation changes in 2003, which elicited intense protest from the club and gambling commerce when proposed.

In Victoria, tax is assessed on the net cash balance of the operators, the difference between the amounts bet, and the amount paid out in prizes. In the case of clubs, the gaming operator and the venues receive 66.6 per cent (33.3 per cent each), the GST amounts to 9.09 per cent and the government receives the remaining 24.24 per cent. Additionally, a levy of $1,553 applies to each electronic gaming machine. South Australia and Queensland tax on gaming starts at a lower revenue level than in NSW. In Queensland, the taxation starts with 17.91 per cent for a monthly-metered win of $9,501. Monthly wins over $1.4 million are taxed at 35.91 per cent. Australian Capital Territory base its taxation on gross monthly gaming machine revenue and taxation starts from $15,000 with 15 per cent and for gaming revenue over $50,000 until the taxation has reached 27 per cent, which is the highest level of taxation. Northern Territory starts taxation already from $0–$5,000 with 12.91 per cent and from $50,001 the taxation is 32.91 per cent and reach the highest level with 42.91 per cent of a gross monthly profit of $150,000 and over. In South Australia, taxation starts at $75,0001 annual net gambling revenue (NGR) with 21 per cent up to $399,000 rising to 47 per cent for annual net gambling revenue between $2,500,001–$3,500,000 and to 55.0 per cent for annual net gambling revenue above $3.5 million (Australian Gaming Council 2007: 44–6). The different scales used for taxation of gaming machine profits demonstrate the independence of the states and territories in regulating and enforcing taxation of the gambling industry revenue.

---

6 Note the Australasian Gaming Council (2008: 44), gives a slightly higher club taxation figures than presented on the NSW government's website 2009.

4.5 Gaming machine gambling in New South Wales

The scope of gambling in Australia can again be illustrated by using New South Wales as an example. Gaming machines had been introduced in the 1920s, but they were not legalised until much later, in clubs in 1956, while the legalisation concerning modern gaming machines for hotels[7] was not introduced until the first NSW casino was established in Sydney in the mid-1990s. The number of gaming machines reached a peak of approximately 104,000 in clubs and 25,980 in hotels (Australian Gaming Council 2007), before caps were introduced in 2001 (New South Wales Office of Liquor, Gaming and Racing 2007b).

In New South Wales the number of gambling machines was capped to 99,000 gaming machines in 2009. The number of gaming machines in NSW represents approximately 53 per cent of all gaming machines in Australia calculated on 186,468 machines Australia wide (Taylor Nelson Sofres 2006: 17; cf. Chapter 3.1.3, Table 3.3). The number of gaming machines has fluctuated in New South Wales from 99,109 operating gaming machines in clubs and hotels in 2003–04, falling to 98,803 in 2005, 98,326 in May 2006, and in 2007 (31 May) the gaming machine amounted to a total of 98,864 (including casino gaming machines) (New South Wales Department of Gaming and Racing 2004, 2006, 2007b, 2009a).

In 2007–08, there were 1,322 registered clubs in NSW holding a total of 72,819 electronic gaming machines and 1,710 hotels with 23,732 gaming machines, thus the clubs have maintained their dominance in providing gaming machine gambling in NSW. The only casino in NSW (Sydney) had 1,500 gaming machines, thus a total number of 98,051 gaming machines in June 2008 (New South Wales Office of Liquor, Gaming and Racing 2009b).

The gaming industry is a highly profitable business and a source of large tax revenues for governments. Clubs paid $3,176 million in pre tax gaming machine profit and $609 million in assessed tax for the period, 2007–08 (June–May), while hotels paid $1,468 million in pre tax gaming machine profit and $391 million assessed in tax. These figures are slightly different from the previous period, 2006–07, when the clubs' gaming machine profit amounted to $3,507 million with $660.9 million in assessed tax, this represented a small decrease in pre-tax gaming machine profit but no real change in assessed tax. In the same period, hotels generated $1,699 million in pre tax profit and $454.1 million in assessed tax during the period 2007–08 (June–May). Overall, the hotels have increased their profit revenue and taxable profit, while the clubs show a small revenue decline. In 2005–06 as well as in 2006–07, the Bulldogs Leagues Club recorded the highest gaming machine profit for the state; while in 2007–08 it was the Mounties (Mt Pritchard and District Community Club), which registered the highest amount of assessed gaming machine profit (Department of Gaming and Racing 2006; NSW Office of Liquor, Gaming and Racing 2009b). Both of these clubs are situated within the Greater Western Sydney

---

7 In Australia sometimes hotels are also called pubs, for simplicity the concept hotels also includes pubs.

102   *Pathways to Excessive Gambling*

area, the Bulldogs Leagues Club in the local government area Canterbury and the Mounties in the City of Fairfield. The City of Fairfield had the highest per capita gambling expenditure within NSW in 2004–05 (Table 4.10).

The only casino in NSW generated $73.83 million payable in casino duty, $11.61 million payable in a responsible gambling levy, and $610 million gross gaming revenue between 2006 (June) and 2007 (May). For the period 2007–08 the revenue level decreased compared with previous period to $71.67 million payable in casino duty, $11.29 million payable in responsible gambling levy, while the gross gaming revenue increased to $643 million (New South Wales Office of Liquor, Gaming and Racing 2009b).

Keno gambling for the period 2007–08 amounted to $351.5 million in net subscriptions, $38.37 million in commissions earned by agencies/venues and $7.77 million payable in tax (exclusive of GST). While in the previous period (2006–07), the figures were $347.8 million in net subscriptions, $38 million in profit to registered clubs and $7.7 million payable in tax (exclusive GST) (NSW Office of Liquor, Gaming and Racing 2009b), the net subscriptions increased during the latter period, but otherwise keno gambling showed a decline. The latest figures (with some exceptions) might reflect the early global financial downturn already being experienced in 2008. The same trend can be found in relation to lottery products. In the 12 month period ending 30 June 2008, public lottery products in NSW generated $1,211 million in sales, $55.69 million in profit and $411.53 million in duty/dividends. This is a noticeable decrease from the figures for previous periods, which showed $1,124.4 million in sales, $50.28 million in profit and $334.37 million in duty/dividends.

The overall NSW gaming machine pre-duty between 1999 and 2004 is shown in Figure 4.1, where it can be seen that the trend has been a consistent increase in gambling profit with variations due more to seasonal variations than any real downturn in the gambling pre-duty profit. Overall there has been a considerable increase in gambling profit since 1999.

Interviews with club representatives revealed a fear that gambling revenue was declining and would be further eroded with increased competition from hotels and casino gambling, gambling taxation and the smoking ban. However, the fear is unfounded, since 1999 gambling pre-duty profit for clubs and hotels has increased for gaming machine gambling. Clubs' strategies to diversify their activities to revenue sources other than gaming were already in place in 2004–05. Despite gambling revenue continuing to underpin all other club activities (cf. Productivity Commission 2009), there has been growing recognition that other club activities should also be profitable. Revenue statistics for the last 10 years do not indicate a decline of revenue in the immediate future. This is of course apart from the usual exposure to seasonal and economic variations, and amendments to legislation and taxation that may occur but which affect any business.

Even with a slight downturn in expenditure in conjunction with the aim to reduce the overall number of machines, it is really the sophistication of the machines that

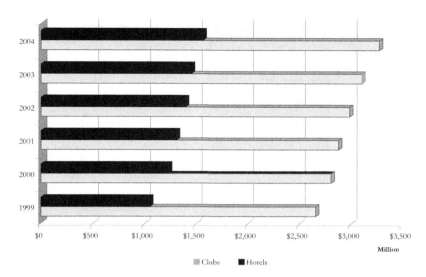

Figure 4.1 Total clubs and hotels electronic machine gaming pre-duty profit in New South Wales between 1999 and 2004

Source: New South Wales Department of Gaming and Racing 2005.

is the major factor in any potential increase in gambling activity. Machines that can handle multiple lines of games, the possibility of networking machines and the speed with which a machine can handle money, is of far more importance for gamblers, in particular excessive gamblers. All these sophistications speed up the process of the gambler losing his or her money (Productivity Commission 2009). In Delfabbro's (2008) South Australian survey, the number of gaming machines seemed to be more than sufficient – there appeared to be no lack of machines in most gambling venues for gamblers to use; the wait for an available machine on which to gamble was non-existent or at worst, negligible.

Approximately 59.1 per cent of the total gambling expenditure in Australia in 2005–06 was spent on gaming machine gambling, while in NSW the corresponding figure was 71 per cent of the total gambling expenditure (see Table 4.7; Figure 4.2). Casino gambling was the second highest gambling form for Australia as a whole (15.6 per cent) while wagering was the next highest for NSW (12.0 per cent), however, still lower than for Australia as a whole (13.6 per cent). Lottery products[8] expenditure had a higher percentage of all gambling for Australia as a whole than for NSW (9.6 per cent and 7.5 per cent, respectively). The gambling

---

8   'Lottery products' include lotteries, lotto, pools and instant scratch-its. Gaming machines refers to machines in clubs and hotels. 'Casino gaming' includes wagers on table games, gaming machines and keno systems in the casino. 'Other' includes keno, interactive and minor gaming.

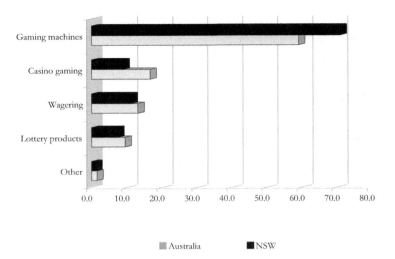

Figure 4.2 Aggregate gambling expenditure for the whole of Australia and NSW 2005–06

Source: Extrapolated from Office of Economic and Statistical Research 2007; Australasian Gaming Council 2008: 20.

form that was smallest in Australia as a whole and in NSW as well was sports betting, it registered only 0.74 per cent in 2004–05 in NSW and 0.96 per cent in 2005–06, an increase from 2004–05 with 0.59 per cent for NSW and 0.81 per cent for the whole of Australia, thus a small increase (Australasian Gaming Council 2008; Australian Gaming Council 2007).

Table 4.10 shows the local government areas with the highest pre-duty profit in 2004–05 in New South Wales. The local government areas with the highest pre-duty profit were Fairfield, Bankstown, Canterbury, Blacktown, and Parramatta followed by Penrith. Fairfield had the highest gambling expenditure of all local government areas in New South Wales with $307.664 million gambled during a 12-month period (New South Wales Department of Gaming and Racing 2005).

Gambling activities attract local residents and visitors from surrounding local government areas as well as visitors from further away, thus the calculation of individual expenditure is 'an estimation'. An estimation of gambling expenditure at clubs and hotels in relation to adult residents, 18 years of age and older, shows that in Fairfield the average expenditure per adult resident was $2,318 during the year 2004–05. In Bankstown the average adult spending on gaming machines was $1,439 followed by Blacktown with $971 (Australian Bureau of Statistics Census 2006; NSW Department of Gaming and Racing 2005). These expenditures were all higher than the average for NSW ($964) and Australia ($663) (cf. Table 4.7). As discussed in relation to gambling in the Northern Territory, the pre-profit gambling duty for the Sydney local government area is not representative for the

Gambling in Australia 105

Table 4.10   The clubs and hotels with the highest electronic gaming machine pre-duty profit in New South Wales local government areas (LGA) the period February/March 2004 to January/February 2005

LGA/pre-duty profit	Club $	Hotel $	Total $
Fairfield	246,623,097	61,041,344	307,664,441
Sydney*	64,862,617	214,585,632	279,448,249
Bankstown	130,018,856	46,812,163	176,831,019
Blacktown	120,745,273	52,962,790	173,708,063
Canterbury	116,731,107	52,939,364	169,670,471
Parramatta	107,168,678	60,796,304	167,964,982
Penrith	121,880,828	38,567,803	160,448,631
Wollongong	109,519,665	29,942,116	139,461,781
Newcastle	97,150,688	39,221,540	136,372,228
Wyong	111,703,599	14,751,191	126,454,790
Randwick	69,545,312	36,913,138	106,458,449
Campbelltown	75,708,014	29,577,155	105,285,169
Gosford	77,727,474	23,716,389	101,443,863
Sutherland	75,459,890	25,186,721	100,646,610
Holroyd	67,358,977	27,453,364	94,812,342
Tweed	83,446,854	9,119,331	92,566,185
Lake Macquarie	72,183,354	20,373,263	92,556,616
Liverpool	51,500,608	36,039,831	87,540,439
Warringah	63,431,613	18,551,652	81,983,264
Rockdale	48,395,686	28,474,172	76,869,858
Ryde	50,035,957	23,078,104	73,114,060
Kogarah	51,714,675	18,644,357	70,359,033
Marrickville	27,215,756	39,942,557	67,158,312
Shoalhaven	54,767,428	10,050,298	64,817,726
Auburn	35,456,758	28,913,622	64,370,380
Waverley	40,737,315	19,029,532	59,766,848
North Sydney	25,427,703	30,894,431	56,322,134
Hurstville	28,512,169	27,517,412	56,029,581
Ashfield	42,392,357	10,315,163	52,707,519
Albury	41,592,295	10,672,357	52,264,653

Note: * National and international visitors, not representative for permanent residents in Sydney local government area.

Source: NSW Department of Gaming and Racing (2005).

residents as the Sydney local government area has a high concentration of hotels with gaming machines and New South Wales' only casino, the StarCity Casino, is located within this area, thus attracting a wide range of national and international visitors (cf. Chapter 4.4, Northern Territory gambling expenditure).

In the local government areas where more than $100 million is spent per year, an exceedingly high figure, are all in the Greater Western Sydney area. These include Fairfield, Bankstown and Blacktown. The Greater Western Sydney area has large pockets of low income households, recent migrants and a higher than average unemployment rate and within each area, a large sports club with extensive gambling facilities is located.

4.6 Conclusion

The chapter presented statistics describing Australians' propensity to gamble and the range of gambling opportunities available in the states and territories. The situation in New South Wales was used as an example for a more detailed examination of gambling opportunities that are present in the local community. As in many other countries, there has been an extensive expansion of gambling in Australia, particularly over the last few decades, with the majority of the adult population participating in some form of gambling – anything from the purchase of a lottery or raffle ticket to gambling on gaming machines and casino tables. It was pointed out that there were marginal differences in the personal characteristics of non-gamblers and occasional gamblers and also between occasional gamblers and regular gamblers. The propensity to gamble was much higher among males than females and people with lower educational levels.

Community clubs are often established around a community need to support a local community issue or cause, in doing so they also create a meeting place and often a place around which local sports activities can come together. As such they fulfil an important social and recreational function. The affordable meals and leisure activities on offer are heavily subsidised by the gambling opportunities they make available. In New South Wales, the highest proportion of all gambling relates to gaming machines in clubs and hotels. State and territory governments have facilitated the activities and increase in the gambling industry thus also created a source of high tax revenue. This is particularly the case for New South Wales where the gambling industry has been given a lower scale of taxation than in the other states and territories and enforcements of harm minimising strategies have been slower. An example is the introduction of the smoking ban which gave the gambling industry a long introduction period and the acceptance of smoking in areas where 25 per cent of the indoor area could be re-classified as open space by opening up one wall to the outdoor area (New South Wales Department of Health 2009). Although the financial contribution by clubs to the Community Development and Support Expenditure Scheme introduced by New South Wales is a commendable project, the cost to participating clubs is negligible as the cost to them is tax deductible. Despite a part of the gaming profit being reinvested into the community, it does little to alleviate or minimise the adversity caused by excessive gambling.

Despite the recent broadening of the market for electronic gaming machines with their legal introduction into hotels, the registered clubs in NSW have retained their domination of electronic gaming machine gambling. The club's income is based on revenue from electronic gaming machines and other gambling activities, other facilities such as health and fitness centres and only to a lesser extent on income from food, beverages and other services. The chapter discussed in detail the real concern posed by the concentration of intensive gambling within the local government areas of Greater Western Sydney. Those areas show the highest gambling expenditure per adult resident in Australia. This is particularly true for Fairfield, a mainly lower socio-economic area, where the expenditure is 2.4 times higher than the state average and 3.5 times higher than the Australian average. Fairfield is well serviced with many clubs and hotels and thus has a high number of gaming machines per capita. It was noted that overall the Greater Western Sydney Area has large pockets of low-income households, recent migrants and a higher than average unemployment rate.

Despite some attempts to regulate the profit levels of the gaming industry, tax revenue statistics show that it is a highly profitable industry and an important tax revenue resource for governments. Industry profit is supported by extensive and easy access to gaming opportunities through long opening hours and less staff intensive operations compared with other entertainment alternatives like restaurants that are only open four to six hours six days a week. Thus gaming is an ideal business with a high degree of utilisation of time and space. The concentration of gambling venues to residential areas with a lack of alternative affordable entertainment opportunities also increases the likelihood that people will gamble as a social entertainment activity and that eventually some will gamble to excess.

The question is would people participate in gambling activities if there were alternative recreational opportunities? This will be explored in Chapter 5 where young people's introduction to gambling as part of family social recreation time is analysed. The research is based on a survey of young people in rural and regional Australia.

Chapter 5
Youth Gambling

5.1 Introduction

It is commonly recognised that young people not only gamble well before the legal age but experience problems with excessive gambling before they are legally old enough to gamble. Research into young people's gambling experiences started much later than research about adult gambling and prevalence studies still focus mainly on the adult gambling propensity (Productivity Commission 1999; Delfabbro 2008; cf. Chapter 2.1–2.2). As examined in Chapter 2, Volberg (2004) highlighted the difficulties with prevalence studies and especially when governments and mass media focus on a single percentage figure to assess adversity caused by gambling. Volberg emphasised that gambling is a complex issue involving a number of players, the government, the gambling industry, the individual, the social environment and access to gambling opportunities, a series of interrelationships that cannot be explained by a single figure.

Research methodology, including sample selection and the type of scale used (SOGS/SOGS-RA, CPGI, DSM-IV-J/DSM-IV-MR-J) to measure gambling propensity, the extent of gambling, and people's perceptions of their gambling are all factors that influence how the prevalence of gambling is assessed. Further, it makes global comparisons more difficult. Prevalence percentages for adult problem gamblers vary between 1 and 2 per cent, while they are somewhat higher for young people, between 1 and 4 per cent or even 5 per cent in some research findings (Gambling Research Australia 2008).

The Moore and Ohsuka (1997) study of 1,000 school students was the first large Australian study of young people. This research was followed by further youth gambling studies in other Australian jurisdictions (Gambling Research Australia 2008: 63–4). More recently internationally, Moodie and Finnigan (2006) surveyed 2,043 young people between 11 and 16 years of age in Scotland, albeit with a broader focus than gambling activities. They concluded that 9 per cent of the surveyed young people demonstrated gambling problems and a further 15 per cent were deemed at risk gamblers, when using the DSM-IV-J scale to assess gambling prevalence. In this study fruit machines were the preferred gambling activity. Nevertheless, this study presented higher percentage values for both problem gamblers and at-risk gamblers among youth than had been indicated when using other scales (cf. Chapter 2.1). In Huang and Boyer's (2007) study of 5,666 Canadian young people between 15 and 24 years of age, they establish a gambling prevalence rate of 2.2 per cent using the CPGI scale.

Dickson, Derevensky and Gupta (2008) found in their study of 2,179 students aged between 11 and 19 years of age that family and school connectedness influenced the youths' risk taking behaviour and gambling propensity. They identified predictor variables that corresponded with gambling at risk levels and possible future pathological gambling. Dickson, Derevensky and Gupta (2008: 25–6) identified the following variables: 'anxiety and risk propensity, experiencing school problems, having a sibling and/or friend with gambling problems, being male and knowing a significant other with a substance use problem', as related to risk taking behaviour and gambling inclination. Goldstein, Walton, Cunningham, Resko and Duan (2009: 113) examined 1,128 African-American (58.0 per cent) and non-African-American young people in the USA between 14 and 18 years of age presenting at an emergency hospital department. They found that non-African-American and African-American youths' gambling correlated with 'lower academic achievement, being out of school, working more than 20 hours per week, alcohol and marijuana use, alcohol problems, severe dating violence, moderate and severe general violence, and carrying a weapon'. This was especially the case for males of African-American heritage who had gambled for the largest amounts of money and gambled frequently. Furthermore, gambling was related to other risk taking youth behaviour, such as crime, violence and truancy. These studies did not solely concentrate on gambling, but researched gambling in relation to other behaviours such as violence, crime, drugs and alcohol. The findings highlight the circumstances that gambling is often one of several problems the young people are dealing with in their formative years.

The following presents gambling research undertaken in Australian rural and regional communities in early 2000. The sample includes young people between 14 and 25 years of age living in two Queensland communities. This research, just as the studies cited above, had a broader focus than solely gambling experience; it also looked at young people's overall leisure activities, their community belonging and future aspirations.

5.2 Research methodology and design

The youth research focused on young people's gambling experiences with gambling seen as a social recreational activity, but also included questions about the youths' everyday life in regional and rural communities, their community affiliation, and leisure activities. A survey was undertaken with the young people, while personal interviews were conducted with elected local councillors, and with government and community organisations, people who were involved with and managed youth services and activities.

The two Queensland regional and rural communities were selected on the basis of their gambling expenditure, demographic profile and the existence of high schools for the Years 10, 11 and 12 within the communities' boundaries. The two communities researched are presented as one sample, except in cases where the gambling opportunities were different (Community A; the mainly agriculture centred community, and Community M; the mainly mining industry centred community). The populations in the communities were between 10,000 and 13,000 residents.

Two high schools in each community were approached and invited to participate in the research and all four schools accepted the invitation to be part of the research project. The self-administered survey was carried out during school time and lasted approximately 20 to 30 minutes. The sample includes students attending their high school on the day of the research. The collated sample represents 98 per cent of all young people attending school on the research day and 84 per cent of all youths enrolled in the participating schools.[1] The research was undertaken in 2003.

Surveys were distributed outside of the school environment to try to include older young people, such as youths who had left school and were within the workforce or enrolled in further education. Unfortunately, the distributed surveys were rarely returned. The youth sample is thus based on young people attending the local high schools with only 0.4 per cent not attending the high schools. The sample is considered representative for young people attending high schools, experiencing comparable social circumstances and living in regional and rural communities (cf. Fabiansson and Healey 2004).

The concept 'participate' was used in relation to all leisure activities in which the young people participated, gambling being only one of them and being defined as part of a leisure or recreational activity; as being one of the team, to share the activity with the team, the family or with a group of friends. In regard to gambling, 'participate' has been used in the same way, as being part of a social leisure pursuit, which is not necessarily to imply that the youths have in person undertaken the financial gambling transaction, made the bet or bought the lottery ticket, but the respondents have defined themselves when participating in gambling, as being the gambler. The research focused on the social context in which the leisure activity was undertaken and the main gambling question was:

> The table below lists many different forms of wagering and gaming activities; some of them can be played in your local community; others can be undertaken over the internet or in the bigger cities. We would like to know which gambling activities you have participated in during the last five years. Please tick all the activities you have taken part in.

The table listed most known types of gambling pursuits; the list was based on information from earlier studies of gambling pursuits[2] (cf. Productivity Commission

---

1 The data was analysed by the Statistical Package for Social Sciences [SPSS] (2007 version 16.0).

2 Raffle tickets, instant scratch tickets, lotto (lottery games, gold lotto, Ozlotto, Powerball, \$2 jackpot lottery, \$2 casket, \$5 jackpot lottery, tatts Keno, pools, sweepstakes, golden casket) table games at a casino (roulette, blackjack, baccarat, mini baccarat, Jupiter

1999). The response could only be 'yes' or 'no' without any recording of the number of times the youths had undertaken the activity during the past five years. To enhance the reliability of the survey, questions were included regarding who bought the ticket and placed the bet – themselves, parents, friends or other adults, and they were asked which game they had most often played and which game they thought was most fun to play.

The definition of gambling used in the research was broad; it included most types of gambling, from raffle tickets to casino and internet gambling. The survey questionnaire listed most known forms of wagering and gaming activities that could be played in the local community, be undertaken over the internet or at special gambling venues such as at casinos in metropolitan cities or abroad. The survey included both familiar types of gambling and more obscure forms of gambling that would require detailed knowledge of available gambling activities. The obscure gambling types were included to determine whether they were part of the young people's knowledge of the area and if they had experience of these gambling types. The respondents were also encouraged to write down other forms of gambling and wagering activities they had undertaken in addition to those listed in the questionnaire. The findings presented are based on the youths' experiences and recollections of gambling pursuits, and not a record of how many times they may have played the particular game.

While the survey had this broad approach to gambling the reality was that very few of the young people participating in the survey would be able to legally undertake the presented gambling activities, except buying raffle tickets. It is permissible for people under 18 years of age to buy raffle tickets, while other forms of gambling for money are not legally accepted in the Queensland jurisdiction, the same as in other Australian jurisdictions.

5.3 Youths' gambling experiences

5.3.1 Background

It is well documented that gambling activities are a common recreational pursuit and children are introduced to different forms of gambling within the family environment, these include board games and card games. Board and card games are played for fun as a family activity, but also as a tool to help children count and to memorise colour and the value of the card played or those still in the stack.

21/treasury 21, roulette tables, card poker, electronic gaming machine, sic-bo, pai gow, Caribbean stud poker, craps, treasury wheel), Keno, bingo, bet on horse races, and greyhound races, sporting events (rugby league ARL football, rugby union football, Australian rules AFL football, soccer, cricket, tennis, boxing, casino games on the internet, games privately played for money (cards, mah-jong, board games, coins – 2ups, dice games, arcade games, video games).

This form of gambling is rarely an introduction to excessive gambling, but it raises the question of when the interest in gambling activities moves beyond this initial stage. Hence the purpose of the youth study was to explore young people's participating in gambling activities within the family environment, with friends and by themselves. The young people were asked about their introduction to gambling, what form of gambling they participated in, with whom they gambled, how much money they spent on gambling, and how they felt about their gambling, especially how they felt about losing money.

Raffle tickets are often seen as an excellent way to raise money for the local school, local community activities and to promote good causes in the wider society. We might question whether buying a raffle ticket to support the local community, local charities and health foundations should be seen as gambling, however, raffle tickets were included in the survey as they were the only legal gambling avenue for 97.5 per cent of the respondents.

The research results are, where relevant, related to gender and four age groups. The sample includes 55.8 per cent females, thus a smaller group of males (44.2 per cent). In age groups, the 14 year olds, the 15 year olds and the 16 year olds are presented as separate age groups, while the 17 year olds are grouped together with the 18 to 25 year olds. The sample included only 19 people who were in the age bracket between 18 and 25 years, they are of the legal age to undertake gambling activities. This age group was too small to be treated as a separate age group, thus it was combined with the 17 year olds (N=132). The 17 year olds were anticipated to be more comparable to this oldest age group than with the 16 year olds age group. The 18 to 25 year olds represent 2.5 per cent of the total sample, thus will have minor influences on the total percentages.

Nearly three quarters of the youths (74 per cent) classified their living standard as good or very good (middle-class or above), and 96 per cent lived in family like situations, thus this research group can not be deemed as disadvantaged or participating in more than 'normal' youth risk taking behaviour, the types generally related to weekend excessive drinking (cf. Goldstein et al. 2009; Modie and Finnigan 2006; Huang and Boyer 2007; Dickson, Derevensky and Gupta 2008).

The results from the youth survey show young people's gambling experiences and gambling patterns, but the results also reflect their families' gambling interests and experiences, as the respondents in the majority of cases, were below the age where they themselves could buy tickets or put a bet on a horse. The youths in these communities were likely to be well known to shopkeepers, newsagents, hotels, clubs and betting officers, which made it unlikely that they could get away with buying lottery tickets by themselves or bet in person, if they were below 18 years of age. Thus, it is assumed that these results represent not only the youths' gambling habits, but also those of their families.

In cases of research where illegal activities are explored, it is essential to consider the whole picture to get a proper perspective – the underage gambler can very well undertake gambling with their parents and older friends, the financial

114 *Pathways to Excessive Gambling*

transaction occurs where the seller and buyer are all over 18 years of age. However, young people frequently challenge the legal regulations and are very inventive and resourceful in their methods. It has always been exciting for young people to do things that are not legally allowed: underage people will smoke, drink alcohol, take drugs, and drive motorbikes and cars. Gambling should not be seen as an exception.

Gambling is a complex subject as it ranges from a social leisure activity to a deeply problematic societal issue. Gambling has a long tradition within many societies; to win is deeply entrenched in the ethos of societies' survival. For the individual, the drive to win is integral to both work and recreational pursuits. This drive to win naturally also underpins gambling but government regulations, gambling industry initiatives and individual freedom must be addressed in a way that balances with the adverse consequences of excessive gambling. A fundamental difficulty in finding the required balance is the fact that gambling is a strong and profitable business activity which generates vast income for governments through taxation on gambling revenue. Additionally, the gambling industry provides employment to people, is legal and it is a popular recreational pursuit for many people. 'Few other forms of problematic consumption in society, with the possible acceptation of alcohol, have such a complicated foundation' (Fabiansson 2003: 8).

5.4   Gambling for money

The research findings describe the youths' gambling experiences over the previous five years, gambling activities they classified as personally participating in. The percentages represent the youths who had participated in a gambling game at least once, they might have gambled only once, several times on a gambling type or on several of the presented games. Only a small percentage of the youths had participated in the majority of the listed gambling types. In summary, 22.1 per cent of the responding 754 youths had not participated in gambling for money, 59.6 per cent had participated in between one and nine games, and 12.1 per cent had participated in between 10 and 19 of the listed games. A smaller group, 3.4 per cent had gambled on between 20 and 29 of the presented games involving money and a further 2.8 per cent had participated in between 30 and 42 games. In total 77.9 per cent of the respondents had gambled for money at least once during the last five years. The percentages are lower in this research than the percentages reported by the Spelinstitutet (2000), where 95 per cent of the respondents had gambled for money at least once, not restricted to the past 12 months, and Rönnberg et al. (1999) reported that 90 per cent had gambled with money also during an unrestricted time period (cf. Jonsson, Andrén, Nilsson, Svensson, Munck, Kindstedt and Rönnberg 2003). A Canadian survey of 585 college students found that 72.1 per cent of the sample reported gambling in the past six months (Williams, Connolly, Wood and Nowatzki 2006). Research about young people's gambling in Australia found that between 60 and 70 per cent of the surveyed young people had gambled at least once during the past year (Delfabbro 2008: 62) and between 10 and 15 per cent had gambled on a weekly basis (cf. Delfabbro and Thrupp 2003; Delfabbro, Lahn and Grabosky 2005).

Research shows that young people's gambling rate is higher than for the adult population. This of course should be expected when gambling is classified as risk taking behaviour like alcohol and drug use, dangerous driving and unsafe sex (Volberg 2006; Powell, Hardoon, Derevensky and Gupta 1999; Derevensky and Gupta 1996). The lifetime gambling rates among American and Canadian college and university students range between 70 to 94 per cent (Adebayo 1998; Devlin and Peppard 1996; Engwall, Hunter and Steinberg 2004; Kang and Hsu 2001; Ladouceur, Dube and Bujold 1994; Lesieur, Cross, Frank, Welch, White, Rubenstein et al. 1991; Oster and Knapp 1998). As in the adult population, young females have a lower rate of gambling than young males (cf. Jonsson et al. 2003). Thus, the Australian youths' gambling experiences in this study are within the range of the gambling frequency of other youth gambling research with 78 per cent gambling and 22 per cent not gambling at all.

However, all gambling figures should be seen as indicative and not absolute in that they are based on confidential responses to survey questions and people's memory of gambling pursuits are not the same as factual observations. Acknowledgement of some gambling activities might be made without considerations, but to admit excessive and problematic gambling might be more difficult. Thus, an underestimation of excessive and problematic gambling cannot be ruled out. Nevertheless, the opposite situation with exaggerating of gambling pursuits can be a factor among young gamblers, thus gambling figures should be considered as approximations of gambling pursuits and not as absolute figures (cf. Derevensky and Gupta 2006). Furthermore, gambling studies are often single issue focused with small samples drawn from one jurisdiction or group of people e.g. high school students, thus generalisations from the results are limited and not always representative for other groups, nor situations outside the researched groups and the special conditions that pertain to the research. The following sections present the findings from the survey of young people's gambling experiences in Australian rural and regional communities.

5.5 Non-age restricted gambling

5.5.1 Raffle tickets

It is a common practice to sell raffle tickets to support the local school and the community and this is sometimes one of the few possibilities for local organisations to financially support local community projects, school buildings and equipment, local services, community sports events, charities and health services. More than two-thirds of the high school students (69.4 per cent) had supported the school through buying raffle tickets (Table 5.1). Female respondents were more inclined

Table 5.1 Young people's experiences of buying raffle tickets by age and gender

Bought raffle tickets to support/ age groups, gender	14 year olds	15 year olds	16 year olds	17–25 year olds	Females	Males	Total average %	Total N^
School activities	70.7	62.5	73.3	73.8*	75.2	62.0***	69.4	514
Sports events	57.6	60.5	66.0	65.8	61.9	64.4	63.0	467
Community projects	52.2	49.8	54.3	55.0	56.1	48.3*	52.6	390
Health foundations	58.7	56.5	67.2	75.2**	70.9	55.6***	64.1	475
Total sample N	94	255	254	151	421	333		754

Note: Pearson Chi-Square; level of significance: $p \leq 0.001***$ – strong; $0.001–0.009**$– moderate; $0.01–0.05*$ – weak; ^ The gambling categories and percentages are independent of each other.

to support school activities through buying raffle tickets, 75.2 per cent compared to 62.0 per cent of the males. In relation to age groups, the differences were minor. The lowest percentage was among the 15-year-old youths, with 62.5 per cent and the highest was among the oldest age group respondents with 73.8 per cent.

While male youths were more involved in sports events and physical activities, their support for these events was only marginally more, through their buying of raffle tickets compared to the female youths. Sixty-four per cent of male respondents had bought raffle tickets to support local sports events, compared to 61.9 per cent of the female respondents; however, the difference was not significant.

Sixty-four per cent of youths had bought raffle tickets to support a health foundation while 52.6 per cent had supported a community project. The female respondents were more active in supporting community projects as well as giving support to health organisations. Older respondents had the highest percentage in supporting different health projects, 75.2 per cent. The gender differences were strongly significant ($p \leq 0.001$) in relation to supporting school activities and health foundations. Overall, the raffle ticket purchasing percentages were highest for supporting school activities, followed by support for health related services, sports events and community projects.

It is permissible for young people to be involved in community activities by collecting money through selling and buying raffle tickets, even if this practice has been questioned lately with parents and schools becoming concerned about the ethical conduct of using young people to collect money for school and community projects. The research findings demonstrate that young people in the two communities showed a strong commitment to their school and to their local community. However, a councillor in one of the communities noted a change in the community with growing difficulties in engaging residents in local raffles, even when the prize was a car. The decline in interest was seen as a lack of 'small change' which was more likely to be spent on gambling than on local raffles for community projects (Fabiansson and Healey 2004).

5.5.2   Card, board, arcade and video games

Most young people will play card games during their childhood together with their family and friends, as a social recreational activity. Card games can be a fun way to learn to count for young children within the family environment, but card games are also used for educational purposes in schools to help children count and to memorise the cards' colour and values that have been played. For older children and young people card games such as poker are often played among friends at school or at home. Even if card and board games are played at an early age, these games are activities where an element of gambling is involved; however, it is questionable whether any indication of future gambling interests can be derived from playing board games and cards as children with family and friends.

It was more popular for males to play card games with friends with money involved (41.0 per cent) than for females. Approximately one third (33.6 per cent) of the female respondents indicated that they had played cards with money. The oldest age group, 17 years and older, and the 15 year olds had the highest percentage of players of cards with money (43.0 per cent and 40.3 per cent, respectively). One third of the 16 year olds had played cards with money while only 27.2 per cent of the youngest age group, the 14 year olds, had played cards with money.[3] Thus playing cards with money was played among friends, but it was still an activity that less than half of the responding youth had participated in, attracting more of the males and particularly the older males. The older youths had, through part time work, larger amounts of their own money than the younger youths, thus for the younger youths playing cards without money was presumably more attractive.

Similar to card games, board games are a classic family leisure activity that is both fun and educational, and hardly related to gambling. It is rather a family social event undertaken within the family environment. These games with no age restriction are family friendly games, where family and friends come together to have fun. Card and board games do not need to involve money, but may be seen as more 'exciting' if the winner can pocket some money, some other prizes or the loss is paid for by losing clothing (strip poker) which commonly include mixed gender groups. Money is more likely to be introduced among older young people and among friends rather than within the family environment. Nonetheless, among teenage friends, the introduction of money makes family board games more attractive, especially in an environment where winning and being rewarded for success such as at school or on the sports field are encouraged, even among young children. A significant difference between the age groups was shown in relation to board games with the age groups 15 years and the 17 years and older (25.7 per cent and 22.1 per cent, respectively) having the highest percentages of the young people playing board games followed by the 14 year olds and the 16 year

---

3   In both cases, the significance level was weak p≤ 0.01–0.05.

Table 5.2   Young people's experiences of betting on games by age and gender

Gambling for money/age groups, gender	14 year olds	15 year olds	16 year olds	17–25 year olds	Females	Males	Total average %	Total N^
Video games	18.5	22.1	15.0	20.8	13.6	25.8***	19.1	141
Arcade games	10.9	19.8	11.8	20.8*	10.7	23.1***	16.2	120
Total sample N	94	255	254	151	421	333		754

Note: Pearson Chi-Square; level of significance: p≤ 0.001*** – strong; 0.001–0.009** – moderate; .01–0.05* – weak; ^ The gambling categories and percentages are independent of each other.

olds (17.4 per cent and 13.4 per cent, respectively). The difference between males and females playing board games was marginal (20.7 per cent and 19.2 per cent, respectively). Another game not related to money is video games played in the home environment. Video games are more recent family games that are competing with the traditional card and board games.

Arcade games, public games where the player pays for playing specific games, were also the most popular with the age groups 15 years and the 17 years and older (19.8 per cent and 20.8 per cent, respectively, Table 5.2). Arcade and video games were clearly more popular with the males (23.1 per cent and 25.8 per cent, respectively) than with the females (10.7 per cent and 13.6 per cent, respectively). Overall, arcade and video games were most popular among the males and most favoured by the age groups 15 years and 17 years and older youths. The Australian arcade games are different from the UK gaming venues, which also include slot machines where young people can play for money and win money on gaming machines (slot/fruit machines) paying out £8 or less (Griffith 1998; United Kingdom Gambling Commission 2005). The Australian arcade venues do not include such gaming machines. Griffith (1998) has shown that when gambling venues are mixed with age specific and non-age specific gambling machines it is difficult to control what machines young people play on.

All of these games, cards, board and video games played in the home with family and friends, including gambling for money or not, and the public arcade and video games are mostly participated in as social entertainment activities without any deeper reflection that they may be creating a foundation for a potential gambling propensity. Most children and young people are quite familiar with these types of gambling games and many of them will have good memories of family time playing cards and board games and playing games at gaming arcades. At the same time, one should not totally dismiss their influence in nurturing a gambling interest and creating curiosity about other forms of gambling pursuits. A competitive gambling interest can already be nurtured at this stage, but it is hardly an indication on future gambling propensity.

5.6 Age restricted gambling

5.6.1 Lottery products

The more public and regulated forms of gambling, such as lottery and scratch tickets can be bought in local communities from newsagents. Overall, lottery tickets are the most common gambling form in which people participate in Australia and globally. In Australia, all lottery and scratch tickets have an age limit of 18 years of age for purchase. This does not restrict advertising scratch tickets in colours and motifs with popular figures that might entice and appeal to young people and even children. One can assume that most lottery tickets were bought in the local community and a number of players would be registered players with weekly systems of lottery tickets. Additionally, it is highly likely that the young people who had bought lottery and scratch tickets had done so in company with parents, older siblings, or friends, than being able to buy them by themselves being underage.

Twenty-two per cent of the respondents indicated that they had bought a lotto or golden lotto ticket during the last five years; a further 16.9 per cent said that they had bought Powerball tickets (Table 5.3). Twelve per cent of the responding youths had played pools and 11 per cent golden casket winners' circle. Ten per cent had bought Ozlotto tickets, played sweepstakes and $2 jackpot/$2 casket.[4]

The oldest age group had the highest percentage (31 per cent) of buying lotto tickets, followed by the 15 year olds (23 per cent). The oldest age group also bought Ozlotto tickets (19 per cent) and $2 jackpot/$2 casket (15 per cent) more frequently than the other age groups. Thus, the older respondents were more inclined to buy lottery tickets than the younger respondents. The oldest age group obviously also had less restriction on their opportunities to buy lottery tickets than the younger respondents.

Male respondents were more involved in lottery type gambling than female respondents. Most popular with male respondents was buying lotto/gold lotto (27.4 per cent) followed by Powerball (20.4 per cent). Lotto/gold lotto tickets (18.4 per cent) were most popular also with female youths. The males' higher participation in gambling is consistent with observations made in earlier studies (cf. Derevensky and Gupta 2004a; Delfabbro 2008; Goldstein et al. 2009; Productivity Commission 1999, 2009).

Approximately half of the respondents had bought instant scratchies. Instant scratch tickets can be bought in local newsagent outlets and are thus easily available. Fifty-one (50.6) per cent of responding youths stressed that they had bought instant scratchies, and 41.6 per cent of them indicated that they had bought scratch'n'win tickets. The oldest responding age group and males had the highest percentages for buying instant scratchies (57.7 per cent and 52.3 per cent, respectively). Concerning scratch'n'win, the youngest age group and the males

---

4 All monetary values presented are in Australian dollars.

Table 5.3   Young people's experiences of buying lotto tickets by gender

Played lotto or other lottery game/gender	Females	Males	Total average %	Total N^
Lotto/Gold lotto	18.4	27.4**	22.4	166
Powerball	14.1	20.4*	16.9	125
Pools	11.7	13.4	12.4	92
Golden casket winners circle	8.5	14.3**	11.1	82
Ozlotto	7.8	13.7**	10.4	77
Sweepstakes	10.0	10.0	10.0	74
$2 Jackpot lottery/$2 casket	7.5	12.8*	9.9	73
Golden casket super 66	5.8	10.3*	7.8	58
$5 Jackpot lottery	4.9	10.6**	7.4	55
Tatts 2	4.1	7.6*	5.7	42
Tatts lotto	3.4	7.6	5.3	39
Total sample N	421	333		754

Note: Pearson Chi-Square; level of significance: p≤ 0.001*** – strong; 0.001–0.009** – moderate; 0.01–0.05* – weak; ^ The gambling categories and percentages are independent of each other.

were the most frequent buyers (44.6 per cent and 43.4 per cent, respectively). Certain types of scratch'n'win tickets give the buyer the possibility of winning up to $25,000 and sometimes more money and lottery tickets can reward the winner with several millions, even if it is a highly unlikely occurrence, it is nevertheless an enticement to gamble.

Only 19 of the respondents were 18 years of age and over, this means 2.5 per cent of the sample was legally allowed to gamble. This does not include the buying of raffle tickets. The percentages of students who have indicated that they had bought these tickets were well above the number of students that were legally allowed to purchase these tickets, thus help from parents and older friends might have been sought in the buying exercise, however, some of the older youths might look like 18 years of age and might have managed to buy the tickets by themselves.

To buy a raffle ticket is not usually considered as gambling and many people would hardly consider buying a lottery ticket as an indication of future gambling problems (Felsher, Derevensky and Gupta 2004). Additionally, in the Productivity Commission 2009 review lottery ticket gambling was excluded as contributing to problem gambling.

The research shows that the young people bought lottery products and it was a common occurrence, especially lotto, Powerball and scratch tickets. Thus, being underage did not limit the ability to participate in this type of gambling activity. Nonetheless, it is highly likely that the majority of these purchases took place in the company of parents, older siblings and friends or other adults (cf. Griffith 1998). Thus, these results are an indication not only of the youths' gambling behaviour, but most likely also of their parents' gambling patterns. The parents' gambling preferences were well fathomed by their children and the gambling was understood to be a pursuit for the whole family rather than a separate activity for the parents or the young people.

5.6.2 Casino table games

The reliability of a survey can always be questioned, even if the results from the youth survey have indicated high reliability and consistency, it is possible that a somewhat higher percentage of gambling will be presented in some categories. It is also likely that some respondents have been over enthusiastic in their reporting of gambling activities, but it is at the same time expected that some youths have underreported their gambling activities. This is partly because people can hardly remember all the different forms of gambling that they may have participated in over the last five years. Notwithstanding these limitations in this survey, the relationship between different types of gambling should not be influenced by the research design and none of the respondents 'ticked' all listed gambling forms. The gambling forms that are hard to access, such as casino table games, have a significantly lower participation rate than the easier accessible gambling games, such as raffle, lotto products, horse races and Keno playing (Griffiths 1998; Griffiths and Wood 2001; Delfabbro and Thrupp 2003).

Casino gambling is illegal for underage youths, but this is not always a barrier for participation and earlier research has noted its occurrence (Dickson, Derevensky and Gupta 2008; Griffiths 1998; Gupta and Derevensky 1998a; Derevensky and Gupta 1996; Productivity Commission 1999). The initial analysis of the findings from the youth survey concerning casino venue gambling raised questions about the possibility for underage youths to gamble at casinos. The findings were discussed with the Responsible Gambling Manager at a larger Australian casino (November 2003). The manager presented the casino's own data that showed approximately 700 underage young people (representing 0.001 per cent of monthly visitors at the casino) were caught each month within that casino. The casino collates statistics for all cases as well as statistics for drunkenness and other offences. In the age group two years and up to 14 years of age, 95 per cent of the underage came into the casino venue in parents' company. In relation to the older age group, 15 to 17 year olds, approximately 50 per cent of them visited the casino together with their parents, the rest by themselves or together with older friends or siblings. In some cases, especially with young children, the breaches were often due to a lack of knowledge about age limits and gambling regulations. Frequently, their intention was to gain access to the salad bar or to other food outlets within the casino. The underage visits increased during the Christmas holidays, but also during school holidays. Many of these visits by the older underage youths were deliberately aimed at gaining access to the gambling games and trying to outsmart the security guards.

The youths' experiences of gambling at a casino venue show that the most frequently mentioned gambling activities were blackjack and electronic gaming machines (Table 5.4). The three most highly played forms of gambling, blackjack, gaming machine gambling and roulette, (12.3 per cent, 12.2 per cent and 7.2 per cent, respectively) are all games that are easy to join and leave quickly, if the casino staff approach to question the age of the player. These findings correspond with the Responsible Gambling Manager's experiences that underage young people try to get access to the casino gambling area to play games at the venue but are well aware of the risks of detection and the need to quickly leave the gambling, thus blackjack, gaming machine gambling and roulette are the best options for a hasty retreat (cf. Dickson, Derevensky and Gupta 2008; Griffiths 1998; Gupta and Derevensky 1998a; Derevensky and Gupta 1996).

Casino gambling was of more interest for the male respondents than for the females. Overall, the female respondents had a much lower gambling profile than the male respondents at a casino venue. Blackjack was mentioned by 18.2 per cent of the male respondents as a casino game they had played, compared to only 7.5 per cent of the female youths. In general, the female respondents had a much lower percentage of participation in all these forms of casino gambling games. Only in blackjack and gaming machine gambling did females show a somewhat higher participation rate (7.5 per cent and 8.8 per cent, respectively), but still well below the males' rate. The figures indicate that female respondents had been less adventurous about accessing casino venues than male respondents.

Despite regulations, information campaigns, and vigilant control by casino staff, underage youths venture into casino venues. An open floor plan with several access areas with open view of the gaming floor makes the gambling inviting and

Table 5.4   Young people's experiences of participating in casino table games by age and gender

Games/gender	Females	Males	Total average %	Total N^
Blackjack	7.5	18.2***	12.3	91
Gaming machine	8.8	16.4**	12.2	90
Roulette	3.9	11.2***	7.2	53
Craps	3.6	10.0***	6.5	48
Roulette tables	2.9	10.0***	6.1	45
Treasury wheel	3.6	8.5**	5.8	43
Caribbean stud poker	2.9	8.8***	5.5	41
Jupiter 21/Treasury 21	3.9	7.3*	5.4	40
Sic-bo	2.4	8.2***	5.0	37
Baccarat	2.2	8.2***	4.9	36
Mini baccarat	2.2	8.2***	4.9	36
Pai gow	2.2	7.0**	4.3	36

Note: Pearson Chi-Square; level of significance: $p \leq 0.001$*** – strong; 0.001–0.009** – moderate; 0.01–0.05* – weak; ^ The gambling categories and percentages are independent of each other. Total sample 754, 421 females, 333 males.

Youth Gambling 123

tempting to access. Prohibited activities have always been an interesting challenge for young people, and it is rather the rule than the exception that restricted access and prohibited behaviour, become draw cards for young people.

5.6.3 Club and hotel games

One of the most popular gambling games in the local communities was to play Keno. Keno is a numbers game, the player buys a card with for instance 20 numbers, and the player marks the numbers that corresponds to the card numbers the 'caller' announces; the numbers called range from 1 to 80. This is a common and popular game played in Australian clubs and hotels. It is also a game that underage young people can easily play during a family outing at the local club. The children and young people play while their parents socialise with their friends. The parents or other adults buy the card while the youths keep track of the numbers. This is one example of how gambling, especially playing Keno becomes closely related to club visits and family dinners at the local club. The children get something exciting to do and the adults can concentrate on socialising.

The students had played Keno games at both clubs and hotels in the communities. Thirty-eight per cent of respondents had played Keno at a club, 23.1 per cent had played it at a hotel, and 6.6 per cent played it at a casino (Table 5.5). Keno was the most popular gambling game played by the young people, other than horse racing (see below).

The dominance of male gamblers has been consistent in this research and other research supports the notion that males have a higher gambling propensity than females (cf. Derevensky and Gupta 2004b; Delfabbro 2008; Goldstein et al. 2009; Productivity Commission 1999, 2009). However, with regard to Keno gambling, the female respondents showed a much higher percentage of participation compared to other forms of gambling. Thirty-six per cent of the female youths indicated that they had played Keno at a club and a further 22.4 per cent had played Keno at a hotel. The corresponding percentages for male youths were 40.7 per cent and

Table 5.5   Young people's experiences of playing Keno by gender

Played Keno/gender	Females	Males	Total average %	Total N^
at a club	35.5	40.7	37.8	280
at a hotel	22.4	24.0	23.1	171
at a casino	5.4	8.2	6.6	49
at a club, hotel or casino	41.1	43.8	42.3	313
Total sample N	421	333		754

Note: Pearson Chi-Square; level of significance: $p \leq 0.001{***}$ – strong; $0.001–0.009{**}$ – moderate; $0.01–0.05{*}$ – weak; ^ The gambling categories and percentages are independent of each other.

24.0 per cent, respectively. Considering the age of the young people there were no significant differences concerning Keno gambling. The percentages ranged between 36 per cent and 39 per cent playing Keno at a club. The age groups that played Keno the most were the 15 year olds and the 17 year olds and above, both 39 per cent.

Another numbers game is bingo, it is the same type of game as Keno, but is mainly seen as a game for mature people. The winnings are not always money but rather goods (small kitchen appliances, movie tickets, vouchers) and perishables (meat tray, fruit baskets). The high school students indicated that they played bingo at a hall or at a club. Nineteen per cent of the respondents had played bingo at a club and 25 per cent had played it at a hall. It is understandable that gambling games can also be used to encourage learning in schools and to make, maths for instance, more fun and realistic for the students. Bingo was played at some of the high schools as an educational activity without students winning any cash prizes. Thus, bingo is one example of how the gambling construct is applied within the education environment and whether or not the family is gambling, the children and young people will encounter gambling games within the community, the education system and among friends.

5.6.4 Horse, sports and internet betting

A classic form of gambling is betting on horse races. Overall, 41.9 per cent of the respondents indicated that they had bet on horse races. In Community M, the mining community, the percentage was 46.4 per cent. In this community a prominent and modern racetrack was established close to the community within easy access for the community residents. Community A, the mainly agricultural based community, also had a racetrack, but less modern and further away from the town centre, here only 37.0 per cent of the young people had bet on a horse race. It is proposed that easy access to a gambling venue contributes to gambling pursuits (cf. Volberg, Rugle, Rosenthal and Fong 2005; cf. Chapter 6). In this case, the more prominent racetrack was to a greater extent utilised by the respondents than the less conveniently placed racetrack in the agriculturally based community.[5] Furthermore, horse riding is a popular recreational activity among young females and it is interesting to note that betting on horse racing was the only gambling type in which the females had a higher gambling activity level than the males. Forty-two per cent (42.2) of the females had bet money on horses and 41.6 per cent of the responding males. Concerning age groups, the 17 year olds and older reported the highest percentage of horse betting (47.0 per cent), followed by the 16 year olds (44.3 per cent).

If horse racing attracted gambling due to its closeness to residents in Community M, the low percentage of young people gambling on greyhounds

---

5   The significant difference between the communities was somewhat weak ($p \leq 0.01$), with no significant differences between gender and age groups.

could be explained by the lack of greyhound racetracks in the communities. Any interest in betting on greyhound races was much less common than betting on horses among the respondents; only 10.3 per cent said that they had gambled on greyhound races. Thirteen per cent (12.8) of the male respondents had gambled on greyhounds compared to 8 per cent (8.3) of the females.

The possibilities to bet on a horse race or a sports event have changed from being first restricted to place a bet only on the event site, to off site betting, betting offices or agents to interactive gambling through phone, digital television and the internet accessible from the gambler's home. These alternatives have created an unlimited diversity in gambling options. Gambling on sports activities through the internet is increasing internationally and nationally and this increase is helped by easy access to global gambling websites, which gives the gambler nearly endless opportunities to bet without time and geographical limits (Australasian Gaming Council 2008; The Allen Group 2009). Internet betting can be done conveniently through the home computer, by phone or digital television. The diversity in betting options has also increased (cf. Parke et al. 2007). It is possible to place bets not only on final results of matches, but also to bet on the first point or goal, and on the difference in scores between the winner and the loser.

Betting on football matches was the most popular form of gambling among the youth respondents. Approximately 30 per cent of the respondents had bet on the results of football matches, followed by cricket and boxing (13.8 per cent and 12.0 per cent, respectively, Table 5.6). Sports gambling were strongly gender related. Thirty-five per cent of the male respondents had bet on Australian Rules football, Australian Rugby League football or Rugby Union matches. Football, cricket and boxing were all sports that attracted more bets from male respondents than from females. Nineteen per cent of the male respondents had bet on cricket while 17.9 per cent had bet on rugby union and boxing. The highest percentage for female betting was also on football matches (25.8 per cent), this was followed by cricket with 10 per cent. These findings indicate that sports betting in the communities was a highly gender specific area, possibly reflecting team sports and other sports importance especially for males. The communities catered very well for sports interested young people and adults, especially for the male residents, but also for sports interested young females and younger adults. The sports alternatives were fewer for females and they did not have the same alternatives in level of competitions mainly due to fewer females being involved in physical sports and team sports than males (Fabiansson 2005).

Betting on sports was more common in the mining community than in the agriculture-dominated community. This was especially true for football betting (34.2 per cent and 25.1 per cent, respectively) and to lesser extent for cricket (15.3 per cent and 12.1 per cent, respectively). The sports facilities in Community M were extensive, modern and well equipped with large lights making it possible to play after dark. Overall, team sports and physical sports are encouraged in rural and regional areas and for males, it was nearly a must to be involved to be accepted in the community. To belong to a winning team creates a special sought

Table 5.6   Young people's experiences of betting on sports by community and gender

Sports event/ community/gender	Community A	Community M	Females	Males	Total average %	Total N^
Australian football*	25.1	34.2**	25.8	35.0**	29.9	221
Cricket	12.1	15.3	10.0	18.5**	13.8	102
Boxing	11.0	13.0	7.5	17.6***	12.0	89
Tennis	9.3	9.3	8.0	10.9	9.3	69
Soccer	8.2	10.1	6.8	12.2*	9.2	68
Total sample N	357	397	421	333		754

Note: Pearson Chi-Square; level of significance: p≤ 0.001*** – strong; 0.001–0.009** – moderate; 0.01–0.05* – weak. * Rugby League football (ARL), Rugby Union, or Australian Rules (AFL); ^ The gambling categories and percentages are independent of each other.

after status by males in the community and it can compensate for lack of school performance and academic interest (Fabiansson 2005).

Sports betting is well suited to interactive gambling and internet technology as the bets can be launched and recorded instantaneously during matches. This form of gambling can be undertaken at home and at any time during the day or night. Eighteen per cent of youths responded that they had gambled through the internet. Internet gambling was more common among the male respondents (22.0 per cent) than for females (15.3 per cent).[6] In relation to age groups, there was no real difference between them; the highest users were among the 15 year olds and the 14 year olds (19.0 per cent and 18.5 per cent, respectively). The lowest percentage was among the 16 year olds (17.5 per cent). Overall, only 135 of the 754 young people (17.9 per cent) indicated that they were gambling on the internet (cf. Australian Council of Social Services 1997).

Through the internet technology the gambler does not need to interact with others and it is one of the most anonymous forms of gambling (Griffiths and Barnes 2008). Concerns have been raised that it would be easy to over commit oneself in this form of gambling (Nelson et al. 2008; Broda et al. 2008). A debit card is needed to pay for online gambling in Australia; however, the majority of sites are based abroad, where a credit card might be accepted. In the regional communities, internet gambling among young people was not seen as a problem. If it happened, it was assumed to be in a controlled minor way and only one case was reported where a young person had had access to a debit card and gambled over the internet without the parent's knowledge.

Gambling on the internet is an area where it is assumed gambling pursuits will increase and especially in geographically isolated areas. The affordability of computer technology has increased, computers are found in many homes and

---

6   The level of significance was weak, p≤ 0.01.

computers have nearly become mandatory for students doing research and school homework. Access to computers and internet services has thus increased and made it easier for computer literate people to also use the computer to place bets from home rather than to visit a betting office or an agency (Griffiths and Barnes 2008; Productivity Commission 2009).

Overall, the interviewed councillors did not associate gambling with young people and youth gambling was not considered a problem in either of the communities. The young people in the community were not seen as gamblers, either due to the fact that gambling was part of an acceptable social leisure activity in company with parents or that youth gambling was not seen as causing any trouble for the young residents and the community, thus not of any concern for the councillors.

5.7 Summary of older youths' gambling experiences

The sample includes 19 young people who could legally participate in gambling activities, as they had reached 18 years of age, which is the legal age of gambling in Australia. As this older age group includes too few participants to give significant statistical differences these older youths were grouped together with the 17 year olds in the age group related analyses. Nonetheless, to explore if there exist any substantial differences between the 18 years old and older young people in the sample that legally can participate in gambling activities and the underage young people, who cannot legally participate in gambling activities, the sample was grouped into two groups, 14 to 17 year olds and 18 to 25 year olds. Overall, the small sample in the age group 18 to 25 year olds would only marginally influence the total average percentages for the whole sample (Table 5.7).

The older respondents have an overall higher gambling participation rate than the younger respondents. The older youths can also buy lottery tickets without any age restrictions. The higher gambling propensity is especially noticeable for lotto, scratch, Powerball and Ozlotto tickets. With scratch tickets, scratch'n'win and instant scratchies, being the most often bought type of lottery ticket. Even if the percentages of the older youths do not influence the average percentages, the older youths' gambling was overall at a higher level than the gambling percentages of the younger respondents. The same trend was present in relation to casino venue gambling, where playing on gaming machines and blackjack were the most popular. The higher percentages for the older respondents in casino venue gambling should be seen in the light that they could legally patronise these venues not only for gambling, but also for socialising with friends (cf. Tanasornnarong, Jackson and Thomas 2004).

Keno is one of the gambling types where even the younger respondents at 14 to 17 years of age had a high gambling rate (overall 42.0 per cent), but it is interesting to note that the older respondents played Keno at a higher rate (overall 52.6 per cent) than the younger youths at clubs, hotels and especially at casino venues. On the whole, the largest percentage differences were associated with gaming machine

128 *Pathways to Excessive Gambling*

Table 5.7   Summary of age limited gambling games by age groups in per cent

Age restricted gambling/age groups	14–17 year olds	18–25 year olds	Average total per cent^
Lottery games			
Instant scratchies	50.4	57.9	50.6
Scratch'n'win	41.0	63.2*	41.6
Lotto/Gold lotto	21.7	47.4**	22.4
Powerball	16.2	42.1**	16.9
Pools	11.9	31.6*	12.4
Golden Casket Winners Circle	10.5	31.6**	11.1
Ozlotto	9.4	47.4***	10.4
Sweepstakes	9.7	21.1	10.0
$2 Jackpot lottery/$2 Casket	9.4	26.3*	9.9
Golden casket super 66	7.5	21.1*	7.8
$5 Jackpot lottery	7.1	21.1*	7.4
Tatts 2	5.5	10.5	5.7
Tatts lotto	5.1	10.5	5.3
Casino venue games			
Roulette	6.7	26.3**	7.2
Blackjack	11.5	42.1***	12.3
Baccarat	4.7	10.5	4.9
Mini baccarat	4.4	21.1**	4.9
Jupiter 21/Treasury 21	4.9	26.3***	5.4
Roulette tables	5.5	26.3***	6.1
Electronic gaming machine	11.1	52.6***	12.2
Casino venue games (cont.)			
Sic-bo	4.6	21.1**	5.0
Pai gow	4.0	15.8*	4.3
Caribbean stud poker	5.1	21.1**	5.5
Craps	5.7	36.8***	6.5
Treasury wheel	5.0	36.8***	5.8
Club and hotel gambling			
Keno (club)	37.4	52.6	37.8
Keno (hotel)	22.9	31.6	23.1
Keno (casino)	5.7	42.1***	6.6
Total Keno	42.0	52.6	42.3
Bingo (club)	19.0	26.3	19.2
Bingo (at a hall)	24.7	31.6	24.9
Sports betting			
Horse racing	41.6	52.6	41.9
Greyhound	9.4	42.1***	10.3
Rugby	29.5	42.1	29.9

Youth Gambling   129

Table 5.7   Continued

Age restricted gambling/age groups	14–17 year olds	18–25 year olds	Average total per cent^
Soccer	8.9	21.1*	9.2
Cricket	13.3	31.6*	13.8
Tennis	9.0	21.1	9.3
Boxing	11.8	21.1	12.0
Internet gambling	18.1	26.3	18.3
Total sample N	735	19	754

Note: Pearson Chi-Square; level of significance: $p \leq 0.001***$ – strong; $0.001–0.009**$ – moderate; $0.01–0.05*$ – weak; ^ The gambling categories and percentages are independent of each other.

gambling, with the 14 to 17 year olds percentage of 11.1 per cent compared to the 18 years and older with 52.6 per cent, followed by Ozlotto (9.4 per cent and 47.4 per cent, respectively) and Keno at a casino venue (5.7 per cent and 42.1 per cent, respectively). The highest frequency for a gambling pursuit was instant scratchies (50.4 per cent) among the 14 to 17 year olds, while the scratch'n'win showed the highest percentage (63.2 per cent) for the 18 year olds and older (Table 5.7).

Keno was the overall preferred gambling type by all young people. The younger respondents had possibility to play Keno during family dinners at the local club. Additionally, the oldest age group also outnumbered the younger counterparts in sports, especially greyhound betting and internet gambling, thus gambling was well established within the 18 years and older age group's everyday social entertainment pursuits. These results indicate that young people continue to gamble when they have reached the legal age for doing so. Thus, the older youths were most likely to continue and increase the gambling pattern they had when gambling together with their parents. In no instances had the oldest youths a lower percentage rate of gambling participation than the young respondents.

The findings show that gambling as a social leisure activity undertaken within the family was following the same pattern for the young people and continued into adulthood. The 18 year olds and older had comparable gambling patterns as their younger counterparts. However, when they could decide their leisure preferences by themselves, the older youths showed an increased gambling propensity relative to the younger age groups (cf. Derevensky and Gupta 2006).

5.8   Youths' gambling intensity

Of all the games that were available in the two communities, in metropolitan cities, and on the internet, the games the respondents thought were most fun to play and

Table 5.8 Gambling activities most frequently played and most fun to play

Games mentioned most frequently	Games most often played	Most fun games
Cards	87	92
Keno	77	60
Scratchies, Lotto, Powerball, Gold lotto	50	36
Sports (Rugby, Soccer, League, Golf, Tennis)	29	31
Raffle tickets	28	3
Horse race	24	29
Blackjack (at venue, computer)	20	19
Bingo	15	24
Video games	12	14
Board games (Mah-jong, Chess, Monopoly)	10	25

Note: The respondents could give more than one alternative.

which they played most frequently were card games[7] (Table 5.8). As mentioned before, playing card games with the family does not necessarily involve playing with money. However, if it is played among friends at high school level it is more likely that money is part of the card game.

The most frequently named public gambling game was Keno, followed by buying lotto or scratch tickets. These gambling types were clearly the most popular and fun games for the respondents. Keno, scratchies and lotto games were also the most often played games, after card games. A distant third was sports betting. Sports activities are the dominant leisure activity for school aged and older males in rural and regional communities. The high focus on physical sports is to a degree carried over to sports betting. However, only 0.03 per cent of the household disposable income (HDI) expenditure was in 2005–06 spent on sports betting, while 1.73 per cent was spent on gaming machines Australia wide. Sports betting as a proportion of HDI was 2005–06 in New South Wales, 0.03 per cent, Victoria 0.04 per cent, whilst only 0.01 per cent in Queensland, where the survey was undertaken (Australasian Gaming Council 2008: 25, 29). Sports betting is increasing in New South Wales and Victoria, but less so in Queensland, Australian Capital Territory, Northern Territory and Western Australia (Australian Gaming Council 2007: 30; cf. Chapter 4).

Buying raffle tickets was the fifth most common gambling form but the least fun, only three students thought it was fun to buy raffle tickets, thus buying a raffle ticket was done more to support the community, the school or a good cause, not for fun. Betting on horse racing was more fun, but less often played by the respondents, even if the highest percentage of all gambling forms for females

---

7 The question specified playing cards with money, but this can have been forgotten at this question, thus the figure is likely to include all card games with or without money.

Youth Gambling

was betting on horse races. Horse race betting was done mostly when races were arranged in the home community thus not a weekly event or even a monthly event, but more related to the spring carnival and larger race meetings.

5.9 Youths' arrangement for gambling payments

Gambling for money can be a cost intensive activity with uncertain returns. Some of the young people in the research sample had part time work and therefore their own money. The research participants who were 18 years of age and older could make the financial transactions by themselves, while the underage needed to rely on parents, older siblings and friends. For the underage gamblers their gambling was often a shared activity with family and friends. Only 37.7 per cent of the participating youth (N=284) in the survey clarified how they paid for their gambling. Sixty-three per cent of the responding youths stated that their parents, older siblings, or an older friend placed the bets or bought lottery tickets. The high involvement of parents in the young people's gambling shows that the youths' introduction to gambling activities was done with help from and condoned by their parents, siblings and friends. Thus the gambling was not done in secret, but as an accepted family and friend activity, a socially endorsed activity. Females (73.3 per cent) were more inclined than males (52.2 per cent) to rely on parents, older siblings or friends for the payment.

Thirty per cent placed their bets at their local club, hotel or at the TAB. The males were more inclined than the females to use the TAB, club, hotel or pub to place a bet (37.7 per cent and 22.6 per cent, respectively). Only 7 per cent placed their bets by using the phone or the internet; 10.1 per cent of the males and 4.1 per cent of the females used this option to place a bet. The different age groups did not show any significant differences in how and where they placed their bets. However, the youngest age group, the 14 year olds, had the highest percentage, 72 per cent, indicating that parents, older siblings or friends placed their bets. For this age group it would also be most difficult to pretend to be over 18 years of age, thus the need to rely on parents, older siblings and friends.

A clear majority of the survey participants responded that they placed their bets by using cash. Eighty-seven per cent of the respondents paid cash for their bets while only 13 per cent used credit or debit card, or used an agency account. There were no significant differences in any of the categories of gender, age groups or communities. Paying cash for bets was the dominant payment method.

5.10 Youths' spending structure

The amounts of money that youths spent on gambling during an evening ranged from less than $5 to more than $50. Forty-six per cent of the respondents who gambled indicated that they spent less than $5 on gambling during an evening and

132 Pathways to Excessive Gambling

Table 5.9   Average spending on gambling activities during an evening by age groups and gender in per cent

Spent on gambling/ age groups, gender	14 year olds	15 year olds	16 year olds	17–25 year olds	Females	Males	Total average %	Total N
Less than $5	50.0	50.5	49.5	32.8	54.6	37.6*	45.9	125
Between $5 and $9	36.4	23.7	21.8	20.9	21.2	25.5	23.4	64
Between $10 and $49	4.5	15.5	20.7	26.9	15.9	22.0	19.0	52
$50 or more	9.1	10.3	8.0	19.4	8.3	14.9	11.7	32
Total respondents %	100.0	100.0	100.0	100.0	100.0	100.0	100.0	
Total respondents N	22	97	87	67	132	141		273

Note: Pearson Chi-Square; level of significance: $p \leq 0.001^{***}$ – strong; $0.001–0.009^{**}$ – moderate; $0.01–0.05^*$ – weak.

a further 23.4 per cent said that they spent $9 or less (Table 5.9). Another fifth of the respondents said that they spent less than $50 during an evening gambling. Overall, almost 90 per cent of the responding youths spent less than $50 on an evening gambling.

There were differences in spending patterns between female and male gamblers. More than half (55 per cent) of the females spent less than $5 during an evening compared to 37.6 per cent of the males. The males were thus more inclined to spend a higher amount of money than the females on gambling (cf. Lambos, Delfabbro and Puglies 2007). This was also the situation for the highest spenders in that, overall, 8 per cent of the females indicated that they could spend on average more than $50 during an evening, compared to 14.9 per cent by the males. The spending amount increased with age with 19.4 per cent of the age group 17 years and older indicating that they spent more than $50 an average evening on gambling activities. In many cases, the youths had part time jobs (a small group were in full time employment) and had access to money for entertainment, thus for them to spend $50 on entertainment once or twice a week or less frequently would not drastically impede on other social leisure activities. However, to spend more than $50 on an average evening would still be a considerable amount of money, especially if it was spent several times during a week.

There was a difference between the communities in the spending pattern on gambling activities. In Community A, 53 per cent of the responding youths spent less than $5 an evening on gambling, while in Community M, 40 per cent of the youth stressed that they spent less than $5. The other notable difference between the communities was the spending pattern for amounts between $10 and $49. Fourteen per cent of the youths in Community A and 23 per cent in Community M spent between $10 and $49 an average evening. The youths in the mining community (Community M) had a higher spending pattern than their counterparts in the agriculture based community (Community A). In Community M with a large group of well paid wage earners or contractors working within the mining industry the available disposable income was presumably higher than in the agriculture based community. The assumption that more discretionary money was available in Community M was corroborated by the Australian Bureau of Statistics Census data for the average household income, which showed a higher income level in Community M than in Community A (Australian Bureau of Statistics Census 2001).

The average evening spending on gambling activities seems relatively modest if the youths had part time work and earning a regular income, if they got enough pocket money or had access to other funds. However, if all available money were spent on gambling even this moderate spending pattern would be of concern. Social recreational gambling implies that the gambler has control over the spending pattern and set limits for the gambling, thus the youths needed to have control over their money otherwise their participation in other paid recreational activities would be limited. Eighty-seven per cent of the respondents who gambled said that they never lost so much money that it affected their everyday normal life. Seven per cent indicated that they needed to be careful with money and 6 per cent said that they were always short of money after an evening of gambling. In this respect, there were no significant differences between female and male respondents.

A higher percentage of youths in Community A indicated that they always had problems with money, 9 per cent compared to 3.7 per cent for youths in Community M. Nearly 10 per cent (9.6) of the youths in the mining community (Community M) responded that they needed to be somewhat careful with spending after losing money on gambling activities. This was the case for only 3 per cent of the youths in Community A (the level of significance was weak $p \leq 0.01$, total N=236). Concerning age groups, it was the youngest age group who indicated that they had most problems with losing money after participating in gambling activities. This group is also the one less likely to have part time work and an income outside any allowances from the parents.

More than half of the respondents (56.3 per cent, total N=284) said that they had never lost too much money on gambling. A further two fifths (38.4 per cent) said that they had rarely or only sometimes lost too much money on gambling. Only 5 per cent of the respondents indicated that they often or always lost too much on gambling. Female gamblers were least inclined to feel that they had lost too much money. Sixty-five per cent said that they had never lost too much money; the corresponding percentage for male respondents was 47.9 per cent. Seven per cent (6.9) of the males said that they often or always lost too much money compared to 3.6 per cent of the females. However, the indicated differences were not significant for gender, age groups or communities. The management of money in relation to gambling was controlled by the majority of the respondents, except for a small group of males and an even smaller group of females.

As discussed in Chapter 3, an important aspect of management of money in relation to gambling is to play within a set limit, to only play with the amount of money intended. Seventy per cent of the respondents said that they had never played with more money than they had planned for during the evening. Fifteen per cent said that they occasionally had played with more money than intended and the same percentage indicated that they had played frequently with more money than intended (total N=343).

These findings show consistency among the respondents. If the youths had control over how much money they intended to play with, the risk of losing too much was much lower than if they did not plan their gambling. The consistency in the young people's responses in relation to management of money and the feeling of control in their gambling, both in how they felt about losing money and the control they exercised over how much money they could play with, indicates a strong reliability and consistency in their responses.

The line between social recreational gambling and excessive gambling can be arbitrary and for a social gambler to occasionally gamble for more money than anticipated will not make them a problem gambler, if it happens only occasionally and as long as they do not attempt to chase the money lost (Neal et al. 2005; Nower and Blaszczynski 2004). Nonetheless, the potential negative feelings that money lost can incite, might be an early indication of future attitudes towards gambling. The majority of the respondents who participated in gambling activities never lost too much money (56.5 per cent, N=147) and if they lost money it did not matter to them, while for 43.5 per cent (N=113) of the respondents, it mattered and they got angry about losing the money.

Furthermore, the group of young people who responded that they never lost too much money and did not get angry if they lost the money were in majority (40.8 per cent, N=106). They played for fun and the money was an expected expense for the gambling activity, thus they were not overly concerned about their gambling losses. Even so, a small group of respondents who played within their set limits and never lost too much money got angry about losing their money (15.8 per cent, N=41) (Figure 5.1, the level of significance was weak $p \leq 0.01$). Overall, the respondents accepted that gambling with money would include losing money and even among respondents who often or always lost too much money (43.4 per cent, N=113), 25.0 per cent (N=65) did not get angry, while 18.5 per cent (N=48) of them got angry about losing their money.

The overwhelming majority of the respondents who gambled said that being with friends was more important than to continue to gamble. Over three quarters of the respondents said it was more important to be with friends than to gamble but a quarter indicated that winning and playing were more important than to be with friends (total N=321). Female respondents emphasised more than the male respondents the importance of being with friends rather than gambling (84.5 per cent and 69.3 per cent, respectively), thus females acknowledged the importance of the social occasion more than males. For male respondents it was more important to win and play than to be with friends, compared to female respondents (30.7 per cent and 15.5 per cent, respectively). There were no differences between age groups except that the 15-year-old group was more inclined to stress the importance of gambling over being with friends and having fun. Competition and the focus on winning are very much related to sports activities which have a high priority especially among males in rural

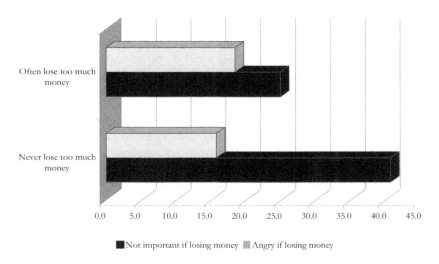

Figure 5.1 Youths' reactions to losing money on gambling activities in per cent

and regional communities, where winning is the ultimate goal, rather than the social occasion and the importance of belonging to a team. The quest for winning might be transferred to the gaming situation where the gambling activity becomes more important than friends. To win becomes the significant issue, not what you win and as long as there is a small win at the end of a session, even if the win does not compensate for the total loss, the gambling session is seen as a success (cf. Chapter 6).

Figure 5.1 illustrates young people's reaction to losing money and gambling within set limits. It is of course easy to get upset when losing money and many people get angry and disappointed about losing their money. However, in gambling it is given that a person is much more likely to lose money than to gain money, thus gambling with money involves a high risk of an overall loss (cf. Chapter 3.4, Table 3.5). As discussed above, a group of young people in the research sample got angry when they lost money and to further elucidate the characteristics of this group of youths, their attitudes towards gambling as a social activity or a gambling to win activity, was explored. The sample includes 277 young people who responded to the questions, 'what is important with gambling, winning, playing or being with friends', and 'reactions to losing money'. One quarter (24.5 per cent) of the respondents were committed gamblers that gambled to win while three quarters (75.5 per cent) were social gamblers that gambled to have fun with friends. In the latter group that gambled to have fun most did not get upset if losing money (51.6 per cent). However, nearly a quarter of them (23.8 per cent) got angry when losing money but still gambled to be with friends. Of the 68 young people who gambled to win, approximately half of them got angry when they lost money (12.6 per cent of the total), while the other half

(11.9 per cent of the total) thought it did not matter (the level of significance was moderate, p≤.003). In summary, the youths who got angry about losing money on gambling comprised of 36.5 per cent of the total number of respondents including participants from both social and committed gamblers (N=101). From this it can be concluded that the majority of young people preferred to gamble as a social recreational activity and the money lost was nothing to be too upset about.

The group of 35 youths who responded that it was more important to win than to be with friends and who expressed anger if they lost money can be seen as being at risk of having possible future problems with gambling activities. These young people might show an early indication of future gambling problems, even if high gambling pursuits among young people do not necessarily translate into high gambling propensity as adults (Derevensky and Gupta 2006; Productivity Commission 1999; cf. Chapter 6).

The youths who preferred winning over social time with friends and who got very angry when they lost money, represent 4.6 per cent of the total sample (N=754) and they correspond to 6.0 per cent of the responding young people in the sample who indicated that they were partaking in gambling activities (N=587).[8] These self-assessment percentages are higher than reported in the Gambling Research Australia (2008: 61–2) review of youth gambling research in Australia. The research review showed that the percentages of youths' gambling problems ranged between 3.1, 3.5 and 3.8 per cent (Delfabbro and Thrupp 2003; Delfabbro, Lahn and Grabosky 2005; Moore and Ohtsuka 2001). All these surveys were undertaken within the school environment, similar to the survey reported above.

As noted above, Moodie and Finnigan (2006) found even higher rates for problem gamblers and at risk gamblers (9.0 per cent and 15.1 per cent, respectively). These differences in the percentage of problem gambling can to a certain degree be explained by differences in the applied research methodology, selection of sample, if a screen was used or not, and which screen was used. Additionally, the present research used the young people's own assessment of their gambling behaviour and of how they reacted if they lost money. The youths also assigned the status of their gambling in relation to the importance of socialising with friends. If the youths' self-assessment can be used as an early predictor of future problems, this needs further examination, – the youths' behaviour and attitudes to gambling is partly mirrored in the case studies of excessive gamblers' gambling pathways (cf. Chapter 6).

5.11 Conclusion

This youth research showed that young people actively participated in gambling activities well before they were legally permitted to gamble for money. Young

---

8 Total sample 754 respondents, 22.1 per cent indicate they did not gamble for money (N=167), 587 young people had gambled for money during the last five years.

people participated in gambling through buying lottery tickets and scratchies by themselves, together with parents, siblings or older friends. They played board and card games for money with family and friends, they played Keno games at clubs and hotels during family dinners and they bet on horse races and sports events. Young people participated in casino games in person and over the internet. These research findings correspond with previous research about young people's participation and experiences of gambling (cf. Derevensky et al. 2007; Derevensky and Gupta 2004a; Delfabbro and Thrupp 2003; Johansson and Götestam 2003; Griffiths and Wood 2001; Rönnberg et al. 1999; National Research Council 1999).

The research findings showed significant gender differences in the majority of gambling games. Overall, the males had a significantly higher gambling propensity than the females, except for buying raffle tickets, betting on horse racing and playing Keno. In most cases the respondents were under 18 years of age, and not legally allowed to gamble for money, yet more than three quarters responded that they had gambled for money. The research showed that young people were introduced to gambling activities well before they reached 14 years of age. They had by that age, already developed their attitudes to and understanding of gambling as a natural part of their everyday social recreational activities. The early contact with gambling activities before 14 years of age was supported by the fact that their attitudes to and experiences of gambling rarely showed significant differences between the age groups.

Gambling inclination and the young people's approach to gambling showed that the young people participating in the research were well aware of the forms of gambling available in the community and in the wider society, they were also well informed about their parents' gambling. Gambling activities were undertaken within the family environment and as a part of the family's social recreational time at the local club; a club that supports the community and perhaps manage the young people's sports activities. Clubs' hospitality and entertainment activities are more or less subsidised through gambling revenue (Productivity Commission 2009: xix), this makes a club dinner affordable for large family groups. Ideally, families should be able to afford to have dinner at a local club, where the food and beverages are not subsided by the club's gambling revenue and exposure to gambling activities were not seen as an acceptable (or unfortunate) trade-off between a club dinner and a dinner at home.

It can be concluded that overall female youths showed more control over their gambling limits than male players, females were less likely to gamble over their financial limits and were more interested in having fun with friends than playing to win. Male youths were more inclined to stress the importance of winning rather than having fun with friends. However, it was also noted that a small group of young people took gambling too seriously and got upset when they lost money, a group of young people that might in the future develop problems with gambling and have difficulties with setting limits for their gambling.

In small regional and rural communities, the likelihood that people are more easily recognised makes it more difficult for young people to participate in unlawful actions. The local shopkeepers were likely to be well aware of the age of the youths trying to buy lottery tickets or taking part in adult gambling activities. The social control of young people through being known in the communities was a factor in itself that was expected to deter youths from participating in gambling activities or other activities of which they could legally not be part. The social control factor was anticipated to be more prevalent in regional and rural areas where most people know or at least recognise each other rather than in urban and metropolitan population dense environments (White and Wyn 2004).

The general perception given through interviews with community residents was that young people did not participate in gambling activities in the local communities and youth gambling was not seen as an issue of concern (Fabiansson and Healey 2003). In regard to gaming machines, only a few of the young people mentioned that they had played on gaming machines outside a casino venue. However, it was noted by one youth that some young people or young adults with a regular work income had been seen to gamble away half their pay packet during a night.

Even if there were few mentioned cases of gaming machine gambling the gambling machines were part of the youths' social recreational environment at the local club where the family dinner habitually took place and where community residents met to socialise. Although the parents paid for the Keno games it was often the children that kept track of the numbers, while the adults socialised. The young people were thus familiarised with the club and the gambling environment and the progression from Keno gambling to gaming machine gambling could be a simple transition.

As emphasised by Dickson, Derevensky and Gupta, (2002) and Wood et al. (2002) family acceptance, as well as the legality and social acceptance of gambling in many jurisdictions, contribute to young people's positive attitudes to gambling, attitudes that are predominantly not much different from adults' attitudes to gambling. Adults are presumed to have a better understanding of the risks associated with excessive gambling however, Hardoon, Derevensky and Gupta (2003) noted that it was commonly independent of age, that people had difficulties in comprehending that they may have a problem with gambling. Problematic attitudes to gambling were highlighted by the young people who got upset and angry about losing money both among the social and the committed young gamblers. The combination of positive attitudes towards gambling, the legality of gambling, an enticing and safe club environment, easy access to community clubs with extensive gambling opportunities and family friendly clubs, encourage participation in gambling activities for underage young people, where gambling pursuits are one of several socially accepted leisure activities.

The high percentages of young people who had parents, older siblings, friends or other adults placing their bets show that gambling was carried out with parents acceptance and as a social family activity, thus the gambling was undertaken with parents' knowledge and assistance. Parents' involvement in the youth gambling was documented by Dickson, Derevensky and Gupta (2008) who found that family and school relationships influenced the youths' risk taking behaviour and gambling propensity. They highlighted especially that anxiety and risk propensity, if young people experienced school problems or had siblings or friends with gambling problems and being male, influenced the likelihood for gambling. The research of Goldstein's et al. (2009) among non-African-Americans and African-Americans highlighted, for instance, that gambling was correlated with lack of academic achievement, with truancy from school, with extensive work commitment, with alcohol and drug use, and with dating violence and general violence.

Additionally, Jackson, Patton, Thomas et al. (2000) concluded that the youths' gambling behaviour, knowledge and attitudes to gambling, were not related to the researched youths' ethnic background, rural or urban residency or socio-economic living standard. Nonetheless, they found in the focus groups that young people differed in their attitudes and experiences of gambling. Children and young people who had a wide experience of gambling (defined as: gambling in more than three ways in the last year) were more likely to come from lower socio-economic circumstances, would be less focused on academic achievements, had been involved in antisocial behaviour, and had used alcohol or drugs. Overall, they were more prone to take part in risk taking behaviour. A finding that was also reflected in Goldstein et al. (2009) survey where gambling was only one aspect of their risk taking behaviour, which also included crime, violence alcohol and drug taking.

This youth research sample was not from a disadvantaged social environment. Nearly three quarters of the young people classified their living standard as good or very good (middle-class and above), and 96 per cent of them lived in a family like situation, thus this research group did not show excessive risk taking behaviour and were not involved in crime or violent acts. The gambling they participated in was a family social activity and not part of risk taking behaviour. Furthermore, the participating high schools had introduced school programs to help students who were not academically inclined to gain work related vocational training before they left school, thus trying to lower the truancy level and future unemployment. Nonetheless, young people's alcohol consumption is acknowledged as a special problem among young people in rural and regional communities, often related to low self-esteem (cf. Duhig, Maciejewski, Desai, Krishan-Sarin and Potenza 2007; Martins et al. 2007; Hardoon, Derevensky and Gupta 2004). Whether the young people who gambled to win and got angry about losing money were also abusing alcohol or drugs was not examined in this study.

The following chapter discusses gamblers' experiences, gamblers who have progressed from social recreational gambling to excessive gambling and where they have reached a stage where they require outside support to handle their personal, family and financial situation. The case studies describe the pathways from the gambler's point of view with comments from gambling counsellors.

Chapter 6
Adults' Excessive Gambling Pathways

6.1 Introduction

There are several ways to describe the pathways to excessive, problem or pathological gambling. Research about adult gambling has hitherto mainly focused on an individual's mental state and symptoms of addictive behaviour as explanations for problem or pathological gambling (cf. Gambling Research Australia 2008; Blaszczynsk and Nower 2002; Productivity Commission 1999, 2009). However, gambling pathways can also be explored from a holistic health perspective where gamblers' mental state is understood as only one part of a person's overall health (Borrell and Boulet 2005; Korn and Shaffer 1999). Additionally, gambling pathways can be examined from a community perspective where access to gambling opportunities and gambling venues and lack of alternative affordable social recreational activities influence gambling propensity (Fabiansson and Healey 2004), and where changes in an individual's life circumstances influence their penchant for gambling (Fabiansson 2007; Neal et al. 2005).

For the majority of adult people their everyday life is divided between paid employment, non-paid work, such as child minding and household work, and recreational activities (Goodin et al. 2005). These different activities coexist very well and each activity is given an allocated time, as work and leisure are both essential provisions for a well balanced life. If the healthy balance is disrupted by unemployment, family relationship problems or ill health, it is likely to influence not only the work situation and family environment, but also the time spent on social recreational activities.

If gambling is part of a person's regular leisure activities a change in employment status, relationship problems or a personal loss might change the gambling behaviour from being moderate to becoming excessive. Gambling is a leisure activity, but can act as an activity to relieve stress for people under pressure, it can help them to forget problems, or be a way to financially compensate for loss of paid employment. When gambling becomes the person's core focus and where work and free time are more or less taken up with thinking about and participating in gambling activities, the social recreational component of gambling has disappeared (Neal et al. 2005).

Cultural traditions and religious beliefs prohibiting gambling do not insulate people from engaging in gambling pursuits when people are relocated to very different societies where gambling is legal and a prominent presence in their local community. The situation in Australia with legalised gambling, easy access to gambling venues in local community areas, and with gambling pursuits highly promoted and advertised in mass media as the gateway to a glamorous future, traditional bearings against gambling are challenged. The prominence of gambling in Australian society competes with traditional and religious beliefs (Fabiansson 2007). Nevertheless, people can very well manage to undertake conflicting activities, thus gambling does not necessarily interfere with time spent on family, work, cultural or religious activities. The time required to purchase a lottery ticket for example, is minimal although of course this activity is less often related to excessive gambling.

The local clubs and hotels are the main providers of gambling opportunities in Australian communities. The clubs present a welcoming atmosphere for everyone where gambling is undertaken in a relaxing and convivial environment. The long opening hours makes it a place where local residents can easily visit, eat, drink and/ or gamble. It is also a place to pass time for a person experiencing unemployment or underemployment and it is a convenient place to visit if someone would like to avoid going home when the home environment is complicated. The local clubs are safe and friendly places to seek sanctuary from everyday problems. Many clubs have created an atmosphere where people can leave their troubles behind, socialise in a positive but artificial way (i.e. with a gaming machine), in a happy and noisy milieu. They are in company with other gamblers without the need for direct social communication or interaction, but are part of a loosely connected group. An environment where people can feel respected and everyday problems can be forgotten.

This chapter presents case studies about gamblers who have sought help for their gambling; a gambling habit that has created problems for themselves, their families and their employment situation. The research is based on the participants' own accounts of their gambling pathways, from the introduction to gambling up to the time when the gambling got out of hand. The gamblers resided within Greater Western Sydney or in neighbouring communities. These New South Wales communities have a concentration of gambling venues and the available possibilities to gamble are almost endless, especially gambling on electronic gaming machines (cf. Chapter 4).

6.2   Research methodology and design

The research aimed to elucidate gambling pathways from social recreational to excessive gambling, from the introduction phase to the point where the gambling activity is a serious problem. The research is derived from case studies based around a set of questions to gain insight into people's journey from gambling as part of the overall social entertainment environment to excessive gambling. It looked at the gambler's everyday life and where the gambling has evolved into a daily struggle associated with stress and financial problems.

The Multicultural Problem Gambling Services (MPGS) in New South Wales Australia collated the case studies in 2005. The sample includes 21 case studies.

The case studies are not randomised but chosen by the gambling counsellors, being cases they became involved with during the research period. The information is collated from people seeking help for their gambling behaviour, help they themselves have sought from the Multicultural Problem Gambling Services or a contact initiated by concerned family members or employers.

The case studies give an insight into the pathways from the early introduction to gambling towards the situation where the problem has gone out of hand and the gambler seeks help from professional organisations. The findings should not be generalised, or perceived as universal for excessive gambling pathways, as each person's circumstances are unique. However, common scenarios emerge in the case studies, where social recreational gambling with friends and work colleagues develops into a problem beyond the control of the individual who must then seek external help to save him or herself and the family, but also to keep friends, work colleagues and employment.

The Multicultural Problem Gambling Services cater for people born outside Australia and second generation Australians from a non-English speaking background. Their client group is mainly gamblers who feel more comfortable with a counsellor who is also from a non-English speaking background and familiar with their cultural background. The gambling counselling program offered includes eight one-on-one counselling sessions. The majority of the clients however, do not attend the full program of eight sessions, on average attendance ranges from three to five sessions, with some only attending one session (Fabiansson 2007).

The majority of the people in the sample were from the Greater Western Sydney area[1] or Sydney's inner west. To seek help from your local support group and ethnic counsellor can however be complicated, there is the possibility of being recognised by someone in the local community or even to know the counsellor socially, thus people who seek help for their gambling problems often seek help in neighbouring suburbs, regions or even in other cities. The people helped by a particular counselling service do not therefore necessarily represent that area's problem gamblers. The case study sample is not representative of people living within the Greater Western Sydney area, but it describes people who have sought help for excessive gambling who are living in residential areas with easy access to gambling venues in their local community.

The case studies include both direct client quotes and the counsellors' descriptions of the clients' gambling problems, and how their everyday situations are affected by excessive gambling. The information is based on the clients' recollection, information volunteered by them and from their perspective. It does not identify individuals except to nominate their gender, approximate age,

---

1 Greater Western Sydney is a growing multicultural residential area outside the metropolitan Sydney, New South Wales. The socio-economic statuses of the residential areas are diverse, but predominately classified as low middle to low socio-economic status, however, with pockets of affluent areas. Greater Western Sydney comprises of a high proportion of first homeowners with large mortgages, public housing, and renters.

employment status and residential area. Any information that may have provided clues to a person's identity was adjusted; this included changing the name of a workplace or suburb. The information is derived from answers to questions that were developed by the research team. The questions focused on the introduction phase of gambling, pathways towards excessive gambling, the clients' employment and socio-economic situation, relationships with family and friends, community affiliation, and their well being in the community.

6.2.1 Sample

The sample is diverse both in age and nationality. The sample includes 43 per cent (N=9) females and 57 per cent (N=12) males. Despite the small sample size, a comparison with the eighth survey of Problem Gamblers Receiving Counselling or Treatment in New South Wales gives a benchmark for people seeking counselling for excessive gambling (Walker, Shannon, Blaszczynski and Sharpe 2004). The eighth survey had a gender distribution of 37 per cent females and 63 per cent males seeking help for gambling problems. The percentages are based on interviews with 184 counsellors who provided information on 806 individuals seeking counselling for excessive gambling.

The ages of the people in this study ranged between 24 years and 65 years of age with the largest group between 24 years and 34 years (47.6 per cent, N=10) followed by the age group between 35 years and 49 years with 28.6 per cent (N=6). The smallest group was people between 50 and 65 years old (23.8 per cent, N=5). The average age was 39 years, which is lower than the average age recorded in the 2004 survey of problem gamblers receiving counselling or treatment in New South Wales (Walker, Shannon et al. 2004: 1), where the mean age was 42 years, an increase from 39 years in the 1998 survey. Most people would seek help only when the gambling caused serious problems for themselves and their family, friends and broader personal situation, thus the age when the gambling problems started would be lower than the recorded average age for people seeking counselling.

The high percentage of young people in the sample indicates that the transition from social gambling to problem gambling is quite rapid, taking only a few years in some cases, this was especially true for the male gamblers with 75 per cent (N=9) of them being under 35 years of age. This age profile differs for the females, who were more likely to be in their 50s or older (55.6 per cent, N=5). Only one female was younger than 35 years of age, while none of the males were older than 49 years of age. Three females and three males were between 35 years and 49 years of age. The age characteristics of the people in the sample, show that the males developed gambling problems that needed professional counselling earlier than the females and that they also probably began gambling at an earlier age (cf. Gambling Research Australia 2008; Productivity Commission 1999).

Just over half the people in the case studies were married (52.4 per cent, N=11) with nearly a quarter (23.8 per cent, N=5) divorced, separated or widowed, and a further quarter (23.8 per cent, N=5) single. The females were equal in being married or having previously been married (both 44.4 per cent, N=4) while males were more likely to be married (58.4 per cent, N=7) or never have been married (33.3 per cent, N=4). One female and four males were single and one male was separated. Thus, the sample shows that the males were both younger and more likely to be married than the females at the time when the social recreational gambling changed to become excessive and a problem requiring professional help.

The information was provided by the Multicultural Problem Gambling Services which has a predominantly multicultural client base. This is not an indication that people from ethnic backgrounds present more gambling problems than those who are English speaking and/or Australian born. The Productivity Commission (1999: Table 3.4; Chapter 4.3) found that the regular gambler was more likely to be an Australian born person than a person born outside Australia (80.2 per cent and 19.8 per cent, respectively). Consequently, the Multicultural Problem Gambling Services' sample reflects their client base rather than representing any ethnic or cultural bias among problem gamblers in the broader population. The sample includes a wide variation in ethnicity and ethnic belonging with representatives from: Argentina (1), Australia (1), Cambodia (1), Chile (3), China (3), Colombia (2), Greece (2), Indonesia (1), Iran (2), Italy (2), Lebanon (2), and Sri Lanka (1). Seven of them were born in Australia while the other 14 were born in their respective home-countries. The gamblers who were born outside Australia had been in Australia at least four to five years or the main part of their adult life, thus they were well familiar with and adjusted to the Australian culture and leisure milieu.

The sample reflects the multicultural landscape of the Greater Western Sydney area, notwithstanding, a higher representation of people born outside Australia (66.7 per cent). For example, in Fairfield, which in 2006 had the highest spending on gambling in New South Wales per adult resident (cf. Chapter 4.5), 58.5 of the residents were born overseas, while for NSW as a whole the corresponding percentage was 31.0 per cent and for Sydney 39.6 per cent (Australian Bureau of Statistics, Census 2006c). The 2004 eighth survey of problem gamblers receiving counselling or treatment recorded 77 per cent of the help seekers having an English-speaking background, 13 per cent with a non-English-speaking European background, 7 per cent an Asian background, and 2 per cent an Aboriginal speaking background (Walker, Shannon et al. 2004: 1).

6.2.2 Employment status

A regular income from employment or other sources of income is a prerequisite for gambling and especially for gambling beyond a social recreational level. Australia's or any country's unemployment and social welfare benefits are not generous enough to sustain excessive gambling, thus to maintain gambling beyond a recreational activity people need a regular cash flow such as a work-related income. Therefore the relationship between gambling and employment status is significant and whether people are employed or not when participating in excessive gambling at the level where counselling help is required. In the sample of the 21 cases, 66.7 per cent (N=14) of the gamblers were employed, 9.5 per cent (N=2) were unemployed, and 23.8 per cent (N=5) were retired or were working with home duties at the time of the research. Thus, two-thirds of the sample had a regular income from employment with only two males indicating that they were unemployed at the time of the data collation. One third of the sample was living on restricted income from age or disability pensions and/or savings. Equal numbers of the females were employed or retired (44.4 per cent, N=4) and one was a home worker. The majority of the males were employed (83.3 per cent, N=10).

The sample shows diversity in employment fields and socio-economic standards. The gamblers were employed as hire car driver, house painter, family business manager, cleaner, travel consultant, real estate agent, public relations consultant, legal clerk or as a chef. The participants described their employment and working situations in the following ways:

> I have always been employed. I have never missed days work due to gambling. I work as a house painter [male 36 years old].

> She works as a manager of a prestigious home-decorating company, she gains a good salary and commission, she also has bonus of travelling overseas [female 32 years old].

> He has a permanent full time job as a sales rep and she [the wife][2] is at home on maternity leave for a year, but she works full time and is a good provider, she gets a better income than him, also her family is very supportive and they have a solid financial situation [male 33 years old].

> He is a public relations consultant, full time, he said he is very successful in his work [male 24 years old-a].

The difference between gambling within one's means and moving to excessive gambling may take only a few months but it can also be quite protracted taking several years. The latter was described by a 65-year-old female who had been gambling responsibly together with her husband for many years but when he died her gambling pattern changed to excessive causing her to lose the home and the retirement savings: 'She is a chef and she was retired, she is currently working part time and looking for a full-time job to pay her legal debts and living expenses'.

Notwithstanding, the need to return to paid employment after gambling away all available funds; the gambler also meets difficulties in entering or staying in paid employment depending on age and skills. It is not only access to money which is related to gambling, it is also the situation where a person has too much free time with nothing to occupy him or her self with except to visit the local club:

---

2 Attempts have been made to insert clarification within some of the quotes [ ].

He has had a long lapse of unemployment due to lack of English and opportunities, but currently is working in the construction industry [male 30 years old].

She is no[t] working any more, her husband has a fumigation business, she used to help him but stop[ped] because he was too difficult to deal with in the work situation [female 56 years old].

She is no[t] working, she [receives] ... the disability pension, her husband works full time for the railway, he also work after hours [female 48 years old].

In these cases, access to an income was dependent on availability of work, language skills and work qualifications, but also leaving work because of a difficult work situation within the family business. However, income issues aside, these examples highlight the gamblers' employment situation and partners' work situations which made it possible to continue to gamble and to facilitate the excessive gambling.

6.2.3 Socio-economic status

The socio-economic situations of the people in the case studies were explored with the aim of understanding their living circumstances – whether they struggled with their everyday financial living conditions (low income), whether they felt their situation was acceptable (lower-middle), involved comfortable living (middle), or if their living conditions were very comfortable (higher middle or high income). The information is based on the gamblers' self reports and the counsellors' knowledge about the clients' living conditions. Self-reporting of financial situations has limitations, thus the accuracy of the information might not accurately reflect the sample's socio-economic circumstances.

Overall, the two most commonly described socio-economic status levels were comfortable (middle) 38.1 per cent (N=8), and struggling 33.3 per cent (N=7). The third largest group, 23.8 per cent (N=5), described their circumstances as acceptable (lower-middle), while only one gambler described the socio-economic living condition as very comfortable (higher middle or high income level). The female gamblers were either struggling or comfortable (44.4 per cent, N=4, and 55.6 per cent, N=5, respectively), while the male gamblers were more likely to consider their socio-economic status as acceptable (N=5) or more comfortable (N=3). Three of the men (25.0 per cent) thought their economic situation (being outside the labour market) could be described as struggling compared to nearly half of the women (44.4 per cent). The current situation described by the gamblers does not necessarily represent their socio-economic situation before the gambling became a problem:

Comfortable, because her family can help her if she needs money [female 60 years old].

Comfortable, because husband is well established in his own business for many years and they only have one daughter, who is married and lives in her home [female 56 years old].

Living with his family who has a comfortable situation, but he spend[s] all his money in gambling and [does not] nor pay board [male 24 years old-a].

These gamblers had a comfortable life as their families supported them, thus the gambling was not directly affecting their everyday living and financial situation. They did not risk being homeless or suffer financial ruin at this stage, but the situation would have been quite different if the family did not support them:

Struggling, she is on the disability support pension, husband works many hours but he has two 'wives' and one child, he also is in charge of his fragile father [female 48 years old].

When he works, he gets $500 per week and his wife works in a permanent full time job for the government. Acceptable lower middle [level] [male 30 years old].

Even if the partners are working, it is a struggle for the family and the gambling has a detrimental affect on the family's well being. The excessive gambling has also for this, 45-year-old man, changed from being a very comfortable socio-economic living standard to a struggling situation where the extended family is stepping in to support him, if he gives up gambling:

He has a house in Russell Lea, he has lost a house in Leichhardt, he used to earn a good salary, his wife works full time in a financial institution, they have only one son. It was a comfortable socio-economic situation, he is struggling at the moment but his sister is going to help him, if he stops gambling [male 45 years old].

The situation for a 65-year-old female is similar where she went from a comfortable and independent lifestyle to a struggling situation where she lives with her sister, a situation triggered by a change in life circumstances with her partner's death. In these last two cases, it can be seen that the gambling has caused considerable alteration to their socio-economic circumstances, from having very comfortable secure living conditions and income to financial struggle with housing and everyday expenses. These cases demonstrate the detrimental effects the excessive gambling has had for some gamblers.

6.3   Introduction to gambling

The manner in which people are introduced to gambling activities does not necessarily predict future gambling propensity. It is likely that a person inclined to try smoking, drinking alcohol or to gamble would partake in the activity independently of the nature of the introduction process. Nonetheless, an introduction in the company of family, friends and work colleagues can facilitate an earlier starting point than if the person was seeking the activity of their own accord. The youth gambling research (Chapter 5) showed that the young people were introduced to gambling within the family environment. Gambling activities such as Keno and horse betting were part of the family's social recreational time at the local club or in the community and buying lottery tickets was included in the weekly shopping routine.

Even if it was assumed that the participants had gambled for several years they were asked about how they were introduced to gambling and especially the first time they gambled. There were various ways the people in the sample were introduced to gambling, but there was no obvious single link between the manner of introduction and future gambling when the introduction was made by a trusted family friend, relative, social friends or work colleagues. The introduction to gambling was instead related to a social occasion, a located and affordable venue, not primarily for the reason that it was a place for gambling. The gambling that occurred was a side activity to the social get-together.

The case studies showed that the introduction involved family, partners, friends, or a young friend's father, and work colleagues. However, there was a small group of young males who visited a club on their own initiative with the purpose of gambling and not principally to socialise. It is interesting to note that each of the people represented in the case studies could identify and describe the first introduction or early introduction to their gambling activities, this being a significant event in their lives. None of the gamblers said that they could not remember the first time they gambled.

The most common introduction was via a visit to a local community club or a club close to the workplace with work colleagues and/or friends to have lunch, dinner or a drink after work, a social occasion to end the day or week. These social gatherings, for the majority of club patrons, continue to be just that, social events where they might enjoy some limited gambling, but the gambling would not encroach on the social purpose of the get-together. Nonetheless, for some people this initial introduction to gaming activities developed into a solitary gaming pursuit where the social aspects of having lunch or an after work drink with work colleagues or friends disappeared. The purpose of visiting the club changed from being centred on the social entertainment aspects to become an exclusive gambling pursuit. The visit to the local club thus turns into a solitary non-social leisure affair with the original leisure occasion initiating the progression into an excessive gambling pursuit.

One of the case studies demonstrated how a person's gambling interest was initiated by a group of work colleagues who regularly visited the club. After a while, the person who had been introduced to gambling by the friends became more interested in playing alone on the pokies (electronic gaming machines) than being with the friends. In this case, the friends became annoyed by this change

150 *Pathways to Excessive Gambling*

of behaviour, as their purpose was primarily a social occasion, even if it included gambling in a minor way. The turning point for this 60-year-old female player was when the visit to the gaming venue changed purpose and became a solitary activity and where the social event at the club with work colleagues was forgotten, replaced by her growing gambling interest.

The question is, did the focus on gambling develop because the person visited a club with gambling facilities or was the club visit an incident that hastened the introduction to gambling. There are many factors influencing a person's behaviour, the social and physical environment, employment and community affiliation circumstances, their relationships with friends and work colleagues. Additionally, a person's own state of mind, susceptibility to addictive behaviour, earlier experiences, and lack of competing recreational activities, are factors that interrelate to influence a person's actions. These are all factors that influence the decision to continue gambling or not. For some people in the sample, excessive gambling was only one aspect of their everyday problems.

After the introduction to gambling, the experience can vary from good to bad. A 36-year-old man, who at the time of the first gambling experience had recently arrived in the country, describes a situation where the pathway to excessive gambling was based on experiences of a loss. A loss that he became determined to recoup, which is a familiar excessive gambling scenario. The young man expressed this in the following way:

> I started gambling four years ago, shortly after arrival in Australia. My brother took me to Star Casino one night. He lost $150[3] and I became determined to win that money back. That night I lost $2,000.

Another situation described in the case studies is where a person who already had a problem with excessive gambling introduced a 48-year-old female to gambling. She was aware of the friend's gambling problems and this knowledge might have worked as a deterrent to others, however this was not the case in this situation. She had additional mental health problems and attended a related service where she met her friends:

> ... it was one of the [group] outings of the Rehabilitation service to go to the club for the $2 lunch ... She was initiated by her friend who had a gambling problem; they used to pay for her to play, because she refused to spend her money in the beginning.

Despite knowing that one of her friends was gambling at unsustainable levels, she did not see the possibility that she could fall into that category. The fact that she was not prepared to use her own money for gambling could be an indication that she was well aware of the pitfalls of gambling. As others paid for her gambling,

---

3   Throughout this chapter the dollar values refers to Australian dollars.

she was detached from the loss of the money and did not see it as wasting her own money. The friends were unwilling to pay for her gambling more than occasionally, at which stage she needed to start spending her own money. She continued to gamble and became mesmerised by playing the poker machines. However, it was not made clear from the case study transcript if this outing was sanctioned by the rehabilitation service or if the group itself initiated the visit. It is well documented that people with gambling problems frequently also experience health, relationship and addiction problems, thus these group members might be in the risk group for excessive gambling and visiting gambling venues creates an additional temptation to play (cf. Gambling Research Australia 2008; Neal et al. 2005; Blaszczynsk and Nower 2002; Korn and Shaffer 1999; Productivity Commission 1999).

The situation with new establishments locating close to workplaces and having promotional offers with cheap lunches and free drinks encourages people to frequent the club. A new club close to a work place increases the choice of lunch outlets and social entertainment, but also creates the temptation to gamble. This was the situation in one case study. After some time he started to go by himself at every possible opportunity. The closeness and the temptation to gamble became too much for the 29-year-old. Here the geographical proximity of the club was a determining factor that made gambling effortlessly accessible where before there were geographical restrictions on access (Lester 1994; Abbott and Volberg 1999).

In another case study, the person started going to the Catholic Club with friends to take advantage of the $1.00 lunch. Everyone, irrespective of financial circumstances, likes a good deal, particularly when cheap food is offered. The friends of a 63-year-old female started to gamble during their lunch break and she followed their actions. It became a regular event to go with friends to play on the poker machines; a gambling situation that escalated into a problem for her.

Four of the young men in the sample, all under the age of 35 years, started gambling independently without outside introduction, by visiting a club with gaming facilities. These four males were all in their 30s, when their problems with gambling required professional gambling counselling. In these cases the young males did not need someone to introduce them to gambling as they were interested enough to start gambling by themselves.

6.4   Age of independent gambling

Research shows that young people enter into gambling activities well before the legal age of gambling. Commonly, this introduction to gambling takes place through the family, older siblings, older friends or together with work colleagues (cf. Chapter 5). Studies have also shown that gambling is negatively related to age, with older people gambling less than younger people (Kallick, Suites, Dielman and Hybels 1979; Li and Smith 1976; Feeney and Maki 1997), except for people who gambled before retirement (Welte et al. 2002; Stitt et al. 2003). In the sample, the age when people started participating in gambling activities by themselves ranged from their

152 *Pathways to Excessive Gambling*

teenage years up to 57 years of age. The most common starting age was between 24 and 34 years of age (38.1 per cent, N=8), followed by people aged between 35 and 49 years of age (N=5); with equal percentages of the sample starting before 24 years of age and older than 50 years of age (19.0 per cent, N=4).

Overall, females started gambling later in life than males. Almost 90 per cent (N=8) of the females were over 35 years of age at the start compared to two-thirds of the males (N=8). None of the females were below 24 years of age, while nearly one in three of the males had started gambling independently at an age younger than 24 years old (N=4) (Gambling Research Australia 2008; Productivity Commission 1999). For the younger people in the sample it only took a few years for the gambling to escalate to unsustainable levels, while for the older people in the case studies, especially women, it took a longer time before they became trapped by gambling (cf. Gambling Research Australia 2008; Productivity Commission 1999).

6.4.1 Age, gender and gambling preferences

In the Greater Western Sydney area as in the rest of New South Wales, local community clubs and hotels have electronic gaming machines as the dominant form of gambling and as a result it is one of the most accessible forms of gambling for local residents. However, other forms of gambling such as Keno and TAB facilities are also available at most local community clubs and hotels. Sydney's StarCity casino[4] has a diverse range of gaming facilities, including table games such as roulette, blackjack, baccarat and poker. The StarCity casino is located in the Sydney city centre and is easily accessible from the suburbs via public transport and private car.

Effortless access to gambling venues with long opening hours increases the opportunities to take part in gambling pursuits. Despite research showing a negative correlation between age and gambling and a decline in gambling propensity with increased age (except for people who gambled before retirement), people live longer, are healthier and continue to be active consumers (cf. Chapter 4; Productivity Commission 2009). The increased ease of access to casinos and local community gambling venues in clubs and hotels has enhanced the overall rise in gambling opportunities for all ages including the number of people who gamble in excess of available funds (Zaranek and Chapleski 2005; Vander Bilt et al. 2004; Stitt et al. 2003; Welte et al. 2002; Shaffer, Hall and Vander Bilt 1997; Lester 1994; cf. Chapter 4).

The preferred type of gambling and the most often mentioned gambling form was gambling on electronic gaming machines. In the case studies all the females had concentrated their gambling on gaming machines, while the males were also inclined to gamble on other forms of gambling. The males gambled on blackjack, roulette, card games, and horse racing. Even if the men showed variations in their

---

4 New South Wales has only one casino venue, StarCity Casino, situated in the city centre.

gambling, all of them also gambled on gaming machines. Two-thirds of the people in the case studies played only on gaming machines and one third played both on gaming machines and participated in other gambling activities (blackjack, roulette, cards and betting on horses). Fifty-nine per cent of the total gambling expenditure in Australia is spent on gaming machines; while in New South Wales the corresponding figure was 71 per cent of the gambling expenditure in 2005–06 (cf. Chapter 4, Table 4.7 and Figure 4.1; cf. Australasian Gaming Council 2008; Productivity Commission 2009).

According to the eighth counselling and treatment survey, 86 per cent of the clients gambled to excess on gaming machines. Wagering on horses and dogs were reported by 8 per cent of the clients as gambling types contributing to excessive gambling. Casino games, excluding electronic gaming machines, formed 2 per cent of gaming activities, and sports betting was also mentioned by 2 per cent of the clients (Walker, Shannon et al. 2004: 1). Subsequently, it is gaming machine gambling that creates most problems for the majority of people visiting local community clubs and hotels and it is this gambling type that most often gets people into financial, legal and social troubles (Productivity Commission 2009). The design of the gambling environment contributes to this. It is easy to be absorbed by the machine's noise and visual display, which creates a perception or illusion that the gambler is in control, but must play quickly to avoid missing a winning chance. Thus it is easy to lose large amounts of money and become lost in the atmosphere of the gambling environment, where time disappears in front of the machine, a machine that the gambler feels he or she can nearly communicate with, a machine that does not mind broken English or personal 'imperfections'.

Furthermore, the lack of natural light and large clocks make it easy to lose track of the time spent in front of the machine. The whole design of the gaming venue creates a perception of an opportunity to win large amounts of money, where the speed, noise and lights of the machines encourage the gambler to feed the machine continuously. Additionally, gaming venues create an enchanting atmosphere where not only time and money are lost, but an environment where it is easy to forget other problems that make up a person's everyday life. For gamblers with multiple problems, time spent in gambling venues gambling on gaming machines is time when other problems can be briefly forgotten (cf. Chapter 6.13). The design of electronic gaming venues with numerous machines in a limited space, closed off from the outdoors is an environment where time becomes difficult to judge. As a business venue design, few could rival the success of the gaming rooms of clubs, hotels and casinos.

6.5 The first gambling win

The odds of winning in lottery and at gaming machine games (and in many other gambling games) are very small, nevertheless, the thrill of trying is irresistible – even when almost everybody realises that the odds required to win, especially a large win, are stacked against them. However, the feeling of the first win, the size of the win, and the happy feeling of winning something can stay in a person's memory for a long time. The other side of gambling, a person's experiences of a loss and the amount lost before any win, is more likely forgotten, disregarded as a one-off occasion or an unlucky day.

In essence, the gambler tries his or her luck in the hope that it is working in their favour. Legal gambling is based on the principle that on average the main part of the money gambled should be returned as winnings to players. The randomised percentage of returned money varies between jurisdictions, but in New South Wales, the minimum return to a player from a gaming machine must be, according to the legislation, at least 85 per cent. In reality the average return to players in NSW is approximately 90 per cent according to the Department of Gaming and Racing (2006). Thus on average, theoretically, each player is likely to lose only 10 per cent of the money gambled, which of course sounds reasonable, nevertheless, the majority of players will lose more money than they invest most of the time (cf. Chapter 3.4, Table 3.5). The reason is similar to the effect of compound interest. In theory, for the first $100 gambled the gambler would get $90 returned. If the gambler reinvests the win of $90 the gambler would only get $81 returned and so on until most of the money is gone. It is only if the gambler does not touch the winnings that the legislated return becomes a true reflection of reality. In real life most people, and particularly excessive gamblers, do not leave the gambling area until all the funds they have set aside for gambling have disappeared and thus the average legislated return becomes an irrelevant figure.

Due to the randomness of gambling payouts the first major win can be special and treasured by the player, because of its unexpected occurrence and rewarding effect for the player. It can also be interpreted as an indication of the gambler's future chances of success or skills and fuel anticipated good prospects in gambling pursuits:

> She said her friends believed she was [the] lucky one and they gave her their money because she had a 'good hand'. She never won a lot but $20 or $40. However, the fact of winning was a new rewarding experience for her [female 48 years old].

The case studies show that the gamblers enjoyed winning even small sums of money. They expressed positive feelings about their winnings and found it rewarding if they could end the gambling session with a win, even a small one. A win can be associated with a specific gaming machine or a club. The win can create a loyalty to the club as a player might feel that the social and physical environment where the win took place was the reason for the win or the machine will bring more luck in the future. Loyalty to a club was the case for a 24-year-old man who was 19 years old at the time of his first win. He won $450 the first time he gambled and became a regular visitor to the club.

A 60-year-old female gambler recounts not the first time she gambled, but the first time she won any money. She was very happy with her win of $200 and invited all of her friends to dinner. She still thinks she has good luck with playing the pokies, even if it now has created financial difficulties and other problems for her. Another female (56 years old) voiced the importance of winning early in the gambling phase. The first time she played, she had won $200. She had never won anything before in her life, and she was very excited about the win. Consequently, this first win encouraged her to continue to gamble.

Several of the gamblers expressed their satisfaction with winning small amounts of money such as $20. Any gambling success, even a minor win and irrespective of the amount of money gambled, the win becomes a cause for celebration. A 65-year-old female told the counsellor that she had won many times and once she won $1,000 on poker gambling. After many years, she still remembers how she and her husband celebrated the win.

Even if gambling on electronic gaming machines is a solitary activity, a person's good luck and success in winning money is measured against the perceived good fortune of others. It was acknowledged, by a 24-year-old male gambler that he had been lucky to win money on gambling, but it was also emphasised that others were more fortunate than himself, '… he always used to win $100 or $200, but his friends used to win a lot of money'.

It can be seen as good fortune, but it is seldom divulged how much the person has spent on gambling before the win. However, a group of gamblers acknowledged the double edged sword of winning. They highlighted the imbalance between the money they spent on gambling before they had success in winning any money. The gamblers voiced these sentiments:

> I won $2,500. I did not feel very happy as [I] had lost $7,000 before that and the win was not big enough, as [I] was hoping to win back all losses [male 36 years old].

> … $500 and did not feel that great 'cause I had lost $1,000 already and wanted to make that money up [male 42 years old].

A male gambler believed he had good luck with gambling on gaming machines as he had won a lot of money. Although he did not give the counsellor any figures, he indicated that he had both won and lost large amounts of money. The downside for this mid-30s male gambler was that he continued to play after a win because he was 'in luck' and he thought that the good fortune would continue:

> … he has won a lot of money and he is a lucky person. He talks about big amounts of money, and also a lot of money he lost. When he wins, he feels compelled to continue playing because he believes he is in good luck.

The principle of randomness of gaming machines to produce a win or not is not determined by skill or being a 'lucky' person in general. Even if a person wins on a gaming machine and in the end has gained more money than invested, it is the randomness of the machine that decides the payouts and not the person's ability to gamble. A representative for an ethnic community group in Western Sydney told of a woman who had won a substantial amount of money on poker machines at the local club, but before she left the club that evening, she had lost everything. She continued to play as she felt admired by other gamblers and the gambling venue took special care of her after the big win.[5] This scenario, where the winnings are reinvested to continue playing, is beneficial for the venue operators, but not for the gambler, as the winning is transferred back into the machines and it is unlikely that the winning strike will persist for the gambler. If winnings, even the small ones, were not to be reinvested for gambling, the procedure could greatly benefit the excessive gamblers, who often play until all the money is consumed.

To be seen as a lucky person, because of a win, can be transferred to other areas of a person's life. Success in gambling can be seen as the person having a unique knowledge, or skill to play that can be conveyed to other areas. To be seen by friends and others as successful, and being a winner, is very attractive for many people. Being seen as a winner and therefore a person of importance can be an essential way to show one's prestige. For a person who cannot gain prestige and self-confidence through employment in a culturally different society, the status gained at a casino or a club can compensate for lack of social status in other areas. For example, this can be important for young men of Anglo-Australian origin or the majority population, but it is especially significant for young men from non-Anglo-Australian or a minority nationality who do not have a natural status position in Australia, a situation typical for minority groups in most countries. To compensate for lack of status and damaged self-esteem, people might seek to gain status by other means. One way is to be associated with a high status place, be seen as successful by others visiting the high profile venue, and to show that they can afford to visit a popular, high-class establishment. The gambling activity can be minimal but the atmosphere, the friendly staff and the enthusiastic social environment make people feel welcome and respected at the venue (The South Australian Centre for Economic Studies 2005; Tanasornnarong, Jackson and Thomas 2004).

6.6 Factors inspiring gambling propensity

Gambling is a leisure pursuit that has existed in different forms for centuries and in most cultures (cf. Chapter 1.4). The level of competitiveness and the focus on success might differ between cultures, the desire to succeed and to be among the winners are human traits. Even when gambling is seen as an easy way to success, to gain money for a carefree future, it might not be the sole motive for gambling. Gambling propensity raises the question: What drives people to continue to gamble even when the odds of winning are clearly stacked against them? Stories about gambling exploits are more about people winning

---

5 The story is anecdotal and could not be verified; as people are more likely to keep quiet about gambling losses, few would acknowledge such a loss.

than about losing, despite the obvious truth that more people lose than win on gambling activities (Reich 1999; Abbott and Volberg 1999). The case studies give an insight into people's reasoning behind continued gambling. For example, gamblers reminisce about situations where they have tried to recoup money and their emotional attachment to gambling:

> Initially because friends did it and now to try and get ahead and return losses as well as craving for it when feeling tired and distressed [male 42 years old].

> I wanted to buy things that I could not afford. Also, once I started gambling I just wanted to chase my losses [male 36 years old].

The case studies also contained examples of the danger of one partner waiting for the other to finish gambling. The male partner was playing table games and the 32-year-old female partner was waiting for him to complete his gambling session. The waiting time was boring so she started to gamble on poker machines as a way to kill time. In due course these two people separated. The initial reason to gamble was thus removed but the young woman continued to gamble and in fact increased her gambling in an effort to recover the lost money.

The emphasis on winning is strong among excessive gamblers and for some gamblers the gambling is driven by a quest for money to buy things the regular employment salary cannot cover. It is not only gamblers who have difficulty in accepting a loss, it is a common human characteristic, for the excessive gambler however, such a response is more likely to be experienced than for the social recreational gambler. Pursuing the lost money until all available funds are gambled away is a far more frequent behaviour among excessive gamblers. The case of a 45-year-old man who continued to gamble even after he had lost everything – including his house and family, clearly demonstrates this drive. A person, who is convinced that the loss can be turned around, even when the magnitude of the loss becomes unaffordable, is capable of an intensely felt conviction that an imminent turn around in success can still be achieved. This unrelenting confidence in recouping lost money exists among some gamblers, despite their own sorrowful experiences. The phenomenon of chasing lost money is acknowledged in the statements: '… she finds it very difficult to accept the loss. She thinks she can win the money back' [female 60 years old], and '… "I just want my money back", … he is chasing, … he wants to recover all the money he has lost' [male 24 years old-a].

It is well known that a change in a relationship through divorce or death can alter the fine balance between social and excessive gambling (Coman, Burrows and Evans 1997: 238). According to one of the case studies, a couple made regular visits to local clubs, as well as national and international gaming venues and gambled as a social leisure activity, a non-excessive recreational pursuit. The gambling was part of their leisure time together. They used to go to the club once a week; they had dinner and played the pokies. They lived a comfortable and financially secure life together. The social gambling had worked very well over several years because both of them were careful not to gamble to excess and they helped each other to stay within an affordable limit. The 65-year-old woman's world fell apart when her partner died. After he died, she started to visit the local club to gamble on her own. The gambling escalated from being within her financial limits to excessive levels where her financial security, the house and all the savings disappeared. The comfortable lifestyle collapsed and she has now been forced to live with relatives.

Unemployment and loneliness are other factors, presented in the case studies, as the breaking point for excessive gambling. Two males, 30-year-old and 29-year-old, were unemployed and this situation gave them large amounts of free time which they could not occupy meaningfully. Their gambling escalated within a short period of time and after three years the younger man had developed serious gambling problems. The long opening hours of clubs make them appealing places in which to congregate and socialise, especially for people who are unemployed, those without any meaningful activities to occupy them during the day, and those who feel lonely and isolated. Community clubs are social hubs; they are places where people are among other people. Gambling is a solitary activity, undertaken in a social environment, but without much social interaction. The club environment is a safe, secure and a friendly place, where everyone who accepts the club's code of conduct is welcome (Fabiansson 2007). For an unemployed person who is feeling isolated and vulnerable, the club environment is a home away from home, with the added advantage that any gambling win might solve urgent financial problems.

For a 56-year-old female, the one-on-one personal interaction with the poker machine was soothing and problem free and allowed her to forget the real world. Her interaction with the machine and the friendly environment made it possible for her to forget, 'the past, all her problems and concerns' and a chance to feel good about herself. A 48-year-old female expressed the same sentiments about the club environment. It gave her a sought after and valued freedom not found in other places. The club was a place where she was allowed to smoke without restrictions, and no one made her feel uncomfortable. Additionally, 65-year-old female thought the club was a place where she felt disconnected from the reality, gambling relieved emotional pain, isolation and sadness, which was associated with her grief for her late partner.

The combination of problems the gambler experiences is supported by previous research (Blaszczynski and Nower 2002; Marks and Lesieur 1992; Getty, Watson and Frisch 2000) where gambling can be seen as a diversion and a way to help alleviate other problems. This was expressed in several of the case studies where the gambling and the gambling venue had become a 'problem free' zone. This was further emphasised by the Wesley Mission gambling counsellor, who regularly was told by clients that they felt gambling venues had a soothing and comforting effect on them, helping them to cope with other personal issues. Depression and boredom were given by several of the gamblers as reasons for gambling, but also the entertainment and excitement of gambling, to gamble as a way to escape from work and a complicated domestic situation.

The interaction with gambling machines can give people real satisfaction and a release from stress, a situation not gained in interaction with friends, family or through other leisure activities that are less financially detrimental. Within the gambling situation they felt less isolated, less stressed and they felt safe at the local club. It was 'time out' where they were in control of their actions and their time. However, not all excessive gamblers were isolated. They can be highly social and have an extensive circle of friends, but they can still seek solitary time for gambling (cf. Chapter 6.12).

Several of the gamblers in the sample were smokers. The right to smoke without restrictions at the gambling venue was highly valued by smoking gamblers. This situation changed in NSW from July 2007 with the implementation of smoking regulations in hotels and clubs. Gambling areas that are enclosed spaces with no direct access to outdoor areas are covered by the total smoking ban, though in response to this, clubs have placed gaming machines in partly open areas to circumvent the total smoking ban (cf. Chapter 3.3).

6.7 Pathways to problem gambling

A large proportion of the Australian adult population gamble for social and family entertainment (Productivity Commission 2009) and the majority of the gamblers do not experience adverse consequences from their gambling pursuits. However, for a noticeable group of gamblers, the social and entertainment emphasis of gambling is transformed into an independent, solitary leisure activity, which overstretches their financial resources, and strains relationships and the good will of family and friends. The change from social gambling into an excessive activity can be a gradual process with gambling increasing over many years or be triggered by a personal or work related event. A gradual process over many years makes it difficult for a person to realise the extent of their gambling until it has become an urgent problem with financial, relationship and other adverse consequences. Gambling that is a result of a gradual process can remain hidden until the person suddenly realises that the gambling is consuming unaffordable large amounts of money and their debts are ever increasing. In one case the gradual process to excessive gambling had taken 20 years [male 45 years old] in others it took only a few years or even a shorter time:

> It was a gradual process. I did have a physical illness soon after arrival here, problems with my knee and I ended up on bed rest for a few months. I was so exhausted and unhappy I soon started gambling after that. But my gambling slowly increased over time [male 42 years old].

> She started to go to the club in the morning while her husband was working, twice a week and spending $100 or $200, however her gambling was escalating to $550 per week [female 56 years old].

160 *Pathways to Excessive Gambling*

> It has been a five-year process, initially he spent $20. When he started to work he started to spend more and more, he finds himself currently out of control with a big debt [male 24 years old-b].

The case studies illustrate where a particular instance occurs that initiates a change in a person's gambling pattern. The incident or event triggers a pathway where the gambling activity gets out of control and the fine balance between work, family and leisure is disturbed. In one example, one of the family members left for a long holiday giving the remaining partner extra free time. The free time for the partner who stayed at home provided an opportunity to increase their controlled gambling into an excessive gambling pursuit. The sudden realisation that the gambling was consuming the whole pay packet prompted the 31-year-old male to seek help.

> He used to be more under control over his gambling in the past, his wife went overseas with the children for six months to visit relatives and he stayed in Australia, when she came back, she found he was late to pay rent, he did not pay the car repayment and there were late fees incurred with increasing interest, he did not pay the childcare, he had a new credit [limit] of $7,000 in credit [male 30 years old].

> He ... earns $2000 [a] fortnight, he lives with his parents and is single, he does not pay boarding, he has been gambling gradually until he noticed he was spending all his money on gambling [male 31 years old].

Changes in gambling patterns can also be related to disruption of the equilibrium of control in the family, such as a separation. Separation can produce unexpected gambling behaviour as in this case of a 63-year-old female who suddenly had excessive free time and had difficulty finding meaningful activities to fill her new unstructured time – her husband had previously controlled her time and actions:

> ... separation from husband, he was very controlling before and they were married for 25 years. She found herself without an external locum of control from one day to other and could no cope with her freedom.

The case studies also highlighted the situations when the comfort of the partner disappears through death. The gambling that had previously been managed jointly, can get out of control for the partner left behind. The gambling becomes an escape from the personal loss, a circumstance, which this 65-year-old widow realised and acknowledged was caused by the loss of the husband, as explained by the counsellor:

> ... it is interesting he was sometimes the one she had to control, but she never had a gambling problem before, she enjoyed going to the club to the pokies and dinner in the husband's company.

There is also the case of the 25-year-old man who experienced a large win, this win initiated a gambling interest and a perception that the win could be repeated. This perception created a gambling cycle with few boundaries as the big win would repay debts and restore financial equilibrium. However, attempts to recoup losses often get the gambler further into debt, where stealing money is one option to get gambling money. A 63-year-old female with a gambling problem gave in to the temptation to steal from the family, as she did not have her own money.

> She is retired, her ex-husband is retired and very upset with her because she was using all her money, she separated from him because he was preventing her from spending too much money in the clubs, but after separation he stopped seeing her and worrying about her finances. She was struggling for money and offered him to do his cleaning in exchange of [grocery] shopping, he accepted and she stole his credit card.

In summary, the processes of change, from social to excessive gambling, range from 'no time at all', a couple of years, to a gradual process over 20 years. The case studies showed that gambling for some of the people got out of control almost as soon as they started to gamble, but for others it took much longer. For some of the gamblers the increase in gambling can be related to a change in their 'normal everyday situation', by unemployment, relationship problems and isolation, where the dreams of a big win to solve personal and financial problems was further nurtured by personal perceptions of the ability to successfully influence the gaming machine, and advertisements of what a win might do to a person's life situation. Mass and ether media advertisements together with an enticing club environment create an illusion of the possibility to win substantial amounts of money especially through lottery and gaming machine gambling. The win, despite being elusive, would create a luxury lifestyle solving most of life's problems; this is an attractive proposal when other options seem impossible.

6.8 Cultural gambling traditions

The gambling pathways of the people in the case study sample clearly show the influence of the social environment and access to gambling opportunities had on their gambling propensity. Gamblers who were born outside Australia were less likely to have gambled in their country of origin. Nearly half of the sample (47.6 per cent) did not gamble before they arrived in Australia, while 14.3 per cent had gambled prior to arriving in Australia. It was only the males in the sample who had gambled before arriving to Australia, none of the females. The Australian born (38.1 per cent) were naturally familiar with the Australian gambling culture from an early stage. These results indicate that the social environment and access to gambling opportunities are contributing factors to gambling inclination as the

162 *Pathways to Excessive Gambling*

people born outside Australia started gambling only when they came in contact with gambling activities in their local community.

Gambling is acceptable for only males in some cultures, but not accepted for either gender in other cultures. Within the Muslim faith, it is unacceptable for either men or women (cf. Chapter 1.4). Nevertheless, covert gambling occurs in countries despite legal, religious and/or moral restrictions. Thus it can be a culture shock to experience public advertising of gambling and the abundant gambling opportunities in the Australian society accessible to all people 18 years of age and older. Clubs and hotels present a nearly unlimited availability of gambling opportunities in Australian local communities. The clubs, with their inclusive community focus and affordable food and beverage, provide local residents with a place to congregate and socialise, but also to gamble. For community clubs the gambling activities provide the underpinning financial support for other activities such as sports, community programs and live entertainment.

A 60-year-old female, who was born in Argentina, said she did only gamble in Australia, as it was not socially acceptable for a woman to gamble and go to casinos in Argentina. When she visited Argentina on holidays she was unable to go to the casino, despite coming as a tourist. Thus when she was in Argentina she did not gamble, a similar situation was described by another woman about the same age:

> She did not used to gambling in her country, Chile, it is not accepted for women in her country of origin, her husband introduced her to gambling in Australia, he was Australian, they used to travel together overseas and they went to Las Vegas, many casinos in different parts of the world ... [female 65 years old].

In this case, the gambling was restricted to places where both of them could gamble as a social recreational activity. Australian society, with its legal gambling and social acceptance of gambling for all adults, challenges the beliefs of migrants from cultures with different views and acceptance of gambling. Migrants who come from cultures where gambling is restricted, will find it quite confronting when faced with the Australian cultural values and social norms. This situation points to the importance of the easy access to gambling opportunities in gambling venues in the local community, as an incentive for non-traditional gambling groups and especially females to take up gambling in Australia.

Gambling advertisements promote the imagined benefits of a major win, 'a holiday mode' construct, which encourages social acceptance of gambling where money is seen as solving personal, financial, and social problems. The description of the benefits of winning emphasise all the things a person is deprived of by not being a winner. This is especially pertinent for an unemployed person from a non-English speaking background, or a recently arrived migrant with few prospects of gaining employment that will lift the family out of poverty, where isolation and lack of a disposable income can be perceived as being able to be rectified through gambling pursuits (cf. Griffiths and Wood 2001; Derevensky et al. 2007). People outside the paid workforce or with short-term casual work conditions will have limited prospects of changing the present situation in the near future through paid work. Promotion of the perception that anyone can win reinforces the idea that the individual can change their own situation through gambling if they only try hard enough, thus enhancing the belief that independent of living circumstances, ethnicity and gender, everyone can win, become wealthy and happy as a result.

6.9 Monetary cost of gambling

When gambling issues are reported in the media, they often focus on large wins and losses, those in the hundreds of thousands or millions of dollars. The scenario presented is often in relation to unauthorised use of money. For most people, wins and losses are much smaller in terms of their monetary value, but not in their significance to an individual with a gambling problem. For example, when a gambler gambles away his or her last few dollars and wins $20 at a cost of $200, their spending is in fact a 90 per cent loss of the gambling expenditure – this is not newsworthy but is highly significant to the gambler.

The amount of money gambled away varied for the people in the sample case studies, from a few dollars to $3,000 or more per week – money from earnings or income support, money that they could manage to borrow, steal, embezzle, or had access to at that moment. During times when gambling took over the person's life, all their accessible money was spent on gambling pursuits, mainly on electronic gaming machines: 'I was gambling up to $1,000 a week when my gambling problem was bad' [male 36 years old] and '... whatever [was] available, [I would] borrow, $100 to $1,000' [male 25 years old]. The realisation that their spending had increased comes after the event: 'She is spending about $300 per week, but it was a concern [when] she spent $3,000 in one day and she was shocked and very scared' [female 60 years old]. While other gamblers realised too late the excess of their gambling spree:

> He was spending about $600 per week, his gambling was escalating to $2,000 and $3,000 per week, he lost his job and his wife closed the access to the bank funds. Currently he is not gambling [male 45 years old].

> It was escalating from $50 to $200, she sold her jewellery, all her savings, she ... borrowed money from all her relatives and friends, eventually she stole the credit card of the ex-husband and spent his money in an effort to chase the loss and recover the money to pay her debts, she was spending about $500 a week when she had a crisis [and sought help] [female 63 years old].

In these case studies, the gambling level changed from being kept at a reasonable level to becoming excessive, unsustainable and well beyond their present living circumstances: 'Between $5 to $800 per week, escalated to spending her whole salary in a day' [female 65 years old]. In another case, the person had a relatively

164 *Pathways to Excessive Gambling*

high gambling level with $300 per week, but the gambling and the loss increased 10 fold: '... he lost $3,000 the last week, he lost $2,000 only three months ago' [male 24 years old-b].

These losses can seem low or not excessive, but they are not sustainable for a person on a low income or a person on a pension – prolonged gambling requires a high regular income from employment or other financial resources. Making this problem worse is the timing of the spending, the money is often gambled early in the pay period when there are maximum available funds and this creates an extended period of having no money. Gambling to chase and recoup the lost money is almost always futile, especially on gaming machines, which are based on a randomised system and not on skill (cf. Spanier 1987; Gupta and Derevensky 1998a; Johansson and Götestam 2003). A flow-on effect of the gambling is that they limit participation in other social leisure activities with family and friends, thus causing relationship problems – a recurrent problem in gambler's families (cf. Nova Scotia Department of Health Promotion and Protection 2008).

6.10   Reasons for seeking help

Despite gambling being accepted in Australian society, it remains an embarrassment for most people to lose money in any situation, but especially to lose money on gambling activities. It is a big step for a person to acknowledge that there is a problem which cannot be solved by the person themselves or by the family, but to admit that external help is needed. The impetus for seeking help for excessive gambling did not always come from the gamblers themselves in the case studies. The help was sought by employers or concerned family members who became aware of the accumulating excessive debts and the gamblers' feelings of stress, depression and anxiety. According to the case studies, the main reasons for seeking help were financial concerns and demands from the family to seek help to save the family relationship.

Furthermore, in some cases not until the gambler was faced by debt collectors chasing them or was caught stealing did they realise the severity of the problem and the need for external help. Nonetheless, if the gambler does not see their gambling as a problem, the counselling program will have less effect in changing their gambling behaviour. The best results came from gamblers who instigate the contact as a result of acknowledging that their gambling had become a serious problem. In the circumstance where a person close to the gambler initiated the contact with the counselling service, the need was acknowledged, 'My wife contacted MPGS. She was concerned about my gambling and the effect it was having on our family [male 42 years old], in another case the counselling help was refused:

> His wife requested counselling for support and to look at ways of encouraging husband to attend counselling. Unfortunately, he refused and said he can resolve the problem on his own. He accepted to go to Relationship Australia and they both are committed to save the relationship [male 33 years old].

Others echoed the same sentiments – female partners of gamblers, 29 years and 30 years old, had contacted the gambling counselling service on their partners' behalf. Unfortunately, in several of the cases the male partners did not see the urgency for counselling and the need for external help, because their present family situation was not critically threatened. They only agreed to counselling when there were compelling reasons for the gamblers to contact a support organisation. They will have experienced direct demands and ultimatums from family members or employers to stop their gambling as it had reached unsustainable levels and threatened family relationships and the employment situation, as in the case of this woman in her late 40s:

> Her husband has set an ultimatum, he told her she has to stop, she was struggling with debts, ... overwhelmed by anxiety, insomnia, and feels very sick [female 48 years old].

This case study was an example of a situation where the family sought help for a family member because of concern for their well being. In a comparable case, the daughter sought help for her 63-year-old mother because the mother had 'insomnia, panic attacks, depression, and suicidal ideation' problems. Additionally, the gambler could have exhausted all the support available from family and friends, where the initial positive support had changed to hostile attitudes towards the gambler, such as in the case of a 24-years-old young Australian man. However, the family treatment did still not compel him to stop gambling even if the consequences would be even more difficult:

> His parents kicked him out of the house, he is living with his grandfather who accepted him in his house only if [he] would take the control over his money, he agreed with this arrangement and his grandfather has taken him under his wing, however he [is] still borrowing money and gambling without his knowledge. ... he is about to [lose] loss his job.

In situations where the gamblers made contact with a support agency, they themselves have more or less realised the seriousness of the problem and their need for external support to manage the excessive gambling:

> She was struggling with debts and [was] overwhelmed by anxiety, insomnia and depression. The trigger for her [was] to look [for] help [as she] was spending $3,000 in one night [female 60 years old].

> He lost $4,000 in one night; this loss motivated him to seek help. His parents suspected he is gambling but cannot prove it as he has covered up his track very well, but he has noticed his father is following him very close[ly]. He is very anxious and experiences disturbed sleep ... all he can think [of] is ... his gambling problem [male 31 years old].

166 *Pathways to Excessive Gambling*

A middle-aged woman felt relaxed, forgot all her problems and experienced confidence when playing the poker machines. Her spending on poker machines had increased to $550 weekly and she would like to decrease the spending, but not stop gambling. She sought help because of her feelings of anxiety and her partner's disagreements about her gambling, which has created further problems in their relationship:

> ... her husband is very angry towards her because she is spending a lot of money in gambling. She said he is a control freak, stingy, overcritical and emotionally abusive man [female 56 years old].

The shock of losing a large amount of money can be the first realisation that the gambling is excessive as for this 24-year-old Australian born man who was prompted a to seek help after a major loss:

> He just had a big [loss] of $5,000, he is feeling hopeless and helpless, however he said he is trying to think [of] ways to get [the] money to continue gambling to recover his financial losses through gambling, he said he is [not] prepared to stop but to slow down his gambling.

His attitude to handling the problem was only to spend less money not to stop gambling. Both these case studies show that the gamblers only wanted to reduce the money spent, not give up gambling altogether. The question is whether this strategy would have any long term prospects of solving their problems or simply help temporarily, possibly until the next time the gambling became excessive. Chasing losses is an indication that the gambling has become excessive and a major problem for the gambler (Blaszczynski and Nower 2002; Productivity Commission 1999, 2009).

Consequences of not seeking help at a sufficiently early stage can make it much more difficult to reverse a negative situation, as it can be a long way back to a more independent life. A 65-year-old woman's life had changed from being able to travel the world and having her own independent household to having nothing:

> She lost her house, spent all her superannuation, she had to live with her sister whom she doesn't go along with; she was finding it difficult to get a job and to keep a job at her age.

A 45-year-old man acknowledged that his excessive gambling had contributed to the demise of his marriage. He understood for the first time that the consequences of the marriage breakdown would be that his daily contact with his young son would suffer. He had gambled heavily for at least the last 10 years, but had gambled in total for a period of 20 years – this had been at more or less sustainable levels. He thinks of himself as lucky and says he had won large sums of money, but also lost considerable sums. Presently he can lose $2,000 to $3,000 per week through gambling, when the gambling was under control, he only lost about $600 per week.

Other circumstances that can influence a person's propensity to gamble are where the gambling is used as a diversion from other problems. For such a person, it can be seen as one of their few available strategies to cope with other social, economic or mental problems. Breaking the cycle of gambling can be more difficult for a person who has exposure to another person's gambling problems within the family. An example was the case where friends introduced a young man to gambling whose father also gambled excessively on gaming machines and playing cards [male 45 years old]. Another example is where the mother was a gambler and the gambling caused financial problems:

> His mother is a gambler as well. He has been very stressed out because his parents are always struggling with financial problems, he feels responsible for his mother who suffers from bi-polar disorder and is also a heavy gambler [male 33 years old].

These case studies highlight the effects gambling activities have on gamblers and their families. Additionally, relationship problems were a recurrent issue, these can be both an effect of excessive gambling and be a contributing factor to it.

6.11 Gambling's impact on personal and public life

Gambling can be a social activity with family and friends, but it can also be an activity undertaken in secrecy where no one else is aware of the gambling or its extent. The case studies show that excessive gambling with increasing loss of money will lead to ill-health, anxiety, and depression for the gambler and stress for their dependents. Financial losses lead to further gambling to recoup the lost money, deepening the financial and emotional suffering for the family. Where the gambling is not known to the family, feelings of guilt and fear that they will find out, arise – the gambler fears exposure and the consequent loss of partner, children and friends. When gambling funds are obtained unlawfully, exposure and the legal implications of embezzlement and theft carry the frightening risk of going to prison. Two of the case studies involve two men, aged 42 and 36, whose situations included problems that had both legal and family relationship consequences:

> Increasing anxiety about the future [pending legal proceedings]. Also contributing to problems with his wife and daughter, though client believes them to be devoted and utterly patient with him. It is also affecting his health. He gets back pain, headaches and generally feels the stress of it in his life [male 42 years old].

> In a big way. I have had problems in my relationships with my wife. She has contemplated leaving me on several occasions. I also don't get on with my brother and brother in law who both disapprove of my gambling. My mum also

168   *Pathways to Excessive Gambling*

worries about me and could not stand living in Australia and has gone back to Iran [male 36 years old].

Family suffering was highlighted in the following extracts from case studies of a 32-year-old woman and two men aged 30 years and 45 years:

> Her family is very worried and frustrated with her, they are tired [of paying] to pay her mortgage and her mother is the one who is in charge of [and] control her credit cards and limit her expenses, her father is no[t] talking to her any more. She is eating for comfort and then turns to obsessive with losing weight and becoming anorexic. She is a workaholic [female 32 years old].

> Financial problems are placing strain in his relationship. Wife has given him an ultimatum, this is the second chance and there is not going to be a third one, she said. Children, oldest is 7, have noticed mother crying as a result of above problems and they get very distressed and [son] present behavioural problems [male 30 years old].

> He has lost his wife's trust and she is very unhappy in the relationship and has initiated the divorce, ... He has lost his job because he was not performing due to lack of motivation, lack of energy, concentration and memory problems, eventually he was fired. He had to move to a unit close to his house as he wants to be close to his son. His extended family is very worried about his situation. He thinks his son is very upset for the separation [male 45 years old].

In these cases, the gambling changed the lives of the people involved from a comfortable secure family and employment situation to losing everything. Financial problems caused by excessive gambling were an obvious link between many of the gamblers; financial problems that placed pressure on the families and the relationships. Two case studies concerning a 31-year-old man and a 56-year-old woman describe the families' frustration with their gambling pursuits:

> Financial problems are placing strain in the family relationships; he is isolated from his friends and his performance at work is no[t] very good at the moment. His father told him if [he] ... is gambling he has to go to live independent[ly] from them [male 31 years old].

> The husband is very concerned and her daughter doesn't want to talk to her, she is very angry with her mother and can not understand why she insists in only reduce it but continue gambling. Her husband has stopped her access to the bank account. She is very anxious; she describes panic attacks and insomnia [female 56 years old].

The frustration may be expressed in verbal and even physical abuse in the family. Family members may seek to exclude the gambler from social interaction with family and friends. In two case studies, both women aged 48 and 63 years of age, the frustration was clearly described and how it affected the gamblers and their families:

> Husband is very angry with her and the emotional abuse in the relationship is escalating, she is isolated from her family and her friends are all in difficult situations as well. She has put a lot of weight on, she said she is eating for comfort [female 48 years old].

> She has received the strong impact of the family rejection, they are very disappointed and angry towards her, all the lies she has told are being discovered now and husband is so disappointed, he has disclosed to their daughter the [truth] true about her mother gambling problems [female 63 years old].

The situation was not much different when the gambler was the adult child in the family and the parents were also gambling. The difference in this example was that in the parents' case the gambling was not adversely affecting their financial situation, but their 24-year-old son had severe gambling problems that were causing significant problems:

> He is depressed, he is fighting with his mother a lot, she is very frustrated about him, he said to her: 'but you are a gambler' and she always said she earns good money, she can spend it as she wants, sometimes she gets very disappointed after disagreements with her son, … He said his father doesn't talk to him, he is his boss, he only talks to him about the work in the firm [male 24 years old-b].

As these cases show, gambling causes severe problems in the affected families. The drive to continue gambling in these situations is compelling as they risked losing their emotional, social and financial security and the support that living in a family environment provides.

In some cases, the close family knows about the family member's gambling, but this is not always the case. Secrecy surrounding the gambler's gambling activities contributed to their anxiety and stress. As expressed in the case study of a married woman in her 50s:

> No one in her family knows she has addictions. She is struggling to survive with her problems and she has to create a lot of stories to [for] husband and daughter [female in her 50s].

Nonetheless, the case studies showed situations where the gambling was known in the family and the gambler was making attempts to settle debts and to make amends for the gambling. A young man, aged 29 recounted this:

170 *Pathways to Excessive Gambling*

Financial problems are placing strain in the relationship but he [has] compromised to work hard to pay all the money he lost, she is in control of the money [male 29 years old].

An example was also given in the case studies where gambling was the cause of stress and anxiety, but the gambling was used to relieve both of them. This excerpt about a young Australian born man aged 24 also highlights gambling in combination with secrecy and excessive drinking:

He describes a pattern of feeling extremely anxious with sleeping difficulties and inability to relax, he said he can relax only in the club when he is gambling, and alcohol helps as well, he has a tendency to cry and gets very depressed with somatic complaints. His family is disappointed because he spends too much time in the club and they are concerned about his drinking, but they don't know the extent of his gambling [male 24 years old-a].

Family members go to extreme lengths to help and support each other, as in the case of the sister of a 65-year-old woman who, before the excessive gambling spree, lived a very comfortable life, but with the death of her husband started a downward spiral. She has lost all her independence and she was not trusted to handle her own income or even to travel by herself to and from work:

She has lost her status, socially, financially and in her family, she has to work again after retirement. She is now depending on her sister for everything, as she is no[t] paying for her food and accommodation, her sister has control over her finances and takes her to work and picks her up after work to prevent her from going to the club [female 65 years old].

These case studies highlight the pressure excessive gambling imposes on relationships, breakdown in communications, feelings of guilt, and isolation from people and other social leisure activities. Family and friends were both supportive and appalled by the gamblers' behaviour. The families were worried and frustrated with the gamblers and they tired of paying expenses such as mortgage and everyday costs. To help the gamblers and themselves, parents and partners of gamblers took control of credit cards and the finances to restrict further financial losses.

6.12 Social isolation

There is uncertainty about whether or not gambling activities increase or decrease social isolation as gambling can be undertaken quite separately from other social leisure time. Excessive gamblers can be highly socially inclined and have an extensive social circle of friends that meet frequently, while at the same time the gambler prefers to engage in gambling as a separate activity without his or hers friends.

In nine of the case studies, the gambling did not affect the person directly, they were still living well integrated social lives, being actively involved in social networks and feeling comfortable in the community. Even if the three females aged in the 40s and 50s and the three males aged in their 20s and 30s acknowledged they were partly isolated, they did not feel that it influenced their everyday life, as they expressed in these ways:

> He feels well in that regard he has good friends and many relatives, his sister is very supportive [male 45 years old].

> I feel ok. I miss my friends and my homeland at times, but life is easier financially here and my child would have a better future here [male 36 years old].

> She feels well in that regard, she has good friends and is appreciated in the work place [female 32 years old].

It would be a misconception to think that non-gamblers would have more active and larger social networks than gamblers. For many people their social network is limited to the immediate family, a few long time friends and work colleagues. Independent of gambling activities, people can be comfortable with a large or small number of friends or the family can be the main part of their social network. Gambling does not need to influence the social circle of friends and the social comfort of people in the community. However, isolation can be a consequence of excessive gambling when the financial support from family, relatives, friends and work colleagues has been exhausted. Thus, a social network restricted to the immediate family, may be all the gambler has, the support they offer may be qualified by the current level of gambling. Furthermore, the social network and support may be conditional upon the gambler agreeing to restrict his or her gambling or to attending a support service to actively address their habit. Their gambling may also be a substitute for other recreational and social activities. Excerpts from the case studies show different levels of isolation, not necessarily directly related to their gambling:

> Client does feel isolated and alone. His only support is his wife and two daughters [male 42 years old].

> He feels isolated, his family has no[t] many friends and he has friends mainly from work but he is concern[ed] most of his friends have a girlfriend and he doesn't, he has no[t] much opportunities to meet girls, he is also shy with girls … [male 24 years old-a].

> He used to have good friends from school but he has lost contact with them, in his work there is no[t] many young people like him, he is a bit isolated, … [male 24 years old-b].

172   *Pathways to Excessive Gambling*

> He feels isolated from his family, [but] he has good friends, he feels well in this
> society [male 33 years old].

These descriptions clearly show that isolation was a factor for some of the gamblers; they were well aware of their social situation and had even identified areas they would like to improve. They wanted to increase their circle of friends beyond the narrow family circle, to have a girl- or a boyfriend and to be out of debt. Gambling at a local community club was seen as a way to alleviate their social isolation and reduce their stress, it became an escape from an unsatisfactory everyday life where boredom, social isolation and lack of status were very much felt (cf. The South Australian Centre for Economic Studies 2005; Blaszczynski and Nower 2002).

Nevertheless, isolation depends on a combination of situational factors, personal issues such as a person's health status, the social environment and easy access to local gambling venues. The gambling sessions can alleviate or relieve stress, boredom and/or isolation. These quotes indicate difficulties to adjust to the local community:

> She feels isolated and misses her family and friends, but she mostly misses
> her husband with whom she used to spend most of her free time [female 65
> years old].

> She feels isolated and very sad, she always wanted to return to her country but
> husband was against the idea [female 63 years old].

> He feels isolated and in the process of acculturation to Australia lack of English
> makes the situation more difficult for him, particularly to [search for] work ...
> [male 29 years old].

> She misses her family and friends, she never learned English and never felt
> integrated to this society [female 56 years old].

> He feels isolated and is in process of acculturation to Australia, because even [if]
> he [has been] is here 8 years ago, however his English is not yet good enough for
> working in his field of experience, he was an accountant in his country of origin
> [male 30 years old].

> He feels acculturation is not an issue for him. He has a lot of friends but at the
> moment is isolated because he is depressed and doesn't feel like socialising
> [male 31 years old].

Additionally, the risk of the gambling becoming general knowledge might lead the gambler to be dishonest about the requests for and the use of borrowed money and this further contribute to their isolation (cf. Borrell and Boulet 2005). In the following case, the gambler felt very isolated and alone with her problems, especially because she had not disclosed her level of gambling and the size of the debt to her immediate family:

> She feels isolated, she misses her family, she had friends but now she is no[t] seeing any one, because she has debts to pay and she is concern[ed] they may say something to her family [female 60 years old].

Thus isolation can increase if the gambler has borrowed money from family members, relatives, friends or work colleagues, giving false reasons for needing the money. The isolation is fuelled by the risk of meeting someone from whom the gambler has borrowed money and the person asking that the money be returned. When the repayments are not forthcoming, it becomes stressful and difficult to meet with other people, thus isolation can be the preferred option.

6.13   Gambling as part of other personal and social issues

It has been documented in other research that some people who have a problem with gambling also have other problems – they often have various combinations of mental, social and physical problems as well as excessive use of drugs, alcohol or smoking. When such a range of problems is combined with gambling, problems and conflicts arise within relationships and in the home environment. The research shows that gambling problems are related to a combination of psychological and social problems, where gambling pursuits might be used to compensate for other difficulties the person experiences (Blaszczynski and Nower 2002; Marks and Lesieur 1992; Getty, Watson and Frisch 2000). According to the 2007 Adult Gambling Prevalence Study (Nova Scotia Department of Health Promotion and Protection 2008: 123)[6] there emerged a difference between problem gamblers and at-risk gamblers on the one hand and those at no risk for gambling problems on the other hand (non-problem or non-gamblers). Problem gamblers and, to a lesser extent, at-risk gamblers were more likely to have mental health issues and life problems affecting their well being than the non-problem gamblers and non-gamblers.

Such combinations of problems were seen in the case studies. Some of the gamblers were smokers and the ability to smoke while gambling was highly appreciated. Smoking has become more and more restricted in public places and while the laws changed in 2007, smoking was still allowed in clubs at the time of this research. Where smoking and social isolation were given as reasons to gamble by the females, the reasons for male gamblers related to the family

---

6   The 2007 Nova Scotia Adult Gambling Prevalence Study, prevalence study using Canadian Problem Gambling Index, a telephone survey of 2,500 adults, 19 years of age and older living in 1,661 randomly selected households in Nova Scotia an overall response rate of 60.6 per cent.

174 *Pathways to Excessive Gambling*

situation and difficulties in coping with children. The males preferred to leave the family home for the club environment and gambling rather than to help their partners with the children:

> ... she feels she belong to this environment, because this is the only place she is allowed to smoke without restrictions, and no one makes her feel uncomfortable, ... they [her friends] are all heavy smokers and they are allowed to smoke in the club [female 48 years old].

> Disconnection of the reality, relieving emotional pain, isolation and sadness associated with grief [female 65 years old].

> ... he doesn't like to be at home, his relationship with wife has deteriorated since she knew he had an affair while she was on holidays [male 29 years old].

> ... he doesn't like to be at home when the kids are too active or noisy and his wife is in a bad mood, ... [male 33 years old].

> ... he doesn't like to be at home, he has a son who is hyperactive, [an]other 2 sons under 5 years old and his wife is extremely frustrated with the situation. He escapes from the house as soon as possible [male 30 years old].

Additionally, depression runs through several of the case studies, depression based on earlier experiences in the family and depression due to the present situation. In the case of a 32-year-old woman the current family situation and past experiences were affecting her state of mind and gambling behaviour:

> She has a dysfunctional family, her mother was alcoholic ... she is no[t] drinking any more but she was a heavy drinker during her childhood, her brother suffers bipolar disorder and he was addicted to heroin, ... She uses amphetamines time by time. All those factors influence her gambling at some levels, at different times [female 32 years old].

Stress, isolation and family relationships can also drive people to use gambling to alleviate the stress as for a young man who was working in the family business, where he was frequently in conflict with his father. The combination of working within the family company and not fulfilling the father's expectations caused him stress. He turned to gambling as a relaxing activity, perhaps influenced by the circumstance that his mother was also a gambler hence gambling was a source of conflict within the family.

A 60-year-old woman who had never learned English lived a socially isolated existence and her lack of English restricted her ability to develop social networks outside her ethnic group. However, gambling was only one of her problems:

She has a long history of addiction to benzos, in the past she was addicted to amphetamines but she is no[t] using them any more, she is a heavy smoker. She has a long history of abuse in the context of domestic violence, her husband who is a heavy drinker was always very abusive towards her, they are currently separated but live under the same roof, she is always having confrontations with him, ... This lady suffers from major depression.

Family, political and religious issues were other factors that created a drive to escape from a complicated home situation. In this case, a middle-aged woman experienced pressure to follow her husband's faith:

She is confronting a difficult situation as her husband is very intense in his religion, ... and is forcing her to convert ... she doesn't like it but has accepted it to avoid confrontations. He can be very abusive emotionally, ... [female 48 years old].

A complicated family situation where there was great sadness and where the woman knew her child had been abused, created great distress and guilt for her, led her into gambling as a form of escape [56-year-old female]. Old traumas were relived, creating anxiety and distress for a woman in her 60s who had come from Chile [63-year-old female] and the social recreational gambling got out of control for a 65-year-old woman when her partner died:

She has a history of trauma, her father was abusive towards her mother, her first husband was physically very abusive towards her and she divorced for this reason. She migrated to Australia with her 10-year-old daughter, to help her sister who was very sick with terminal breast cancer and she assisted her until her last day; she took care of the family and at the time she was very busy and sad. Living with her sister was very difficult because she [sister] has 2 little children who were very distressed for the situation and the husband of the sister was always drunk. Five years ago her daughter disclosed to her that she was sexually abused by her uncle when they were living in her sister's house [female 56 years old].

She suffers from depression, she has trauma issues of the revolution in her country, the terrorism and the persecutions, many of her friends vanished, her family and friends had to escape as refugees and she manage[d] to immigrate to Australia; but the traumatic experiences she went through are always at the back of the mind ... [female 63 years old].

She is very depressed ... the illness and death of husband were very traumatic experiences, she is confronting trauma of the past she never resolved. She finds gambling alleviating of her symptoms, in terms of helping her forget and rest for a while of the emotional pain, she finds it relieving ... [female 65 years old].

In many of the case studies drug and alcohol addiction, loss of loved ones, in combination with relationship issues, stress and depression occurred with excessive gambling, in such cases, the positive effects of gambling were emphasised. The living circumstances the case studies have portrayed encompass many common themes. Other research shows the same pattern with gambling being part of the gambler's health problems. Health related issues such as generally poor health, smoking and alcohol use and mental health problems affecting gamblers are higher than for the general population – the combination of these factors clearly impacts on the everyday life of the gambler (Taylor, Grande, Delfabbro, Glenn, Goulding et al. 2001: 9). The public health perspective proposed by Korn and Shaffer (1999: 289, 291) insists that gambling should be seen as a health issue and public health professionals should be made more aware of gambling and its consequent risks. For the people in the case studies with health issues, gambling was both a contributor to the problem and an activity that helped to alleviate their complicated and stressful situations – their gambling sessions provided 'time-out' for them.

In the Nova Scotia gambling survey, the interrelationship between health problems and gambling was highlighted in the 2007 survey (Nova Scotia Department of Health Promotion and Protection 2008: 123–4). In the sample of surveyed people 85 per cent experienced at least one life and health issue, while for the problem gamblers the corresponding percentage was higher at 93.2 per cent. Between 2003 and 2007 relationship problems increased for the problem gamblers from 7.5 per cent to 9.0 per cent, the depression rate increased from 7.5 per cent to 12.6 per cent. Nearly a quarter of the problem gamblers (23.0 per cent) and at-risk gamblers (27.5 per cent) had some type of financial problems compared to only about 7.7 per cent for non-gamblers and 8.7 per cent for non-problem gamblers. Nevertheless, the figures showed a decline in financial problems for the problem gambler group since 2003 when 44.6 per cent reported financial problems. The incidences of relationship problems, loneliness and depression increased in the problem gambling group. Almost a quarter of problem gamblers (23.0 per cent) reported experiencing relationship problems and loneliness in the previous year compared to about five to 12 per cent for non-gamblers and non-problem gamblers and 16 per cent to 19 per cent for at-risk gamblers. Additionally, the problem gamblers reported a higher percentage of problems with depression (39.3 per cent) compared to 19.8 per cent of the at-risk gamblers and about 12 per cent of the non-problem gamblers and non-gamblers.

The case studies examined in this chapter show similar complex problems among the excessive gamblers with those presented in the Nova Scotia Department of Health Promotion and Protection (2008) research. The combination of mental, social and health problems and family relationship problems were obvious and for the gamblers the gambling situation both created relief for a stress full situation, time out from their compound problems and contributed to the whole problematic environment.

6.14 Conclusion

The case studies have given an insight into 21 gamblers' pathways from social recreational gambling to excessive gambling where external professional counselling help was sought. In Australian society, gambling opportunities are extensive in metropolitan but also in urban and regional communities. Gambling opportunities are widely advertised in the media where a gambling win is portrayed as giving the winner everlasting happiness and a problem free life. Gambling is legal, thus a legitimate way to pursue financial wealth. The temptation to easily improve one's financial situation is a driver for many people and gambling can be seen as one of several techniques to achieve this. The winners are heard and acknowledged, but rarely the losers.

Electronic gaming machines attract many people, they are easy to play and it does not cost much to play a single game. It is an accessible gambling form, thus attracting social, regular and excessive gamblers, who play for fun, a chance to win money or as a way to forget complex life and living conditions. Gambling opportunities are accessed within a relaxing and convivial atmosphere at the local club or hotel, an environment where the gambler can socialise in a positive and friendly atmosphere, leave their everyday troubles behind and gamble on a gaming machine in a happy and noisy milieu in company with other gamblers without any social demands. Local clubs create an atmosphere where people feel respected and welcome.

The average age of the people in the case study was 39 years with males having a younger age profile than females; the males were also more likely to be married than the females. Females were more likely to be introduced to gambling activities and club visits by friends and work colleagues, while males were also inclined to have initiated the gambling contact by themselves. The pathways from social recreational to excessive gambling had taken shorter time for the males than the females and the males had started their gambling earlier than the females. For the females, gambling on electronic gaming machines was the preferred option, while men were inclined to utilise other forms of gambling. However, it was the electronic gaming machine gambling that had led them down the excessive gambling pathway.

It can be concluded from the case studies that the majority of the male gamblers seeking help for excessive gambling were in employment, from full employment to casual employment, while females were more likely to be outside the paid labour market, mainly due to an older age profile than the males. Two-thirds of the gamblers in the sample were employed, one fifth retired, and one tenth unemployed and one person was a homemaker. Access to a regular income is one of the prerequisites for gambling while income from age pension or social security payments are commonly too low to sustain excessive gambling, although even gambling with small amounts can cause excessive problems. However, no matter what the income source, gambling had become unsustainable for all the people studied.

The excessive gambling pathways were for some people a gradual process, but there were also occasions where loss of employment, relationship problems and death of a partner created an environment where the previous controlled gambling became excessive. All people in the sample remembered their first win, even the small one. The first win was treasured and a cause for celebration, the win was associated with special luck for the person or the club where the win took place.

The sample had an international profile as the Multicultural Problem Gambling Services NSW client group are people with English as a second language and therefore the sample was not representative of the general population who seek gambling counselling (cf. Walker, Shannon et al. 2004). The majority of people in the sample, who were not born in Australia, had not gambled before they arrived. This was especially the case for the women in the sample. This highlights the influence that the ease with which people can gamble, its legitimacy and the extensive variety and possibilities for gambling in Australia have had on these gamblers.

In the case studies the people lost considerably more money than they won and needed help to manage their increasing debt levels, but also the social, mental and physical problems engendered by their excessive gambling. This loss of money created stress both for the gambler and for the gambler's family. It was difficult for the gambler to recognise they had a problem with gambling even when the severity of the problem was clear to their partners or employers. The unwillingness on the part of the gamblers to stop gambling was especially true for those who did not initiate the gambling counselling sessions themselves. One third of the sample was struggling financially even without the gambling, while another third of the sample was earning enough money for a comfortable living standard. However, in all cases the gambling expenditure was challenging their financial situation.

The case studies also indicated that excessive gambling pursuits not only negatively influence the well being of the gambler and their family, it also increases social isolation. This is especially the situation when the family is unaware of the excessive gambling and most particularly when the source of gambling funds has been got through deception or by illegal means. It is true however, that not all gamblers felt isolated despite experiencing stress due to escalating gambling problems.

Electronic gaming machine gambling is undertaken in isolation, but in a social construct where people are together even if they do not communicate with each other. A contributing factor to the attractiveness of poker machine gambling is that the club environment is perceived as very safe, where patrons are left alone, but are in a friendly, entertaining and encouraging social environment with friendly staff. They do not therefore feel lonely and are not seen as alone. Gambling venues are one of the few remaining places where heavy smokers could, at the time of the research, still smoke while gambling and have a drink. The gambling location and activity was associated with the freedom to smoke and have a drink without interference and condemnation from the establishment, family and friends. Gambling venues also have extended opening hours and therefore little time restriction on how long the gambler can stay at the venue. Consequently, a person can patronise a club most of the day and almost all of the night.

Gambling is part of Australian leisure culture, a common leisure activity even if it is restricted for many people to buying a weekly lottery ticket. For the people in the sample, gambling had taken over other forms of leisure and recreational activities, thus precluding other social activities with family and friends. Gambling pursuits had become the main issue that occupied their thoughts and their leisure time.

Several of the people in the sample said the positive effects of gambling were that it helped them to cope with other personal problems. The gambling sessions made it possible to cope with the personal issues, complicated relationships and other problems, even if the gambling as such undoubtedly contributed to an overall problematic picture and made their everyday life and the whole situation more complicated and difficult to handle.

Gambling was pursued for many reasons, but for a significant number of gamblers it was a desire to improve their financial situation. The dream of securing a substantial win was present in all the gamblers. Even when gamblers acknowledge the total money lost on gambling exceeds any current win, there was a strong belief that a major win would compensate for all the losses. The urge to be wealthy was the driving force that clouded their judgement about the small probability of creating wealth through gambling pursuits.

The case studies showed that the loss of employment and/or their partner gave them extensive free time which could be spent at the club engaged in gambling activities. In general however, the loss of their family, employment and home had to occur before they would seek help for their excessive gambling. The loss is accompanied by exposure, either exposure of their hitherto secret activity or their illegal activity to access funds with which to gamble. The latter may result in a prison term.

The case studies give an insight into the problem excessive gamblers experience and what their families go through. The stories told by the gamblers show the depth of despair excessive gambling causes.

Chapter 7
Concluding Discussion

7.1 Introduction

The book aims to contribute to the debate about gambling and to highlight how the current arbitrary distinction between social recreational and excessive gambling has led to misconceptions about the scope of and pathways to excessive gambling. Here gambling is approached from a societal perspective, as a societal issue. It explains gambling beyond the traditional perspective of gambling as an individual problem. Governments, the gaming industry, individual gamblers, their families and friends, and the social environment in which gambling is undertaken are all 'participants' in gambling and must be seen together to be able to properly understand the phenomenon of gambling. The book explores and explains the individual variables and the relationships between them. Gambling is variously enjoyed as a recreational activity while it negatively impacts on other gamblers and their families; it generates large profits for the gaming industry and raises vast revenues for governments. It provides employment and supports sporting and other recreational activities from the local to the national level.

While local sports clubs with gaming machine gambling facilities have a local focus, betting on horse racing and lottery sales reach a population of potential participants from the local to the global level. The internet allows easy access to a global gambling market, where national borders are made redundant. Players can gamble from home through a gaming website located anywhere in the world and anyone can gamble on anything with anybody irrespective of time and geographical location.

The gambling pursuits of individual gamblers generate considerable profits for the gambling industry and governments benefit enormously through gambling licences and taxation revenue. The gambling industry operates on a highly successful business model because while people win sometimes, most people will lose their money – essentially, it is set up so that the 'house can never lose'. Electronic gaming machine gambling is a low investment high return business where there is a high density of gambling machines to a low floor space ratio together with long opening hours in clubs and low staff to patron ratios.

Gambling revenue contributes to government community projects and to social support services as well as to research about gambling's influence on people's well being. However, the gambling revenue does not benefit the highest contributors to the gambling revenue – the regular local gambler who occasionally or habitually gambles until all the money is gone. The use of gambling revenue to fund social benefits and welfare entrenches gambling as an essential activity that enables social services and community leisure activities. The use of gambling revenue to fund support services for problem gamblers and research into gambling, hardly justifies the hardship imposed on people affected by the adverse effects of gambling. It contributes significantly to the problems endured by excessive gamblers but also requires that they pay (in advance) for their own future counselling and gambling support services.

In jurisdictions where gambling is legal and condoned by the population, gambling is widespread. In Australia, the majority of people gamble in one way or another. While most people only buy lottery and raffle tickets, about three out of 10 people gamble regularly and approximately 5 per cent of adults gamble at least weekly on gaming machines (Chapter 4; Productivity Commission 2009). As mentioned above, governments and local communities benefit from gambling commerce through gambling revenue, local employment opportunities and clubs' role as sports and social recreational facilities. Governments have the responsibility of balancing the financial and employment benefits brought by the gambling industry with the potential adverse effects of excessive gambling through the regulation of the gambling industry and the funding of counselling services and social welfare support organisations. Additionally, nations legislate to safeguard against the criminal activities that are attached to gambling, such as money laundering through casino gambling and individual's criminal activities due to excessive gambling (Chapter 3).

The book highlights the global nature of gambling, and the policy and strategies being implemented to safeguard against adverse outcomes for individuals. Policies and regulation strategies (and even the suggestion of abolishing gambling entirely) have been recorded as early as fourteenth century Spain and in Italy in the sixteenth century (France 1902); the adverse effects of gambling were acknowledged even then. Today, the global nature of gambling makes it a difficult industry to regulate. This creates a situation with complex jurisdictional impediments. To develop global gambling regulations and to control activities spanning many jurisdictions is an exceedingly complex issue, not only because of different classifications of gambling activities and regulations but also because of different jurisdictions' legal authority. In the US and Australia, the regulation of gambling is the responsibility of the states, while regulation is at a national level in the UK and Sweden (Chapters 3 and 4; The Allen Group 2009).

In contemporary urban areas, the community construct can be artificial. Normally, to have membership in any community, active participation and involvement are prerequisites. It is quite possible on the individual level to live in a community without active involvement in community life and events and remain anonymous, by preference or otherwise (cf. Wellman 2001). A community becomes what the residents or the individuals wish to make of it; a place to live and sleep or an energetic place that engages an essential part of the residents' everyday life, where what is happening becomes their responsibility and enjoyment. Greater Western Sydney has a growing population, with a broad socio-economic range. It has a mixture of cultures and multiethnic community concentrations. The multicultural population influences and creates a diverse community milieu and street life, including culturally influenced businesses, restaurants and community groups. Community belonging is a balancing act between residents' geographical and social mobility. The community construct often requires a challenging crisis to unite people and get people engaged outside their own private sphere. Local community clubs were established to enhance the community spirit and cultivate local community interests, be it sports, cultural or professional.

In Australia the large clubs have an active community involvement and a concern for the local community and its residents, often this was the original reason for establishing the club. The originally humble clubs have grown into large sports, professional, ethnic or interest specific social recreational establishments. These establishments with vast gambling opportunities are established in mainly low socio-economic residential areas where alternative leisure and recreational activities are limited. In these areas land prices are lower than in established older residential areas, which makes it easier to build large gambling and hospitality complexes. These club complexes create a focal point for social entertainment and hospitality and the associated sports club will be the main supplier and manager of local sports activities, all activities within an affordable price range for the local residents, affordable because they are subsidised by gambling revenue. In these residential areas the unemployment and underemployment rates are highest, areas where the more recent arrivals will congregate due to housing affordability but where perhaps everyday hardship is most strongly felt. These are areas where people become geographically isolated if they do not have access to a vehicle or if public transport is inadequate, areas where the dreams about a better future is strongest, but perhaps most difficult to achieve. Community clubs invite to large memberships because of their low annual fees and attractive membership benefits. These member rich clubs can wield considerable influence in their communities but can also be a successful lobbying force with governments and influence the outcome of proposals for gambling industry related policy and regulations (Independent Pricing and Regulatory Tribunal 2008; Productivity Commission 2009).

The researched local community clubs had developed from modest beginnings to become multimillion dollar businesses. Electronic gaming machines have been and still are clubs' unsurpassed revenue generating business sector (Productivity Commission 2009). The revenue from gaming machines and the taxation governments collect from this revenue are sources of financial support for local community activities through, for example, the Community Development and Support Expenditure Scheme. This scheme provides direct support to community organisations and activities (New South Wales Office of Liquor, Gaming and Racing 2009c).

A perceived advantage of the club environment is that it is considered a safe environment where the patrons are left alone, but at the same time they are in a friendly, entertaining and encouraging social environment with congenial staff. People feel safe and they are not seen as lonely as they are among a large group of people even if they do not socially interact. As gambling venues have extended opening hours, the gambler can stay at the venue for a long time and is not restricted to set hours like they are at a sports event or a movie. This possibility can make the local club an alternative 'home' for some people.

Opportunities to gamble in Australian communities are diverse and easily accessible through the community club culture. The Australian clubs are unique in the respect that they are for all people, local and non-local, the membership fee is low, and they are open for extended hours, catering for all age groups from children and young people through sports training and management to club and elite sports events. They also facilitate local entertainment; provide conference and hospitality facilities and serve affordable food and beverages. Clubs provide a local place for social gatherings as well as for the lone visitor who wishes to have a quiet drink and gamble on the gaming machines. Local clubs are excellent meeting places for groups of people, for people doing shift work and those working irregular hours – the long opening hours make them convenient winding down places after work. The club can be a convenient meeting place without excessive joining fees or entrance fees, only the food and drink need to be paid for and for a person who does not visit the gambling area, the cost for the outing is reasonable; thus local community clubs have an important function as entertainment and social network centres as well as a source of support for local sports activities. Nonetheless, local community clubs are a focal point for gambling and especially electronic gaming machine gambling, where the easy access and convenient location of gambling areas facilitate gambling and make access to gambling opportunities an effortless affair for people who want to gamble and especially for people who have developed a problem with excessive gambling.

Research has conclusively found that excessive gambling causes hardship for the gamblers, their families and the community. To restrict the adverse effects, policy and regulation strategies have been applied; these are continuously revised and amended as a result of new choices for policy direction, research findings, demands from the gaming industry and public pressure. While the economic interests of all the stakeholders – the gambling industry, governments and individuals, remains fixed on the stream of money (a dream for gamblers), gambling will continue to be a part of everyday life and be seen as an essential employment market and revenue source by governments.

A problem needs several strategies to be managed. The policy and regulation approach is just one measure and does not diminish the benefits of early education programs for young people about gambling, odds of losing and winning, the randomness of gaming machines where skills are irrelevant, and the pitfalls and long term consequences of excessive gambling. Such educational programs present information and create knowledge about the real chances of winning and losing, and show alternative ways to gain a comfortable living through education and work, social entertainment where occasional controlled gambling is not excluded. In Australia, Canada, the USA and other countries, programs for primary and high school students are already in place. However, in the Productivity Commission's 2009 (Chapter 6) draft review, questions were raised about the short and long term benefits of such programs and the lack of evaluation of current programs. Understanding the randomness of gaming machines and the real chances of winning may well reduce gambling propensity and the consequent adverse effects of gambling. The value of such educational programs may simply lack a longitudinal perspective. Some people have even questioned whether information about gambling encourages gambling, but thinking that prefers ignorance to knowledge must always remain dubious.

It is obvious that the needs of each of the stakeholders must be met. It is quite clear that policy and regulations alone will not change the present situation; education is a long term approach where the effects are as yet uncertain and finally, regardless of political ideology, the close relationship between the gaming industry and governments will not change because of the two-way financial benefits. Gambling therefore can only be properly understood when it is seen from a holistic perspective.

Gambling, as a recreational leisure activity can be very enjoyable, to go to the races or the sports match and bet on the outcome to create some excitement. For the majority of gamblers, the money lost on gambling does neither interfere with nor create a need for change in their everyday life; neither does it prevent the family from participating in leisure and educational programs. Nevertheless, gambling is a problem when it exceeds the person's financial, social, legal and health limits and when gambling becomes an excessive pursuit that rules the person's life.

The strategy used in relation to long distance driving; 'stop – revive – survive', could also be applied to gambling pursuits. A feasible principle could be to divide gambling sessions into shorter periods, lower the money gambled and enforce limits on lost money to avoid people gambling above their means and chasing lost money. It is for many gamblers difficult to keep track of lost money and time spent gambling. Gaming machines are run by computers and could be programmed in gambler specific ways though personalised cards, even prepaid cards, to control the gambling before the start of the gambling session. The gambler could decide how much money and time to spend before each session or have a fixed scheme applicable to a variety of gambling venues. In addition the machines could enforce a rest period, applicable to all gamblers, as a time to revive and assess the gambling situation away from the machine. Thus, there are possibilities available in reducing and managing the adverse effects of excessive gambling over and above general guidelines and regulation of the gaming business and the individual gambler (cf. Submission to Productivity Commission February 2009: 5; Independent Pricing and Regulatory Tribunal 2008: 1). Nevertheless, it will ultimately become governments' and the gambling commerce prerogative as to how to handle excessive gambling, but it should not be seen as an unsolvable or exceedingly complicated problem.

In the following sections the main points of the research and issues examined in the book will be highlighted. It will focus on young people's gambling, adults gambling and the pathways to excessive gambling that have emerged from the Australian research after a brief reiteration of gambling in a global perspective.

7.2 Gambling in the global society

Gambling is a worldwide recreational activity. Lottery schemes have long been sanctioned by governments around the world as a way to collect money for community projects and special events, such as hospital, community and education facilities, as well as Olympic Games – projects where federal and state governments did not have the available funds to finance the enterprise (Chapter 3). Lottery schemes have a long tradition in being organised for such purposes and are largely acceptable and legally condoned ways to collect money by organisations (Welte et al. 2004). Lottery ticket sales are one of the most common gambling products and lottery schemes can be found in more than 200 jurisdictions. In 2006, Europe was the region with the highest number of lottery sales followed by North America, Asia and Middle East (*La Fleur Magazine* 2007). The individual jurisdictions with the highest lottery sales were the USA, Italy, Spain, France, Germany and China (McQueen 2008; Australasian Gaming Council 2008: 212).

Horse racing has most likely been popular since horses were domesticated and it is thought to have started first in Middle Eastern and Asian countries and then spread to Europe (Parker 1998). While the USA has the largest number of horse races, Japan presents the highest betting turnover (Australasian Gaming Council 2008: 221-2). The highest growths in horse racing were seen in Korea, Turkey and Brazil, while small decreases were lately noted in the USA and Japan (Australian Racing Board 2006; Australian Gaming Council 2007: 230; Australasian Gaming Council 2008: 221).

Even if lottery products and horse racing attracts large numbers of people, casino gambling, and especially gambling on electronic gaming machines, has taken a sizeable share of the total gambling market. The countries with the highest number of gaming machines are the United States and Italy. These countries have three times and twice the number of machines respectively as the next largest group, the United Kingdom, Russia and Spain. However, the number of machines per capita is a more accurate measure in assessing gambling opportunities (cf. Productivity Commission 1999; Griffith 1998; Gupta and Derevensky 1998a). The lowest number of people per machine, excluding smaller countries with an extensive hospitality industry catering for the tourist market, can be found in Australia, Spain and Italy (Taylor Nelson Sofres 2006, 2008). Nonetheless, gaming machines in the different jurisdictions are of various technical sophistication and not always comparable. For example, the low value pay out of slot machines, fruit machines and pachinko machines are not comparable with high technology electronic gaming machines with the ability to play several lines with high stakes simultaneously.

Gaming machines are often considered the type of gambling, which creates most problems for the largest group of people (Productivity Commission 2009; Neal et al. 2005). This is especially the case for people living on low incomes with few uncommitted funds. When people also have limited alternative leisure opportunities in their local community, this compounds the problem. The easy access to gambling opportunities, the venue's long opening hours, and the safe and friendly atmosphere are compellingly attractive features for anyone to visit a local community club. The same attractive factors also contribute to social recreational gambling that might develop into excessive gambling pursuits (Neal et al. 2005; Fabiansson 2007).

Globally, all jurisdictions with gambling facilities and accepted gambling, regulate gambling through laws and guidelines and control gambling venues through licence procedures, but at the same time gambling is one of the best income resources for governments all over the world, thus the regulation of gambling pursuits is adjusted to balance continued high revenue while limiting individual hardship and negative publicity.

7.3 Young people's gambling

Young people's experiences of gambling, how they are introduced to gambling and possible pathways to excessive gambling were explored. The accessibility to gambling venues (Chapter 4), the protection of the gambler, especially vulnerable people and young people through gambling policy, regulation and responsible gambling guidelines were explored in the jurisdictions of the USA, Canada, the UK and Australia (Chapter 3), the presented original research was situated within the Australian society. The youth research was based on a survey of 754 young people living in rural and regional Australia (Chapter 5) while the adult research was based on an urban multicultural sample (Chapter 6). The research elucidated access to gambling opportunities in the local community environment where the accessibility and diversity of alternative leisure activities are limited. It looked specifically at the local sports club's role, both as a facilitator and manager of youth sports and as a family friendly social entertainment and hospitality venue. The survey was mainly undertaken with high school students and explored their experiences of gambling as one of several leisure activities. The youths' current situation was further explored to elucidate similarities in the introduction and attitudes to gambling with case studies of adult gamblers' pathways to excessive gambling requiring professional help to overcome the addiction. These two original research projects were analysed for similarities in people's introduction to gambling and if possible pathways to excessive gambling can be identified among young people's experiences and attitudes towards gambling.

The youth research explored young people's introduction to gambling, what gambling forms they were familiar with, what they thought was most fun to play, how much money they played for during an evening and the reason for playing as a social recreational activity or playing for winning. Particular attention was paid to young people's introduction to gambling at a time when they were under the legal age to gamble for money, and also to gambling as a social recreational activity in a society where gambling pursuits have become a natural and accepted part of everyday social entertainment.

The Australian research about young people's gambling experiences and introduction to gambling showed that 78 per cent of the young people had gambled for money at least once during the previous five years and were well aware of different forms of gambling that existed within the communities and in metropolitan areas. The youths' classified their involvement in gambling as participation, thus an active involvement in the gambling, from buying lottery and raffle tickets, playing card and board games, playing Keno and betting on horses and other sports. None of the gambling games listed, like buying raffle tickets, or playing card or board games, would normally be seen as main contributors to future gambling problems. Nevertheless, they introduce children and young people to gambling games as an everyday acceptable activity. Buying weekly lottery tickets as a common activity and part of family gambling sounds very innocent but is a step in the endorsement of gambling pursuits, even if it is still not strongly connected to excessive gambling.

Gambling games such as Keno might lead more directly to excessive gambling and gambling for money. It is a game especially associated with young people's introduction to gambling as part of a social recreational activity during a family dinner at the local club. Keno was a highly popular gambling type among the young people in the research. Keno and horse betting were the two most popular gambling games, after buying raffle tickets. In relation to Keno and horse betting, these games only showed minor differences between females and males, otherwise the males gambled on more gambling games than the females. The young people played casino table games less than Keno, horse betting and buying lottery tickets.

Casino table games were not available in the communities and it is more difficult for underage young people to access this form of gambling. It was mainly the older youth who accessed these types of games. It has been noted in several studies that young people can look older than they are and it can be difficult to determine age without proof of age identification, which might explain some of the illegal underage gambling. There is a habitual element of young people participating in adult only activities when they are underage, such as drinking alcohol, take drugs and driving cars and motorcycles (Fabiansson and Healey 2004; Dickson, Derevensky and Gupta 2002; Wood, Derevensky, Gupta and Griffiths 2002; Griffith 1998; Productivity Commission 1999).

As the majority of the youth sample was high school students below 18 years of age (97.5 per cent), they could not legally buy lottery tickets or gamble on Keno, horse racing, sports, casino tables or gaming machines. Nonetheless, the high school students were well aware of the family gambling behaviour and gambling activities. Parents, older siblings and older friends undertook the financial transactions, thus the gambling was a family activity where parents and friends considered it an activity that was socially acceptable and condoned. The females were more inclined to gamble accompanied by the family with the parents undertaking the financial transaction, while males relied more on older friends and other adults, thus showing more independence in their gambling pursuits.

Concluding Discussion 189

The importance of gambling opportunities within the local community was demonstrated in relation to horse race betting. Both communities had horse racetracks, but in Community M (the mining dominated community) the horse racetrack was located within the main town area where the race days attracted thousands of local and non-local visitors. For the regional and rural young people, easy access to a gambling venue enhanced their frequency of gambling participation. The percentage of young people who participated in betting on horse races was significantly higher in this community with the race track in the town than in Community A (the agriculture dominated community) where the horse racetrack was further away from the main town with a less modern facility and less utilised racetrack. It is worth acknowledging that in many regional areas entertaining events are rare and when they happen they become a community event where people who normally do not venture into the towns will come together to meet friends and socialise (Binde 2006; Wynne, Smith and Jacobs 1996), not necessarily for gambling on the horses. These results, the easy access to Keno gambling at the local club and horse racing, support the conclusion that easy access and regular gambling opportunities influence young people's gambling participation.

A small group of young people was less focused on gambling as a social recreational activity and took the chance to win money seriously. They preferred to play in isolation rather than to be with friends. The research was done in Australian rural and regional communities where team sports are a dominant part of leisure activities, especially for young males. Winning is important and risk taking is part of their everyday environment (Dickson, Derevensky and Gupta 2008). It is possible that the males' higher focus on winning and gambling are influenced by the intense concentration on winning in sports activities. To be successful on the sporting field can be a way to future success and selection to regional, national and international sports teams, especially for young males, who are less academically inclined, being good at sports can be a beginning of a future career first in sports but later transferred to other areas, an opportunity not always easily achieved by rural and regional young people.

The importance of physical sports activities in rural and regional areas and the imperative involvement in local community organisations and community clubs should not be underestimated. Clubs and community organisations facilitate and support children's and young people's sports activities. They also contribute to social recreational activities that are affordable for families such as subsidised food and beverages, a broad spectrum of entertainment as well as gambling games, which all become an integrated part of the social life that underpin both social recreational activities and community sports activities. Overall, the negative effects of gambling are largely hidden and gambling in rural and regional communities is not seen as overly threatening to neither the residents nor the well being of the community.

Other leisure activities do not need to interfere with gambling activities, but rather become part of the social leisure time with family and friends, for instance when the family visits the local club or hotel and have dinner together. Affordably priced meals are an important incentive when the whole family has a social evening together. The research showed that family time and gambling opportunities intermix. During family outings, gambling activities were an essential part of family social leisure time and for the young people perhaps the highlight of the evening (Fabiansson and Healey 2004).

For the majority of youths, an early introduction to gambling activities is not a problem; for a small group of youths however, this early introduction to gambling activities might create a pathway to future problems. It was stressed by the elected local government councillors that the clubs and hotels were strictly enforcing the age limits for gambling, thus it would be difficult for underage young people to gamble on adult only games. However, there is debate as to whether or not young people gamble more than adults, and even if that were the case, it is suggested that youths' gambling propensity is not always carried on to adulthood (Jacobs 2000; Productivity Commission 1999: 235, 244; Griffiths 1998). Nevertheless, the introduction to gambling by parents or older friends is well documented in research (Fabiansson and Healey 2004; Wynne et al. 1996: 11; Derevensky and Gupta 1996, 1999).

The legality of gambling and the public promotion of gambling activities to young people as well as adults might enhance a positive attitude towards gambling (Dickson, Derevensky and Gupta 2002; Wood, Derevensky, Gupta and Griffiths 2002). Similar to older gamblers, young gamblers have difficulties in comprehending that they have a problem with gambling, even when the gambling causes other parts of their private and public life to suffer (Hardoon, Derevensky and Gupta 2003). Jackson, Patton, Thomas et al. (2000: 13) found that gambling behaviour was not influenced by ethnic background, rural or urban residency, or socio-economic status, but young people differed in their attitudes and experiences of gambling and of other risk taking behaviour. The children and young people who had a wide experience of gambling were more likely to come from lower socio-economic circumstances and being less focused on academic achievements. They were also more likely to have been involved in antisocial behaviour and to have used alcohol or drugs.

In interpreting the results of the youth research the possibility that the construction of the survey with the listing of a wide selection of gambling forms influenced the recorded gambling experience should be considered. However, it can be concluded that the sample did not show any higher gambling experiences than comparable contemporary research and it did not show any extreme results (Gillespie et al. 2007; Rönnberg et al. 1999; Stinchfield and Winters 1998). The fact that the survey was undertaken during a school lesson enforcing the seriousness of the task, the high response rate and the size of the sample, supports the reliability of the results.

In the following sections the youths' attitudes and experiences of gambling will be further elucidated and compared with the adult gamblers whose gambling had become excessive, as presented in the case studies. However, first the adults' introduction and experiences of gambling and what made them develop excessive gambling pursuits are analysed.

Concluding Discussion   191

7.4 Adults' gambling

The adult research explored pathways to excessive gambling from the person's early introduction to gambling to the stage where their gambling had reached unsustainable levels requiring professional help. The research took into account their present family relationship, employment and financial situation, and their social and mental well being. All had come from ethnically and culturally diverse backgrounds and lived in urban communities with easy access to gambling opportunities at local community clubs. The sample included 21 case studies, selected from a specific group of people and was thus not representative of all gamblers or excessive gamblers. The objective of the research was to explore the nature of gambling in local communities within the Greater Western Sydney area, to examine the communities socio-economic, and demographic structure, and the social community life in relation to recreational gambling pursuits. Furthermore, the aim was to elucidate the circumstances behind the change from a social club visit within a relaxing social network environment with family, friends and work colleagues to an individual pursuit of an excessive gambling nature.

The people in the case studies had gone beyond the social recreational gambling stage, as the gambling had become a major problem in their everyday life. As in the youth gambling research, a societal framework was applied where the individuals' situations as well as their social environment's and the local community's role in enhancing or restricting gambling opportunities were explored. A particular emphasis was placed on the circumstances where recreational gambling develops into a destructive activity which creates negative consequences for the individual gambler, his or her family, friends and the community.

The gamblers attended the Multicultural Problem Gambling Services NSW support program. Two-thirds were foreign born and one third Australian born residents. The people in the sample had been in Australia for various lengths of time. None of them were recent arrivals and most of them had been settled in Australia for the main part of their adult life. The people in the sample were quite familiar with Australian society including its leisure and gambling culture. The average age was 39 years with the males more likely to be married than the females. The majority of the gamblers were within the paid labour force. Employment or a secure income source is vital for gambling pursuits and when the gambling is controlled as a social recreational leisure activity among other everyday activities it will often not impose any negative consequences. It is only when the gambling becomes excessive that the employment status is threatened; as was shown in the case studies with gamblers losing their employment because of underperformance, linked by the gamblers to their excessive gambling. The amount of money lost needs to be seen in the context of how much money is available as, regardless of the level of gambling that is undertaken, the loss of the entire accessible amount of money will have the same effect. The common ground for all the people in the sample was that they had gambled beyond their monetary means where the excessive gamblers' social and mental well being were threatened and they were compelled to seek external help to manage their situation.

Friends and work colleagues introduced the people in the case studies to gambling activities and club visits, but males also initiated the gambling themselves by going alone to the local club. The males started gambling earlier than the females and the males experienced problems with gambling earlier than the females (Gambling Research Australia 2008; Neal et al. 2005; Productivity Commission 1999). The preferred gambling form for the females was to play on gaming machines while the males additionally played on horse races and casino table games. However, the gambling form that created the most problem for the people in the sample was gambling on electronic gaming machines. These findings are also emphasised in the Productivity Commission draft report (2009) and the Neal et al. (2005) research, which highlighted the negative effects of gaming machine gambling on a large group of people.

Remarkably, all the gamblers could remember their first gambling win and still, even if it was a long time ago, the first win was treasured; they remembered what they did with their first win. As the gamblers in the sample talked about their winning, it was clear they had lost much more money than what they had won, thus they needed help to sort out the increasing debt they had incurred. This did not necessarily mean that they intended to stop gambling, but rather to restrict their gambling to manageable levels. Approximately one third of the sample was struggling financially even without the gambling while another third of the sample was earning enough money for a comfortable living standard. However, in all cases the gambling expenditure was challenging their financial situation. Excessive gambling pursuits also influenced the well being of the gambler and their family. In some cases the gambling pursuits increased their social isolation, especially if money had been borrowed from family members, work colleagues and friends, and in particular if the family of the gambler was unaware of his or her excessive gambling.

In some cases the adult gamblers viewed their gambling as only one of their problems, they also reported social, physical and mental problems (Gambling Research Australia 2008; ACNielsen 2007; Neal et al. 2005; Abbott et al. 2004; Blaszczynski and Nower 2002; Hardoon et al. 2002; Productivity Commission 1999). Some of the gamblers viewed the gambling as a time where other problems could be forgotten and the gambling relieved their compounded problems, thus gambling created a 'problem free and relaxing' time.

The sample included 21 case studies of people from multicultural backgrounds, it is therefore not possible to generalise beyond people in similar circumstances who seek gambling counselling. The sample is based on people for whom English was a second language and preferred counselling from a counsellor familiar with their ethnic background. The sample is not representative for people seeking gambling counselling from the majority population. The problems presented in the case studies, beyond specific gambling problems, are in some cases more pertinent to this or that ethnic group. It should be emphasised that the majority of

Concluding Discussion   193

excessive gamblers are Australian born. Nevertheless, the case studies highlight the importance of gambling opportunities in the local community, a gambling-accommodating social environment, the legal status of gambling and gambling as an accepted social recreational pursuit (cf. Productivity Commission 2009: 4.43).

7.5 Gambling pathways

The youth and adult research show that pathways to excessive gambling can be diverse despite this however, patterns do emerge. The pathway from social recreational to excessive gambling can be decades long, but it may also take less than five years. The young people's gambling was more a social recreational activity with the family with the majority of them gambling for fun. The adults also gambled for fun, especially in the beginning during the introduction and before they became mesmerised by the gambling environment and the possibility of winning. Most of the young people played with small amounts of money and did not get overly upset when the money was lost. The majority of them did not chase their losses. Except for a few of the people in the adult sample, the adults were initially gambling within their means and the losses were manageable. Clearly, for these people, gambling had a social recreational aim where the intention was to have fun. Even a small win could be the highlight of their life – some of the people in the sample explained that they felt special with the win, never having won anything before.

In the rural and regional communities the young people were introduced to gambling in about the same way, as part of a family dinner at the local club where the children and the teenagers played sports. The youths might gamble on Keno while the adults socialised, thus gambling became a natural part of the family outing. The clubs' profitable gambling business, a common situation for most clubs, supports other club activities thus making their entertainment and hospitality functions affordable to family groups (Australasian Gaming Council 2008; New South Wales Office of Liquor, Gaming and Racing 2009; Productivity Commission 2009). The links between sports and gambling are well established in Australia and sports and physical leisure activities are very much part of young people's everyday life, thus a dinner at the local club becomes a continuation of the residents' sports, social recreation and community participation.

The young people's introduction to gambling is reflected in the adult problem gamblers' experiences. The adults indicated that their introductions to gambling were through work colleagues, friends and family at the local club. For example, an adult gambler remembers being introduced to gambling by a friend's father, others were introduced through parents' gambling, rehabilitation group's outings, social friends, and through work colleagues and by self-introduction. They could all reminisce about when they started to gamble and the venue where they had first gambled.

The excessive gamblers' introduction to gambling appears comparable to other gamblers' introduction, thus it is questionable if it is actually the form of introduction to gambling that is an essential predictor to future gambling. It likely lies in a range of other factors that coalesce for some individuals such as the availability of gambling opportunities, whether the gambler wins or loses on their first or early gambling sessions, if the person becomes upset or not with the loss, their particular personal circumstances and the presence of various health issues. The research also highlighted the importance of the social environment, geographical closeness to gambling opportunities – whether the gambling venue was within the local area or close to work, as factors influencing gambling propensity. Further reasons specifically related to the local club other than its local convenience, were its long opening hours and the affordability to visit the club and not initially at least, because of opportunities to gamble. However, in the adult sample, a small group of young men had ventured into a local club by themselves. These young men gambled excessively nearly from the beginning and needed help with their gambling problem within four to five years.

The adult sample did not divulge any information about underage gambling, as presented in the youth sample. The lack of information about their early introduction phase to gambling by the adults in the case studies may be explained by the fact that a high percentage had been born outside Australia in communities where there was little or no access to gambling opportunities (Australian Bureau of Statistics 2001). Frequently, in such communities, gambling did not exist or was not legal and lacked social approval.

It is possible that the introduction process by work colleagues, friends and family increased people's gambling activities, an activity they perhaps, would not by themselves, have ventured into. While cultural consideration might be a factor that restricts self-introduction, it is possible that even the women in the sample may have come to gambling, with or without introduction as they generally began gambling at a later age than the men; the case studies however, do not provide conclusive information about whether the introduction was active or passive as the reporting of this phase of their gambling is given from the gamblers perspective and would perhaps not be corroborated by others.

The adult sample shows that their excessive gambling was frequently related to other health problems (Korn and Shaffer 1999). It is not possible to determine from the case studies whether all or any of their problems existed prior to the excessive gambling. Nonetheless, it is obvious from the case studies that anxiety, stress, relationship problems, financial and employment issues were present in the lives of these excessive gamblers and that gambling contributed to their overall social, mental, legal and financial problems. The adult gamblers in the case study sample described the gambling sessions as a relaxing time where they felt safe and enjoyed the activity. It took their minds off other problems they experienced, such as stress and anxiety. It was also possible for smokers to smoke without restriction and the gambling provided a way to avoid a complicated home situation with young children and relationship conflicts. The club environment gave the gamblers freedom, security and rights they did not feel they had in other public or even private venues. It is important to recognise that gambling opportunities and an inclination to gamble, family situation, social inclusion and community affiliation all can affect a person's general well being and gambling propensity (Arthurson and Jacobs 2003; Blaszczynski and Nower 2002; Korn and Shaffer 1999; Ni Laoire 1995). The case studies indicated that excessive gambling pursuits influence the well being of the gambler and the family. In some cases it increased isolation, however, not all gamblers felt isolated; some were satisfied with their social environment, especially if they had a good employment situation and family life; this was true for some even as they experienced stress due to their escalating gambling problems.

Parallels emerge between the young people and the people in the case studies with regard to how they were introduced to gambling. The attitudes of a small group of gamblers towards gambling including their response to winning and losing money is common to some people in both groups. The high profile of sports competitions and the significance of competing for a place in the team can be fierce. Even if the majority of the young people did not approach gambling as a winning contest analogous to a sports match, there was a small group that prioritised gambling for winning and got upset when they lost. This small group of young people were more focused on winning and the gambling than on gambling as a social recreational activity. They also wanted to recoup their lost money. It is likely that possible future problem gamblers would belong to this group, as acknowledged by national and international gambling research (cf. Welte 2008; Derevensky et al. 2007; Gillespie et al. 2007; Derevensky and Gupta 2006, 2004a; Delfabbro et al. 2005; Wood and Griffiths 2004; Delfabbro and Thrupp 2003; Productivity Commission 1999).

The Australian gambling culture is freely promoted in society, it is advertised and encouraged in mass media (cf. Griffith 2005) and gambling is a substantial revenue raiser for state governments (Australasian Gaming Council 2008; Productivity Commission 2009). Socio-economic diversity in society is perceived to be widening (Buchanan and Watson 1997) and if you are at the bottom of the income ladder, the dream of changing your situation can be strong. It is in human nature to enhance one's prosperity, personal freedom and choice of living arrangements. Gambling can be seen as a legitimate way to raise funds for a better future for themselves and the family. The dream of creating a better financial situation, and being recognised as a winner were important drivers for some of the adults as well as for the youth gamblers. For the adults with few prospects of securing the level of funds required for the comfortable living to which they aspire, gambling was one alternative in attaining this lifestyle with its independence and status in society (Tanasornnarong, Jackson and Thomas 2004; The South Australian Centre for Economic Studies 2005). For young people who had missed out on the selection to the top sports team, winning on gambling could restore their status in the community. Thus gambling may be seen by some as a possible solution to an unsatisfying situation. The case studies have shown that with the combination of problems the people in the sample presented, gambling both exacerbated the problems and provided an illusionary escape route.

The pathways to excessive gambling are made easier by the local community clubs' support of local community activities. Gaming machines in clubs and hotels generate considerable revenue for state governments. Thus the gambling industry, the local community clubs and hotels and the state government all have common interests in gambling and a vested interest in there being as little criticism as possible about the number of people who gamble to excess. Additionally, the influence the clubs can exert in different areas of the community through their high number of members is evident in their ability to negotiate with the state government about issues influencing their areas of concern (Independent Pricing and Regulatory Tribunal 2008; Productivity Commission 2009).

Gambling pursuits can be related back to the social environment of the young people. When young people feel accepted, appreciated, included in community activities with access to a diversity of leisure activities, they are less likely to develop problems with gambling later in life (Jackson, Patton, Thomas et al. 2000). To be young and to take part in risk-taking behaviour is part of growing up, the risk taking in relation to other vices such as drugs and alcohol is better understood; why young people develop gambling problems is less clear (Derevensky and Gupta 2004b; Stinchfield 2004, 2000; Coman, Burrows and Evans 1997). What is clear is that the social milieu, accessibility and community affiliation must be taken into account as factors that influence gambling propensity (Wynne et al. 1996).

In conclusion gambling is affecting many more people than prevalence figures indicate (Volberg 2004). Prevalence gambling research shows the estimated number of problem and pathological gamblers within the community. Depending on scale and research methodology, approximately between 1 and 2 per cent of the population have gambling problems (cf. Gambling Research Australia 2008; ACNielsen 2007; Volberg 2006; Productivity Commission 1999, 2009), while the percentage of people gambling in excess of their available funds is a much larger group. Gambling is an integrated part of many societies, it gives the gaming industry a high return on investment, it creates excellent tax revenue for governments and the gambling industry creates employment opportunities both for the people directly employed in the industry but also for sectors that service the gambling industry. In addition, it facilitates affordable entertainment for people in communities with limited availability of reasonably priced alternative leisure activities and sports opportunities for young people. It is difficult to find another consumable pursuit with such a potentially damaging effect on people and the community, that also has such strong and complicated financial underpinnings and where attempts to develop effective policy and regulation have been so unsuccessful.

The final chapter asks the question, does societal longitudinal independent gambling research have a future?

Chapter 8
Has Gambling Research a Future?

Gambling research requires a broad interdisciplinary, scholarly and independent framework; research undertaken without constraint from political, commercial, industry and interest groups. A research environment were the terms of reference clearly state the independence of the research, where access to knowledge and information are facilitated by all partners within ethical guidelines and where the findings can be published for public debate, policy and regulation development and to enhance general knowledge. This is perhaps a highly utopian research framework in contemporary research milieu, where the focus is more on commissioned research, short timelines, single gambling issue based research, and restrictions on what can be publicised.[1]

In Australia, the Productivity Commission, a federal body, has conducted two reviews (1999, 2009) of the Australian gambling sector. These are examples of where gambling's advantages, disadvantages and scope have been analysed. However, there have been 10 years between the reviews, and in relation to the most recent one, new independent research was not undertaken, here the Productivity Commission relied upon research previously carried out. During the last 10 years, the growth in the gambling industry and in the range of gambling products available has been extensive and the requirement for the development of policy to regulate national and global gambling is consequently becoming more complex. To make an adequately informed response, there is a need for innovative interdisciplinary research models and strategies which explore national and international gambling, especially as gambling and hospitality is a sector that is itself rapidly responding to the possibilities of enhanced gambling diversity and expanding interactive gambling through internet, phone and digital television facilitated gambling.

The first decade of the twenty-first century started with high employment, a financial and industry boom where leisure and recreational pursuits were affordable and sought after, bigger and ever more luxurious resorts, casinos and community gambling venues were refurbished and developed. Amalgamations of smaller community clubs into larger sports club complexes augmented the gaming market in Australia. The revenue from gaming, betting and especially electronic gaming machine gambling has underpinned this expansion and investment in the hospitality and gaming industry, both in Australia and globally. Legislation and regulation of gambling has been introduced to keep problem gambling within

---

1 The gambling framework discussed is based on Australian circumstances. Other nation states might have different structures and research models and the relationship between scholarly research, funding body, political, commerce and interest groups might be different.

'acceptable levels', that is, without harming the overall value of the gambling commerce, the local employment market and government taxation revenue.

From this perspective it is not surprising that the recent Productivity Commission (2009) gambling sector review questioned whether the legislation and the harm minimising strategies actually have had an effect, observing that excessive gambling and gambling expenditure have continued to grow and perhaps at a scale not anticipated in 1999 at the time of the first review. Thus a scholarly, interdisciplinary, political and industry independent gambling research model has merit. A new model for gambling research was discussed in a special issue of the *Australian National Association for Gambling Studies* journal (2009; Fabiansson 2009). Four discussion models were presented for a national research approach to gambling with the aim of establishing a sustainable research environment for interdisciplinary gambling research. Leaving aside which of the proposed models would be the most useful, the fundamental issues for any scholarly research are the funding structure, independence of the research from commercial and political interests, ability to develop longitudinal high quality multidisciplinary research, and the right to publish scholarly research findings without confidentiality limitations.

The complex relationship between the gambling industry and governments' regulatory authority as well as being recipients of critical tax revenue from gambling profits, require that the whole sector be open to question and critique, especially as the negative consequences of excessive gambling are well known and documented.

The main participants, the gambling industry, governments and gamblers, are all more or less unwilling in sharing detailed, longitudinal statistical data and information about the scope of gambling, for fear of adverse findings. Nonetheless, research is funded and facilitated by jurisdictions and partly by the gaming industry through levies and taxation revenue. Additionally the gaming industry also directly supports individual researchers through consulting projects, research grants or grants that create university positions. Thus the gambling industry is an active supporter, partner and/or financier of gambling research, a relationship where the independence of the research might be queried. Universities' quest for external funding support is also a contributing factor and not restricted to the gambling industry.

As gambling is often issue or situation focused, it gives a less than holistic understanding of people's gambling experiences and the frequency of gambling. The majority of gambling research is restricted to one jurisdiction or part of a jurisdiction. Gambling research is focused on adults or young people and often on a specific type of gambling. This issue and situation based research restricts the possibility of understanding the whole scope of gambling and its influence on society. It also makes comparative gambling research between jurisdictions more difficult. Nonetheless, some scholarly research has been carried out such as regulatory, economic and sociology grounded research, particularly from the beginning of 2000. Research by Slade and McConville (2003), Collins and Lapsley (2003), Chhabra, Lutz and Gonnerman (2005), Mangham, Carney, Burnett and Williams (2005), and Smith and Wynne (2000) have, for instance, tried to ascertain the costs and benefits of gambling for the whole society, but frequently on a minor scale as much of the gambling research is specific to a jurisdiction or to a single gambling issue (Easton 2003).

In addition to limited interdisciplinary gambling research, few longitudinal national and particularly international research projects have been undertaken. There are a few notable exceptions such as the recent global internet gambling research project (Parke et al. 2007). Most jurisdictions regularly commission prevalence studies, but they are restricted in their scope and concentrate mainly on individuals' personal gambling, where the calculated prevalence percentage is between 1 and 2 per cent for adults. Such studies tend to reinforce the view that gambling is a 'marginal problem' in society, affecting only a small group of people (Productivity Commission 1999, 2009; Gambling Research Australia 2008; Volberg 2004).

Gambling research will benefit from a wider interdisciplinary approach. As emphasised, the main part of gambling research has been undertaken within the discipline of psychology with a focus on the individual and addiction. Sociological and societally grounded research has been undertaken where a holistic approach is emphasised, the research presented in this book follows this approach. A sociological approach seeks explanations from the entire gambling environment: the providers of the gambling venues, the design of machines and venues, government regulations and harm minimising guidelines and the social environment and opportunities to gamble, as well as exploring the gambler's social situation. Gambling pursuits have become one of the most accessible social recreational activities in community settings. Thus, the societal gambling research perspective is essential to understanding the scope of gambling in society and to situate gambling in a holistic research framework. Gambling research clearly must therefore be an interdisciplinary and collaborative endeavour.

Hitherto, it has been quite easy to gain small grants from government's gambling bodies, however, these often come with funding contracts which stipulate strict rules for ownership of the data and rights to publish the final report or journal articles from the research. This seems to be the real explanation as to why research within gambling is so issue-based and short-term focussed in Australia. True research independence will provide the required impartiality to entice researchers into developing sustainable gambling research. Without such a research milieu, retaining gambling researchers will become increasingly difficult. Whilst there are the current financial interrelationships between the gambling industry, governments and their regulatory authorities, the prospect of real research independence in this field, is likely to remain elusive.

For multidisciplinary gambling research to gain scholarly status, an independent research organisation with a long term focus and funding that ensures the future of independent researchers and their work, is required. Such an organisation would be the location of commissioned, long term projects, in applied and theoretical gambling research, and the publishing of results would be free from political and commercial sanctions. Thus, research projects scientifically evaluated and independently funded would directly remove both the commercial and political influences over gambling research. It would emphasise national longitudinal research and collaborate with international research organisations with an emphasis on longitudinal research projects to create an empirical and theoretical knowledge base for gambling research.

In conclusion: does gambling research have a future? Undoubtedly, however, the level of interdisciplinary approach, independence of the research, and the openness of the debate, are all factors that have to be addressed if best possible outcomes are to be achieved and to raise the significance of gambling to a societal issue.

List of References

ACNielsen. (2007). *Prevalence of Gambling and Problem Gambling in NSW*, Final Report Prevalence of Gambling and Problem Gambling in NSW – A Community Survey 2006, NSW Office of Liquor, Gaming and Racing, Department of the Arts, Sport and Recreation.

Abbott, M.W. (2001). *What Do We Know about Gambling and Problem Gambling in New Zealand?* Report Number Seven of the New Zealand Gaming Survey, June. The Department of Internal Affairs, Wellington, New Zealand. Retrieved 5 July 2008 from http://www.dia.govt.nz.

Abbott, M., Volberg, R., Bellringer, M. and Reith, G. (2004). *A Review of Research on Aspects of Problem Gambling: Final Report*, October 2004. Prepared for: Responsibility in Gambling Trust, London, United Kingdom. Retrieved 30 March 2009 from http://www.rigt.org.uk/documents/a_review_of_research_on_aspects_of_problem_gambling_ auckland_report_2004.pdf.

Abbott, M.W. and Volberg, R.A. (1999). *Gambling and Problem Gambling in the Community: An International Overview and Critique: Report Number One of the New Zealand Gaming Survey.* The Department of Internal Affairs, Wellington, New Zealand, December. Retrieved 5 July 2008 from http://www.dia.govt.nz.

Adebayo, B. (1998). Luck of the dice: Gambling attitudes of a sample of community college students. *College Student Journal*, 32, 255–7.

Allcock, C.C. (2000). A background to problem gambling. *Australasian Psychiatry*, 8, 253–5.

Allen, D. (1952). *The Nature of Gambling.* New York, NY: Coward McCann.

American Gaming Association. (2009). *2009 State of the States: The AGA Survey of Casino Entertainment.* Retrieved 23 September 2009 from http://www.americangaming.org/assets/files/uploads/aga_sos2009web_FINAL.pdf.

American Gaming Association. (2009). *Advertising.* Retrieved 20 August 2009 from http://www.americangaming.org/industry/factsheets/issues_detail.cfv?id=1.

American Psychiatric Association. (1994). *Diagnostic Criteria for Pathological Gambling*, DSM-IV-Diagnostic and Statistical Manual of Mental Disorders. 4th Edition (revised 2000). American Psychiatric Press; Washington, DC. Retrieved 14 July 2009 from http://www.problemgambling.ca/EN/ResourcesForProfessionals/Pages/DSMIVCriteriaPathologicalGambling.aspx.

Andorka, R. (1987). Time budgets and their uses. *Annual Review of Sociology*, 13, 149–64.

Arnett, J.J. (2004). *Emerging Adulthood: The Winding Road Through the Late Teens to the Twenties*. New York: Oxford University Press.

Arnett, J.J. (2006). Emerging adulthood in Europe: A response to Brynner. *Journal of Youth Studies*, 9, (1) 111–23.

Arthurson, K. and Jacobs, K. (2003). *Social Exclusion and Housing*, Australian Housing and Urban Research Institute, Southern Research Centre, Final report December.

Ashton, J. (1968). *The History of Gambling in England*. New York, NY: Burt Franklin.

Australasian Gaming Council. (2008). *A Database on Australia's Gambling Industry 2008/09*. Published by the Australasian Gaming Council, Melbourne, Victoria.

Australasian Gaming Machine Manufacturers Association (AGMMA). (2009). *Responsible Gambling Fact Sheet*. Retrieved 30 March 2009 from http://www.agmma.com/pdf/responsible_gaming_machine_play.pdf.

Australian Bureau of Statistics. (1996). *Census 1996 Commonwealth of Australia*, Canberra. Retrieved 30 March 2003 from http://www.censusdata.abs.gov.au/.

Australian Bureau of Statistics. (2001). *Involvement in Organised Sport and Physical Activity*, Australia, April 2004, cat. no. 6285.0. Commonwealth of Australia, Canberra.

Australian Bureau of Statistics. (2006a). *Gambling Services Australia 2004–05*, cat no 8684.0. Commonwealth of Australia, Canberra.

Australian Bureau of Statistics. (2006b). *Census 2006*. Commonwealth of Australia, Canberra. Retrieved 30 March 2008 from http://www.censusdata.abs.gov.au/.

Australian Bureau of Statistics. (2006c). *Census 2006 Census of Population and Housing New South Wales (State)*, cat. no. 2068.0-Census Tables 2006. Commonwealth of Australia, Canberra.

Australian Bureau of Statistics. (2009). *National Health Survey: Summary Results 2007–08*, cat. No. 4364.0. Commonwealth of Australia, Canberra.

Australian Casino Association. (2005). *Annual Report 2004–05*. Retrieved 30 March 2007 from http://www.auscasinos.com/assets/files/pdf/ACA-Annual-Report-0405.pdf.

Australian Council for Social Services. (1997). *Young People, Gambling and the Internet.* Paper 28. Sydney, Australia.

Australian Gaming Council. (2007). *A Database on Australia's Gambling Industry 2006/07*. Melbourne, Victoria: Australian Gaming Council.

Australian Institute for Gambling Research. (1999). *Australian Gambling Comparative History and Analysis*. Report prepared for Victorian Casino and Gaming Authority, Melbourne, October 1999. University of Western Sydney.

Australian National Association for Gambling Studies. (2009). Gambling Research. Special Issue. *Journal of the National Association for Gambling Studies, Australia*, 1, (1), May, 3–59.

List of References

Australian Racing Fact Book. (2006). *Australian Racing Fact Book 2005–06.* Retrieved 30 April 2007 from www.australianracingboard.com.au/factbook/05_06_factbook/factbook0506.pdf.

Australian Racing Board. (2007). *Australian Racing Fact Book 2006–07.* Retrieved 30 April 2007 from http://www.australianracingboard.com.au/factbook/06_07_factbook/factbook0607.pdf.

Australian Racing Fact Book. (2008). *Australian Racing Fact Book 2007–08.* Retrieved 30 April 2007 from http://www.australianracingboard.com.au/factbook/07_08_factbook/arbFinalBook.PDF.

Bailey, P. (1987). *Leisure and Class in Victorian England: Rational Recreation and the Contest for Control, 1830–1885.* London: Routledge.

Barnhart, R. (1992). *Beating the Wheel: Winning Strategies at Roulette.* New York, NY: Lyle Stuart.

Beck, U. (1992). *Risk Society: Towards a New Modernity.* London: Sage Publications.

Beck, U. (1999). *World Risk Society.* Cambridge: Polity Press.

Belanger, F., Hiller, J. and Smith, W. (2002). Trustworthiness in electronic commerce: The role of privacy, security, and site attributes. *Journal of Strategic Information Systems*, 11, (3–4), 245–70.

Berger, B.M. (1972). On the youthfulness of youth cultures. In P.K. Manning and M. Truzzi (eds) *Youth and Sociology.* Englewood Cliffs, NJ: Prentice-Hall, 52–68.

Binde, P. (2005). Gambling across culture: Mapping worldwide occurrence and learning from ethnographic comparison. *International Gambling Studies*, 5, (1), 1–27.

Binde, P. (2006). *Why People Gamble: An Anthropological Perspective.* Paper presented at the 13th Global Remote and E-Gambling Research Institute Conference, Amsterdam, Netherlands.

Binde, P. (2007). Selling dreams – causing nightmares? On gambling advertising and problem gambling. *Journal of Gambling*, 20, 167–92.

Blaszczynski, A. (1998). *Overcoming Compulsive Gambling: A Self-help Guide Using Cognitive Behavioural Techniques.* London: Robinson Publishing.

Blaszczynski, A., Ladouceur, R., Goulet, A. and Savard C. (2006). How much do you spend gambling? Ambiguities in questionnaire items assessing expenditure. *International Gambling Studies*, 6, (2), November, 123–8.

Blaszczynski, A. and Nower, L. (2002). A pathways model of problem and pathological gambling. *Addiction*, 97, (5), May, 487–99.

Blaszczynski, A., Walker, M., Sagris, A. and Dickerson, M. (1999). Psychological aspects of gambling behaviour: An Australian psychological society position paper. *Australian Psychologist*, 34, 4–16.

Borrell, J. and Boulet, J. (2005). A theoretical exploration of culture and community health: Implications for prevention, research, and problem gambling. *Journal of Gambling Issues*, 13 March, 1–21. Retrieved 8 July 2009 from http://www.camh.net/egambling/issue13/jgi_13_borrell.html.

Broda, A., LaPlante, D., Nelson, A., LaBrie, R., Bosworth, L. and Shaffer, H. (2008). Virtual harm reduction efforts for internet gambling: Effects of deposit limits on actual internet sports gambling behaviour. *Harm Reduction Journal*, 5, 5–27.

Browne, B.R. (1989). Going on tilt: Frequent poker players and control. *Journal of Gambling Behavior*, 5, (1), 3–21.

Buchanan, J. and Watson, I. (1997). The living wage and the working poor. In Bittman, M. (ed.) *Poverty in Australia: Dimensions and Policies.* Sydney, Australia: Social Policy Research Centre Reports and Proceedings No. 135, May, 17–38.

Bush, A., Martin, C. and Bush, V. (2004). Sports celebrity influence on the behavioral intentions of Generation Y. *Journal of Advertising Research*, 44, 108–18.

Cameron, B. and Myers, J.L. (1966). Some personality correlates of risk taking. *The Journal of General Psychology*, 74, 51–60.

Campbell, A., Converse, P.E. and Rodgers, W.L. (1976). *The Quality of American Life.* New York: Russell Sage.

Campbell, C.S. and Smith, G.J. (1998). Canadian gambling: Trends and public policy issues. *Annals of the American Academy of Political and Social Science*, 556, 22–35.

Campbell, C.S. and Marshal, D. (2007). Gambling and crime. In G. Smith, D. Hodgins and R.J. Williams (eds) *Research and Measurement Issues in Gambling Studies.* Burlington, MA: Academic Press, 541–64.

Canadian Partnership for Responsible Gaming. (2007). *Canadian Gambling Digest 2006–2007.* Retrieved 14 July 2009 from http://www.cprg.ca/articles/Canadian_Gambling_Digest_2006-07.pdf.

Canadian Partnership for Responsible Gaming. (2008). *Canadian Gambling Digest 2007–2008.* Retrieved 14 July 2009 from http://www.cprg.ca/articles/Canadian_Gambling_Digest_2007_2008.pdf.

Canada West Foundation. (1999). *Canada's Gambling Regulatory Patchwork: A Handbook.* Calgary, AB: Canada West Foundation. Retrieved 26 March 2009 from https://dspace.ucalgary.ca/bitstream/1880/311/2/Canada%27s_Gambling_Regulatory_Patchwork.pdf.

Canada West Foundation. (2001). *Gambling in Canada: Final Report and Recommendations.* Retrieved 24 August 2009 from http://www.ccsa.ca/Eng/Statistics/ Canada/Pages/GamblingStatistics.aspx.

Canada West Foundation. (2005). *Gambling in Canada: Statistical Context.* Canada West Foundation. Retrieved 29 September 2007 from http://www.cwf.ca/V2/filres/GamblinginCanada.pdf.

Cassidy, R. (2002). *The Sport of Kings: Kinship, Class and Thoroughbred Breeding in Newmarket.* Cambridge: Cambridge University Press.

Castells, M. (1997). *The Power of Identity.* Oxford: Blackwell.

Centre for Gambling Research. (2004). 2003 *Victorian Longitudinal Community Attitudes Survey.* Gambling Research Panel Report 6, Victoria: Australian National University.

Chhabra, D., Lutz, G. and Gonnerman, M. (2005). *Socioeconomic Impact of Gambling on Iowans: Final Report.* Prepared for the Iowa Legislative Council, Des Moines, IA.

Clarke, J. and Critcher, C. (1985). *The Devil Makes Work: Leisure in Capitalist Britain.* London: Macmillan.

Clubs NSW. (2000). *Registered Clubs Responsible Conduct of Gambling Code of Practice: Best Practice Guidelines*, Clubs NSW, Sydney. Retrieved 5 June 2008 from http://www.cmaa.asn.au/Info/ Code%20of%20Practice.pdf.

Coman, G.J., Burrows, G.D. and Evans, B.J. (1997). Stress and anxiety as factors in the onset of problem gambling: Implications for treatment. *Stress Medicine,* 13, 235–44.

Coleman, J.S. (1974). Youth: Transition to adulthood. *National Association of Secondary School Principals [NASSP] Bulletin*, 58, (385), 4–11.

Collins, D.J. and Lapsley, H.M. (2003). The social costs and benefits of gambling: An introduction to the economic issues. *Journal of Gambling Studies,* 19, (2), 123–48.

Criminal Code of Canada. (2009). *Criminal Code of Canada.* Ottawa: Department of Justice. Retrieved 28 July 2009 from http://laws.justice.gc.ca/en/showdoc/ cs/C-46/bo-ga:l_VII//en#anchorbo-ga:l_VII.

Curliss, A. (2007). School, lottery deals get wary eye: Legislators want to limit ads. *The News & Observer*, May 18. Retrieved 7 July 2009 from http://www. newsobserver.com/politics/lottery/story/575404.html.

David, F. (1962). *Games, Gods and Gambling.* New York, NY: Hafner.

Delfabbro, P.H. (2008). Evaluating the effectiveness of a limited reduction in electronic gaming machine availability on perceived gambling behaviour and objective expenditure. *International Gambling Studies*, 8, (2), August, 151–65.

Delfabbro, P.H., Lahn, J. and Grabosky, P. (2005). Further evidence concerning the prevalence of adolescent gambling and problem gambling in Australia. *International Gambling Studies*, 5, 209–28.

Delfabbro, P.H. and LeCouteur, A. (2006). *A Decade of Gambling Research in Australia and New Zealand: Implications for Policy, Research and Harm Minimization.* (1st Update Edition) Report prepared for the Independent Gambling Authority of South Australia.

Delfabbro, P.H. and LeCouteur, A. (2007). *A Decade of Gambling Research in Australia and New Zealand: Implications for Policy, Research and Harm Minimization.* (2nd Update Edition) Report prepared for the Independent Gambling Authority of South Australia.

Delfabbro, P.H. and Thrupp, L. (2003). The social determinants of youth gambling in South Australian adolescents. *Journal of Adolescence*, 26, 313–30.

Dembski, W.A. (2007). *No Free Lunch: Why Specified Complexity Cannot Be Purchased Without Intelligence.* Lanham, MA: Rowman and Littlefield Publishers.

Dempsey K. (1990). *Smalltown: A Study of Social Inequality, Cohesion and Belonging.* Melbourne: Oxford University Press.

Derevensky, J.L. and Gupta, R. (1996). *Risk-taking and Gambling Behavior Among Adolescents: An Empirical Examination.* Paper presented to the Annual Meeting of the National Conference on Compulsive Gambling (May), Chicago, IL.

Derevensky, J.L. and Gupta, R. (1999). Youth gambling problems: A new issue for school psychologists. *Nova Scotia Psychologist,* 12, (11), 8–11.

Derevensky, J.L. and Gupta. R. (2000). Prevalence estimates of adolescent gambling adolescent: A comparison of the SOGS-RA, DSM-IV-J, and the GA 20 Questions. *Journal of Gambling Studies,* 16, (2), 227–51.

Derevensky, J.L. and Gupta, R. (2001). Le problème de jeu touché aussi les jeunes. *Psychologie Québec,* 18, (6), 23–27.

Derevensky, J.L. and Gupta, R. (2004a). Adolescents with gambling problems: A synopsis of our current knowledge. *eGambling: The Electronic Journal of Gambling Issues,* 10. Retrieved 29 May 2008 from http://www.camh.net/ egambling/ archive/pdf/EJGI-issue10/EJGI-Issue10-derevensky-gupta.pdf.

Derevensky, J.L. and Gupta, R. (2004b). Preface. In J.L. Derevensky and R. Gupta, (eds) *Gambling Problems in Youth: Theoretical and Applied Perspectives.* New York, NY: Kluwer Academic/Plenum Publishers.

Derevensky, J.L. and Gupta, R. (2006). Measuring gambling problems among adolescents: Current status and future directions. *International Gambling Studies,* 6, (2), November, 201–15.

Derevensky, J.L., Sklar, A., Gupta, R., Messerlian, C., Laroche, M. and Mansour, S. (2007). *The Effects of Gambling Advertisements on Child and Adolescent Gambling Attitudes and Behaviors.* Report for Fonds Québécois de la Recherche sur la Société et la Culture.

Devlin, A.S. and Peppard, D.M. (1996). Casino use by college students. *Psychological Reports,* 78, 899–906

Dickerson, M.G. (1984). *Compulsive Gamblers.* London: Longman.

Dickson, L., Derevensky, J.L. and Gupta, R. (2002). The prevention of youth gambling problems: A conceptual model. *Journal of Gambling Studies,* 18 (2), 97–160.

Dickson, L, Derevensky, J.L and Gupta, R. (2008). Youth gambling problems: Examining risk and protective factors. *International Gambling Studies,* 8, (1), April, 25–47.

Duhig, A.M., Maciejewski, P.K., Desai, R.A., Krishan-Sarin S. and Potenza, M.N. (2007). Characteristics of adolescents' past-year gamblers and non-gamblers in relation to alcohol drinking. *Addictive Behaviors,* 32, 80–89.

Easton, B. (2003). *The Analysis of Costs and Benefits of Gambling.* Retrieved 29 July 2009 from http://www.eastonbh.ac.nz/article443.html.

Ekeland, I. (1993). *The Broken Dice and Other Mathematical Tales of Chance.* Chicago, IL: University of Chicago Press.

Engwall, D., Hunter, R. and Steinberg, M. (2004). Gambling and other risk behaviors on university campuses. *Journal of American College Health*, 52, (6), 245–5.

Fabiansson, C. (2003). Gambling and homelessness in New South Wales. *Parity*, 16, (4), May, 6–8.

Fabiansson, C. (2005). Youths' leisure milieu in rural settings – Gender equality in utilisation of leisure opportunities. *Annals of Leisure Research*, 8, (1), 23–37.

Fabiansson, C. (2006a). Recreational gambling – Young people's gambling participation in rural Australia. *Journal of Youth Studies*, 9, (3), 345–60.

Fabiansson, C. (2006b). Pathways to excessive gambling within a social community construct. *Journal of the National Association for Gambling Studies*, 18, (2), 55–68.

Fabiansson, C. (2007). *A Community Study – Employment Status & Gambling Pursuits in Greater Western Sydney, New South Wales.* Sydney: University of Western Sydney.

Fabiansson, C. (2008). Pathways to excessive gambling – Are young people's approach to gambling an indication of future gambling propensity? *Child Indicators Research*, 1, (2), 156–75.

Fabiansson, C. (2009). Why would anyone want to do gambling research? *Journal of the National Association for Gambling Studies [NAGS] Australia: Gambling Research*, 21, (1), May, Special Issue, 25–27.

Fabiansson, C. and Healey, L. (2004). *Young People's Community Affiliation: Final Report.* Sydney: University of Western Sydney.

Fairbairn, J. (1995). *Go in Ancient China.* Retrieved 5 August 2009 from http://www.pandanet.co.jp/English/essay/goancientchina.html.

Fantino, E., Navarro, A. and O'Daly, M. (2005). The science of decision making: Behaviours related to gambling. *International Gambling Studies*, 5, (2), 169–86.

Farkas, S., Johnson, J., Duffett, A. and Bers, A. (1997). *Kids These Days: What Americans Really Think About the Next Generation.* New York, NY: Public Agenda.

Feeney, D. and Maki, T. (1997). *Age, Generational Membership and Their Effect on Gambling Behavior and Attitudes.* Roseville, MN: Minnesota State Lottery.

Felsher, J., Derevensky, J.L. and Gupta, R. (2004). Lottery playing amongst youth: Implications for prevention and social policy. *Journal of Gambling Studies*, 20, 127–53.

Ferentzy, P. and Turner, N. (2009). Gambling and organized crime – A review of the literature. *Journal of Gambling Issues*, 23, June, 111–55.

Ferris, J. and Wynne, H. (2001). *The Canadian Problem Gambling Index: Final Report.* February 19, Submitted for the Canadian Centre on Substance Abuse (CCSA). Retrieved 14 July 2009 from http://www.ccsa.ca/2003%20and%20earlier%20CCSA%20Documents/ccsa-008805-2001.pdf.

Fisher, S. (2000). Developing the DSM-IV-MR-J criteria to identify adolescent problem gambling in non-clinical populations. *Journal of Gambling Studies*, 16, (2–3), 253–73.

Flatt, A. (1998). Overview of Native American Gambling Legal and Regulatory Issues. *National Gambling Impact Study Commission*, July 23. Retrieved 26 March 2009 from http://govinfo.library.unt.edu/ngisc/meetings/jul2998/flatt.pdf.

Fleming, A. (1978). *Something for Nothing: A History of Gambling*. New York, NY: Delacorte.

Focal Research. (2008). *2007 Adult Gambling Prevalence Study*. Nova Scotia Health Promotion and Protection. Retrieved 14 July 2009 from: http://www.gov.ns.ca/ohp/publications/Adult_Gambling_Report.pdf.

France, C. (1902). The gambling impulse. *American Journal of Psychology*, 13, 364–407.

Furlong, A. and Cartmel, F. (2007). *Young People and Social Change*, 2nd ed. Open University Press, Berkshire: McGraw-Hill.

Furstenberg, F.F. (2000). The sociology of adolescence and youth in the 1990s: A critical commentary. *Journal of Marriage and the Family*, 62, (4), 896–910.

Gambling Research Australia. (2008). *Review of Australian Gambling Research*. Department of Justice, Victoria.

Gausset, Q. and Jansbøl, K. (2009). 'Tell me what you play and I will tell you who you are': Values and gambling habits in two Danish universities. *International Gambling Studies*, 9, (1), April, 67–78.

Gershuny, J. (2000). *Changing Times: Work and Leisure in Postindustrial Society*. Oxford: Oxford University Press.

Getty, H.A., Watson, J. and Frisch, G.R. (2000). A comparison of depression and styles of coping in male and female GA members and controls. *Journal of Gambling Studies*, 16, 377–91.

Gillespie, M.A., Derevensky, J.L. and Gupta, R. (2007). Adolescent problem gambling: Developing a gambling expectancy instrument. *Journal of Gambling Issues*, 19, January, 51–69. Retrieved 8 July 2009 from http://www.camh.net/egambling/issue19/pdfs/gillespie1.pdf.

Goldstein, A.L., Walton, M.A., Cunningham, R.M., Resko, S.M. and Duan, L. (2009). Correlates of gambling among youth in an inner-city emergency department. *Psychology of Addictive Behaviors*, 23, (1), 113–21.

Goodin, R.E., Rice, J.M., Bittman, M. and Saunders, P. (2005). The time-pressure illusion: Discretionary time vs. free time. *Social Indicators Research*, 73, (1), 43–70.

Griffiths, M.D. (1998). Youth gambling – Where is it heading. Paper presented at the *National Association for Gambling Studies Practitioners Conference*, November, Adelaide.

Griffiths, M.D. (2005). Does gambling advertising contribute to problem gambling? *International Journal of Mental Health and Addiction*, 3, 15–25.

Griffiths, M.D. and Barnes, A. (2008). Internet gambling: An online empirical study among student gamblers. *International Journal of Mental Health and Addiction*, 6, 194–204.

Griffiths, M.D. and Wood, R. (2001). The psychology of lottery gambling. *International Gambling Studies*, 1, 27–44.

Gupta, R. and Derevensky, J.L. (1997). Familial and social influences on juvenile gambling. *Journal of Gambling Studies*, 13, 179–92.

Gupta, R. and Derevensky, J.L. (1998a). Adolescent gambling behavior: A prevalence study and examination of the correlates associated with excessive gambling. *Journal of Gambling Studies*, 14, 319–45.

Gupta, R. and Derevensky, J.L. (1998b). An empirical examination of Jacobs' General Theory of Addictions: Do adolescent gamblers fit the theory? *Journal of Gambling Studies*, 14, 17–49.

Hall, G.S. (1904). *Adolescence: Its Psychology and its Relations to Physiology, Anthropology, Sociology, Sex, Crime, Religion and Education.* New York, NY: D. Appleton.

Hardoon, K., Derevensky, J.L. and Gupta, R. (2002). *An Examination of the Influence of Familial, Emotional, Conduct and Cognitive Problems, and Hyperactivity Upon Youth Risk-taking and Adolescent Gambling Problems.* Report prepared for the Ontario Problem Gambling Research Centre, Toronto.

Hardoon, K., Derevensky, J.L. and Gupta, R. (2003). Empirical vs. perceived measures of gambling severity: Why adolescents don't present themselves for treatment. *Addictive Behaviors*, 28, 933–46.

Hardoon K.K., Gupta R. and Derevensky, J.L. (2004). Psychosocial variables associated with adolescent gambling. *Psychology of Addictive Behaviors*, 18, 170–79.

Hing, N., Dickerson, M. and Mackellar, J. (2001). *Australian Gaming Council Summary Responsible Gambling Document*, Australian Gaming Council, Melbourne.

Hing, N. and Mattinson, A. (2005). Evaluation of the NSW ClubSafe responsible gambling program: Opportunities and challenges for New Zealand clubs. *eCommunity – International Journal of Mental Health and Addiction*, 3, 61–9.

Horbay, R. (2004). *Slot Tutorial Treatment Guide.* Ontario: Game Planit Interactive Corp.

Huang, J-H. and Boyer, R. (2007). Epidemiology of youth gambling problems in Canada: A national prevalence study. *The Canadian Journal of Psychiatry*, 52, (10), October, 657–65.

Independent Pricing and Regulatory Tribunal [IPART]. (2003). *Review Into Gambling Harm Minimisation Measures.* Independent Pricing and Regulatory Tribunal of New South Wales. Retrieved 28 July 2007 from www.ipart.nsw. gov.au.

Independent Pricing and Regulatory Tribunal [IPART]. (2004). *Gambling: Promoting a Culture of Responsibility.* June, Independent Pricing and

Regulatory Tribunal of New South Wales. Retrieved 28 July 2007 from www. ipart.nsw.gov.au/files/Gambling04.pdf.

Independent Pricing and Regulatory Tribunal [IPART]. (2005). *Gambling: Promoting a Culture of Responsibility Consequential Report on Governance Structures.* February, Independent Pricing and Regulatory Tribunal of New South Wales. Retrieved 28 July 2007 from www.olgr.nsw.gov.au/pdfs/ Promoting_Culture_of_Responsibility_2.pdf.

Independent Pricing and Regulatory Tribunal [IPART]. (2008). *Review of the Registered Clubs Industry in NSW.* Other Industries. Draft Report. February, Independent Pricing and Regulatory Tribunal of New South Wales. Retrieved 28 July 2007 from www.ipart.nsw.gov.au/files/Final%20Report%20-%20%2 0Review%20of%20Registered%20Clubs%20Industry%20in%20NSW%20- %20APD%20-%20Website.PDF.

Ipsos Reid Public Affairs and Gemini Research. (2008). *British Columbia Problem Gambling Prevalence Study.* Gaming Policy and Enforcement Branch, Ministry of Public Safety and Solicitor General. Retrieved 5 June 2008 from http:// www.bcresponsiblegambling.ca/responsible/docs/rpt-rg-prevalence-study- 2008.pdf.

Jackson, A.C., Patton, G., Thomas, S.A., Wyn, J., Wright, J., Bond, L., Crisp, B.R. and Ho, W. (2000). *The Impacts of Gambling on Adolescents and Children.* Melbourne: Victorian Department of Human Services, 92.

Jacobs, D.F. (2000). Juvenile gambling in North America: An analysis of long-term trends and future prospects. *Journal of Gambling Studies,* 16, (2–3), 119–52.

Jacques, C. and Ladouceur, R. (2003). DSM-IV-J criteria: A scoring error that may be modifying the estimates of pathological gambling among youths. *Journal of Gambling Studies,* 19, (4), 427–31.

Jessor, R. (1998). New perspectives on adolescent risk behavior. In R. Jessor (ed.) *New Perspectives on Adolescent Risk Behavior.* Cambridge: Cambridge University Press.

Johansson, A. and Götestam, K.G. (2003). Gambling and problematic gambling with money among Norwegian youth (12–18 years). *Nordic Journal of Psychiatry,* 57, 317–21.

Johnston, L.D. (2003). Alcohol and illicit drugs: The role of risk perceptions. In D. Romer (ed.) *Reducing Adolescent Risk: Towards an Integrated Approach,* 56–74. London: Sage Publications.

Jones, G. (2009). *Youth.* Cambridge: Polity Press.

Jonsson, J., Andrén, A., Nilsson, T., Svensson, O., Munck, I., Kindstedt, A. and Rönnberg, S. (2003). Spelberoende i Sverige – vad kännetecknar personer med spelproblem? Rapport om andra fasen av den svenska nationella studien av spel och spelberoende. Statens Folkhälsoinstitut. Report no 2003: 22. Retrieved 25 May 2008 from http://www.speletsbaksida.se/files/spelberoende_i_sverige- vad_kannetecknar_personer_med_spelproblem.pdf.

Kallick, M., Suits, D., Dielman, T. and Hybels, J. (1979). Gambling participation. In M. Kallick, D. Suits, T. Dielman and J. Hybels (eds), *A Survey of American*

Gambling Attitudes and Behaviour. Ann Arbor, MI: University of Michigan, Institute for Social Research, Survey Research Center, 1–44.

Kang, S.K. and Hsu, C.H.C. (2001). University students' perceptions on legalized gambling and their casino gaming behaviors. *The Consortium Journal*, 5, 5–16.

Kavanagh, T.M. (1993). *Enlightenment and the Shadows of Chance: The Novel and the Culture of Gambling in Eighteenth-Century France.* Baltimore, MD: Johns Hopkins University Press.

Khalifa, R. (1989). *QURAN: The Final Testament.* Authorized English version with Arabic text. Islamic Productions, Tucson, Arizona. Chapter/Sura 5:90-91832/57696, *Intoxicants and Gambling Prohibited.* Retrieved 30 September 2009 from http://www.submission.org/suras/sura5.html.

Kim, S. and Stoel, L. (2004). Apparel retailers: Website quality dimensions and satisfaction. *Journal of Retailing and Consumer Services*, 11, (2), 109–17.

Korn, D. and Shaffer, H. (1999). Gambling and the health of the Public: Adopting a public health perspective. *Journal of Gambling Studies*, 15, (4), 289–365.

Kusyszyn, I. and Rutter, R. (1985). Personality characteristics of heavy gamblers, light gamblers, non-gamblers, and lottery players. *Journal of Gambling Behavior*, 1, 59–63.

Kweitel, R. and Allen, F.C.L. (1998). Cognitive processes associated with gambling behaviour. *Psychological Reports*, 82, 147–53.

Ladouceur, R., Bouchard, C., Rheaume, N., Jacques, C., Ferland, F., Leblond, J. and Walker, M. (2000). Is the SOGS an accurate measure of pathological gambling among children, adolescents and adults? *Journal of Gambling Studies*, 16, 1–24.

Ladouceur, R., Jacques, C., Chevalier, S., Sevigny, S. and Hamel, D. (2005). Prevalence of pathological gambling in Quebec in 2002. *The Canadian Journal of Psychiatry*, 50, 451–6.

Ladouceur, R., Sylvain, C. and Gosselin, P. (2007). Self-exclusion program: A longitudinal evaluation study. *Journal of Gambling Studies*, 23, 85–94.

Ladouceur, R., Dube, D. and Bujold, A. (1994). Prevalence of pathological gambling and related problems among college students in the Quebec metropolitan area. *Canadian Journal of Psychiatry*, 39, 289–93.

La Fleur's Magazine. (2005). *May.* TLF Publications.

La Fleur's Magazine. (2007). *May/June.* TLF Publications.

Lambos, C., Delfabbro, P. and Puglies, S. (2007). *Adolescent Gambling in South Australia.* Department for Education and Children's Services, Adelaide. Report prepared on behalf of the Department for Education and Children's Services for the Independent Gambling Authority of South Australia.

Langhinrichsen-Rohling, J., Rohde, P., Seeley, J.R. and Rohling, M.L. (2004). Individual, family, and peer correlates of adolescent gambling. *Journal of Gambling Studies*, 20, 23–46.

Lesieur, H. (1985). Alcohol, other drugs and gambling: A study at South Oaks Hospital. *The National Council on Compulsive Gambling Newsletter*, 1, (13), 3–4.

Lesieur, H.R. and Blume, S.B. (1987). The South Oaks Gambling Screen (SOGS): A new instrument for the identification of pathological gamblers. *American Journal of Psychiatry*, 144, 1184–8.

Lesieur, H.R., Cross, J., Frank, M., Welch, M., White, C.M., Rubenstein, G., Moseley, K. and Mark, M. (1991). Gambling and pathological gambling among university students. *Addictive Behaviors*, 16, 517–27.

Lester, D. (1994). Access to gambling opportunities and compulsive gambling. *International Journal of Addiction*, 29, 1611–16.

Li, W.L. and Smith, M.H. (1976). The propensity to gamble: Some structural determinants. In W.R. Eadington (ed.) *Gambling and Society*. Springfield, IL: Charles V. Thomas.

Lowenfeld, B.H. (1979). Personality dimensions of the pathological gambler. *Dissertation Abstracts*, 40, (1-B), 456.

Lowie, R. (1975). *Indians of the Plains*. New York, NY: The Natural History Press.

Magnusson, M. (1985). *Reader's Digest Book of Facts*. London: The Reader's Digest Association Limited.

Maher, A., Wilson, N., Signal, L. and Thomson, G. (2006). Patterns of sports sponsorship by gambling, alcohol and food companies: An internet survey. *BMC Public Health*, 6, 95–104.

Mangham, C., Carney, G., Burnett, S. and Williams, R. (2005). *Determining Socio-economic Impacts of New Gaming Venues in Four Lower Mainland Communities: Socio-economic Issues and Impacts Baseline Report*. Victoria, BC: Ministry of Public Safety and Solicitor General, Government of British Columbia.

Mann, K. (2003). *'Sit Anywhere You Like, We're all Friends Together': Reflections on Bingo Culture*. London: Goldsmith College.

Marks, M.E. and Lesieur, H.R. (1992). A feminist critique of problem gambling research. *British Journal of Addiction*, 87, 549–65.

Martins, S.S., Storr, C.L., Ialongo, N.S. and Chilcoat, H.D. (2007). Mental health and gambling in urban adolescents. *Journal of Adolescent Health*, 40, 463–5.

Mason, W.D. (2000). Indian gaming: Tribal sovereignty and American politics. Norman, OK: University of Oklahoma Press, 189–206.

McQueen, P.A. (2008). At $230 B. and Climbing, It's Another Banner Year for the World's Lotteries. *International Gaming and Wagering Business*, September 2. Retrieved 4 November 2008 from www.igwb.com/copyright/BNP_GUID_9-5-2006_A_10000000000000412283?view=print.

Messerlian, C. and Derevensky, J.L. (2005). Youth gambling: A public health perspective. *Journal of Gambling Issues*, 14, September, 1–20.

Mok, W.P. and Hraba, J. (1991). Age and gambling behavior: A declining and shifting pattern of participation. *Journal of Gambling Studies*, 7, 313–35.

Monaghan, S. (2009). Responsible gambling strategies for internet gambling: The theoretical and empirical base of using pop-up messages to encourage self-awareness. *Computers in Human Behavior*, 25, 202–207.

Monaghan, S., Derevensky, J.L. and Sklar, A. (2008). Impact of gambling advertisements and marketing on children and adolescents: Policy recommendations to minimise harm. *Journal of Gambling Issues*, 22, 252–74.

Moodie, C. (2008). Student gambling, erroneous cognitions, and awareness of treatment in Scotland. *Journal of Gambling*, 21, July, 30–56.

Moodie, C. and Finnigan, F. (2006). Prevalence and correlates of youth gambling in Scotland. *Addiction Research & Theory*, 14, (4), August, 365–85.

Moodie, C. and Reith G. (2009). Responsible gambling signage on electronic gaming machines, before and after the implementation of the United Kingdom Gambling Act: An observational study. *International Gambling Studies*, 9, (1), April, 5–17.

Moore, S.M. and Ohtsuka, K. (1997). Gambling activities of young Australians: Developing a model of behaviour. *Journal of Gambling Studies*, 13, (3), 207–36.

National Research Council. (1999). *Pathological Gambling: A Critical Review.* Washington, DC: National Academy Press.

Neal, P., Delfabbro, P.H. and O'Neil, M. (2005). *Problem Gambling and Harm: Towards a National Definition.* Report prepared for the National Gambling Research Program Working Party, Melbourne.

Neighbors, C., Lostutter, T.W., Cronce, J.M. and Larimer, M.E. (2002). Exploring college student gambling motivation. *Journal of Gambling Studies*, 18, (4), Winter, 361–70.

Nelson, S., LaPlante, D., Peller, A., Schumann, A., LaBrie, R. and Shaffer, H. (2008). Real limits in the virtual world: Self-limiting behavior of Internet gamblers. *Journal of Gambling Studies*, 24, 463–77.

Nelson Rose, I. (2000). *Minimum Legal Age to Place a Bet.* 15 June 2000. Retrieved 25 March 2009 from http://rose.casinocitytimes.com/articles/966.html.

New South Wales Department of Gaming and Racing. (1999). *Gambling Legislation Amendment (Responsible Gambling) Act 1999.* Retrieved 5 June 2008 from http://www.austlii.edu.au/au/legis/nsw/repealed_act/glaga1999450/.

New South Wales Department of Gaming and Racing. (2004). *Gaming Machine Tax Act 2001, Community Development and Support Expenditure (CDSE) Scheme Guidelines*, March. Sydney: New South Wales Government.

New South Wales Department of Gaming and Racing. (2005). *Gambling Statistics 2004–2005.* Requested statistical data collated by NSW Government.

New South Wales Department of Gaming and Racing. (2006). *Industry Statistics at a Glance*, for the year ended 30 June 2005, www.dgr.nsw.gov.au (February), Department of Gaming and Racing 2006; Industry at a glance fact sheet. Retrieved 29 May 2008 from http://www.olgr.nsw.gov.au/pdfs/ industry_stats_ 05.pdf.

New South Wales Department of Arts, Sport and Recreation. (2000). *Registered Clubs Amendment (Responsible Gambling) Act 2000 NSW.* The NSW Office of Liquor, Gaming and Racing. Retrieved 5 June 2008 from http://www.olgr.nsw. gov.au/pdfs/leg_bull_clubs_leg_april_00.pdf.

New South Wales Department of Arts, Sport and Recreation. (2007). *Gaming Machine Review.* The NSW Office of Liquor, Gaming and Racing. Retrieved 5 June 2008 from http://www.olgr.nsw.gov.au/pdfs/Gaming_Machines_ Review.pdf.

New South Wales Department of Health. (2009). *Smoke-free Environment Amendment Regulation 2009*, 2009 No 297, under the Smoke-free Environment Act 2000. Retrieved 2 October 2009 from http://www.legislation.nsw.gov.au/ sessionalview/sessional/sr/2009-297.pdf.

New South Wales Government. (2005). *Towards a Culture of Responsibility in Gambling,* May. Response by the NSW Government to the Reports of the Independent Pricing and Regulatory Tribunal: "Gambling: Promoting a Culture of Responsibility" and "Consequential Report on Governance Structures". Sydney: New South Wales Government.

New South Wales Office of Liquor, Gaming and Racing. (2007a). *Fact Sheet, Gambling Regulation.* Retrieved 7 September 2008 from http://www.olgr.nsw. gov.au/gaming.

New South Wales Office of Liquor, Gaming and Racing. (2007b). *Report on the five-year statutory review of the Gaming Machines Act 2001.* December 2007. Retrieved 7 June 2008 from http://www.olgr.nsw.gov.au/pdfs/gaming_ machine_act_review_report_061207[1].pdf.

New South Wales Office of Liquor, Gaming and Racing. (2008). *Gaming Machines Amendment Act 2008.* Retrieved 7 September 2009 from http://www.olgr.nsw. gov.au/gaming.

New South Wales Office of Liquor, Gaming and Racing. (2009a). *Fact Sheet, Gambling Regulation.* Retrieved 7 April 2009 from http://www.olgr.nsw.gov. au/olgr_default.asp.

New South Wales Office of Liquor, Gaming and Racing. (2009b). *Industry Statistics at a Glance.* Retrieved 10 August 2009 from http://www.olgr.nsw. gov.au/gaming_info_taxrates.asp.

New South Wales Office of Liquor, Gaming and Racing. (2009c). *Community Development and Support Expenditure Scheme Guidelines*, February 2009, Gaming Machine Tax Act 2001. Retrieved 2 October 2009 from http://www. olgr.nsw.gov.au.

New South Wales Office of Liquor, Gaming and Racing. (2009d). *Gaming tax rates.* Retrieved 20 October 2009 from http://www.olgr.nsw.gov.au/gaming_ info_taxrates.asp.

New Zealand Government. (2009). *Gambling Statistics.* Retrieved 15 April 2009 from http://www.dia.govt.nz/Pubforms.nsf/URL/Expendstats08.pdf/ $file/Expendstats08.pdf.

Nielsen, J., Molich, R., Snyder, C. and Farrell, S. (2000). *E-commerce User Experience: Trust.* Fremont, CA: Nielsen NormanGroup. Retrieved 28 July 2009 from http://www.nngroup.com/reports/ecommerce.

Ni Laoire, C. (1995). *Conceptualising Rural Youth Migration.* Paper presented at the Annual Conference, Institute of British Geographers, University of Northumbria, Newcastle, 3–6 January 1995.

Nowatzki, N.R. and Williams, R.J. (2002). Casino self-exclusion programs: A review of the issues. *International Gambling Studies,* 2, 3–25.

Nova Scotia Department of Health Promotion and Protection. (2008). *2007 Adult Gambling Prevalence Study.* Halifax, Canada. Retrieved 25 August 2009 from http://www.gov.ns.ca/hpp/publications/Adult_Gambling_Report.pdf.

Nower, L. and Blaszczynski, A. (2004). A pathways approach to treating youth gamblers. In J.L. Derevensky and R. Gupta (eds) *Gambling Problems in Youth: Theoretical and Applied Perspectives.* New York: Kluwer Academic/Plenum Publishers, 189–210.

Office of Economic and Statistical Research. (2005). *Australian Gambling Statistics 2005.* Brisbane: Queensland Government Treasury.

Office of Economic and Statistical Research. (2006). *Australian Gambling Statistics, 2006.* Brisbane: Queensland Government Treasury.

Office of Economic and Statistical Research. (2007). *Australian Gambling Statistics 1980–81 to 2005–06,* 24th Edition 2007. Brisbane: Queensland Government Treasury.

Olason, D.T., Sigurdardottir, K.J. and Smari, J. (2006). Prevalence estimates of gambling participation and problem gambling among 16–18-year-old students in Iceland: A comparison of the SOGS-RA and DSM-IV-MR-J. *Journal of Gambling Studies,* 22, (1), 23–39.

Orford, J. (2003). *Gambling and Problem Gambling in Britain.* New York, NY: Brunner-Routledge.

Orford, J. (2005). Disabling the public interest: Gambling strategies and policies for Britain. *Addiction,* 100, 1219–25.

Orford, J., Griffiths, M.D., Wardle, H., Sproston, K. and Erens, B. (2009). Negative public attitudes towards gambling: findings from the 2007 British Gambling prevalence survey using a new attitude scale. *International Gambling Studies,* 9, (1), April, 39–54.

Oster, S.L. and Knapp, T.J. (1998). Underage and pathological gambling by college students: Emerging problem on campus? *Psychology and Education,* 38, 15–19.

Parke, J. and Griffiths, M.D. and Irwing, P. (2004). Personality traits in pathological gambling: Sensation seeking, deferment of gratification and competitiveness as risk factors. *Addiction Research & Theory,* 12, (3), 201–12.

Parke, J. and Griffiths, M.D. (2006). The psychology of the fruit machine: The role of structural characteristics (revisited). *International Journal of Mental Health and Addiction,* 4, (2), April, 151–79.

Parke, J., Rigbye, J., Parke, A., Wood, R.T.A., Sjenitzer, J. and Vaughan Williams, L. (2007). *The Global Online Gambling Report: An Exploratory Investigation into the Attitudes and Behaviours of Internet Casino and Poker Players.* eCOGRA (e-Commerce and Online Gaming Regulation and Assurance). Retrieved 28 July 2009 from http://www.ecogra.com/Downloads/eCOGRA_Global_Online_Gambler_Report.pdf.

Parker, M. (1998). *A Brief History of Horse Racing.* Retrieved 14 April 2009 from http://www.mrmike.com/explore/hrhist.htm.

Plutarch. (1883). *Moralia.* Published in 1960 by Heinemann, Harvard University Press, London, Cambridge, Mass, in 15 volumes, English translation by Frank Cole Babbitt.

Productivity Commission. (1999). *Inquiry into Australia's Gambling Industries.* Final Report, No 10. Canberra: AusInfo.

Productivity Commission. (2009). *Gambling. Draft Report.* Canberra October, www.pc.gov.au.

Powell, J., Hardoon, K., Derevensky, J.L. and Gupta, R. (1999). Gambling and risk taking behavior among university students. *Substance Use and Misuse,* 34, 1167–84.

Queensland Government Treasury. (2004). *Report on the Implementation Review of the Queensland Responsible Gambling Code of Practice.* Research and Community Engagement Division Queensland Office of Gaming Regulation, Queensland Treasury. Retrieved 30 March 2009 from http://www.olgr.qld.gov.au/resources/responsibleGamblingDocuments/responsibleGamblingReportOnTheImplementationReview04.pdf.

Queensland Government Treasury. (2007). *Queensland Household Gambling Survey 2003–2004.* Brisbane. Prepared by the Office of Economic and Statistical Research, Queensland Treasury.

Registered Clubs Association of NSW. (1994). *Directors Guide.* Sydney: Registered Clubs Association of NSW.

Registered Clubs Association of NSW. (1999). *Directors Guide.* Sydney: Registered Clubs Association of NSW.

Reith, G. (1999). *The Age of Chance. Gambling in western culture.* London and New York: Routledge Taylor and Francis Group.

Robinson, J.P. (1977). *How Americans Use Time.* New York, NY: Praeger.

Rodda, S. and Cowie, M. (2005). *Evaluation of Electronic Gaming Machine Harm Minimisation in Victoria.* Report prepared for the Victorian Department of Justice. Melbourne, Caraniche Pty. Ltd.

Rojek, R. (1985). *Capitalism and Leisure Theory.* London: Tavistock.

Rojek, R. (2000). *Leisure and Culture.* London: Macmillan.

Rönnberg, S., Volberg, R.A., Abbott, M.W., Moore, W.L., Andrén, A., Munck, I. et al. (1999). *Gambling and Problem Gambling in Sweden.* Report No. 2 of the National Institute of Public Health Series on Gambling. Stockholm: National Institute of Public Health Sweden.

Room, R. (2005). The wheel of fortune: Cycles and reactions in gambling policies. *Addiction*, 100, 1226–7.

Roy Morgan Research. (2005). *The Fourth Study into the Extent and Impact of Gambling in Tasmania with Particular Reference to Problem Gambling.* Report prepared for the Department of Health and Human Services, Hobart.

Shaffer, H. (1989). It's poor state policy to legalize gambling just for the revenue. *Boston Herald*, August, 31.

Shaffer, H.J., Hall, M. and Vander Bilt, J. (1997). *Estimating the Prevalence of Disordered Gambling Behavior in the United States and Canada: A Meta-analysis.* Cambridge, MA: Harvard Medical School.

Shawn, R., Currie, S.R., Miller, N., Hodgins, D.C. and Wang, J-L. (2009). Defining a threshold of harm from gambling for population health surveillance research. *International Gambling Studies*, 9, (1), 19–38.

Sifakis, C. (1990). *Encyclopedia of Gambling.* New York, NY: Facts On File.

Skokauskas, N., Burba, Æ B. and Freedman, Æ D. (2009). An assessment of the psychometric properties of Lithuanian versions of DSM-IV-MR-J and SOGS-RA. *Journal of Gambling Studies*, 25, 263–71.

Slade, P. and McConville, C. (2003). The problem with problem gambling: Historical and economic concerns. *Journal of Economic and Social Policy*, 8, 1–16.

Slowo, D. (1998). Are all gamblers the same? An exploration of personality and motivational characteristics of individuals with different gambling preferences. In G. Coman, B. Evans, and R. Wootton, (eds), *Responsible Gambling: A Future Winner.* Adelaide, SA: National Association for Gambling Studies, 339–51.

Smith, G.J. and Wynne, H.J. (2000). *A Review of the Gambling Literature in the Economic and Policy Domains.* Edmonton, AB: Alberta Gaming Research Institute.

Smith, G.J. and Wynne, H.J. (2002). *Measuring Gambling and Problem Gambling in Alberta Using the Canadian Problem Gambling Index (CPGI).* Alberta Gaming Research Institute. Retrieved 14 July 2009 from https://dspace.ucalgary.ca/bitstream/1880/1626/1/gambling_alberta_cpgi.pdf.

Smith, G., Wynne, H. and Hartnagel, T. (2003). *Examining Police Records to Assess Gambling Impacts: A Study of Gambling-related Crime in the City of Edmonton.* Study prepared for The Alberta Gaming Research Institute. Edmonton. Retrieved 28 July 2009 from www.ncalg.org/Library/Studies%20and%20White%20Papers/Crime%20   and%20Corruption/albertagamblingcrime.pdf.

Smith, S. (1948). Lotteries. *Journal of Criminal Law and Criminology*, 38, 547–56 and 559–69.

Spanier, D. (1987). *Easy Money: Inside the Gambler's Mind.* London: Secker and Warburg.

Spelinstitutet (2000) Ungdomars Spelvanor i Piteå. En undersökning gjord av Spelinstitutet i Piteå. Retrieved 7 January 2004 [unavailable in 2009] from www.spelinstitutet.se/reports/.

Statistical Package for Social Sciences [SPSS]. (2007). *Statistical Analysis*, v16.0.

Stebbins, R.A. (1997). Casual leisure: A conceptual statement. *Leisure Studies*, 16, 17–25.

Stebbins, R.A. (2001). Serious Leisure. *Society*, 38, (4), May/June, 53–7.

Stevens, R. and Beristain, M. (2004). Canada's Risky Business: A Canadian Guide to Selected Gambling Industry Sources, Alberta Gaming Research Institute. *Reference Services Review*, 32, (3), 320–8. Retrieved 26 March 2009 from https://dspace.ucalgary.ca/bitstream/1880/1597/1/Canadian_guide_to_gaming_RSR.pdf.

Stinchfield, R. (2000). Gambling and correlates of gambling among Minnesota public school students. *Journal of Gambling Studies*, 16, (2–3), Fall, 153–73.

Stinchfield, R. (2004). Demographic, psychosocial, and behavioral factors associated with youth gambling and problem gambling. In J.L. Derevensky and R. Gupta (eds) *Gambling Problems in Youth: Theoretical and Applied Perspectives*, New York, NY: Kluwer Academic/Plenum Publishers, 27–40.

Stinchfield, R., Govoni, R. and Frisch, G.R. (2005). DSM-IV diagnostic criteria for pathological gambling: Reliability, validity, and classification accuracy. *The American Journal on Addiction*, 14, (1), 73–82.

Stinchfield, R. and Winters, K.C. (1998). Gambling and problem gambling among youth. *Annals of the American Academy of Political and Social Science*, 556, March, 172–85.

Stitt, B.G., Giacopassi, D. and Nichols, M. (2003). Gambling among older adults: A comparative analysis. *Experimental Aging Research*, 29, 189–203.

Submission to Productivity Commission. (2009). Submission no 5, February, http://www.pc.gov.au/projects/inquiry/gambling-2009.

Tanasornnarong, N., Jackson, A.C. and Thomas, S.A. (2004). Gambling among young Thai people in Melbourne, Australia: An exploratory study. *International Gambling Studies*, 14, (2), November, 199–214.

Taylor, A., Grande, E.D., Gill, T., Delfabbro, P., Glenn, V., Goulding, S., Weston, H., Barton, S., Rogers, N., Stanley, A., Blandy, R., Tolchard, B. and Kingston, R. (2001). *Gambling Patterns of South Australians and Associated Health Indicators*. Paper prepared for Department of Human Services, South Australia, May.

Taylor Nelson Sofres. (2004). *Word Count of Gaming Machines 2004*. Prepared for Australasian Gaming Machine Manufactures Association [AGMMA].

Taylor Nelson Sofres. (2006). *Word Count of Gaming Machines 2006*. Prepared for Australasian Gaming Machine Manufactures Association [AGMMA].

Taylor Nelson Sofres. (2008). *World Count of Gaming Machines 2008*. Prepared for Australasian Gaming Machine Manufactures Association [AGMMA].

The Allen Consulting Group. (2004). *Socio-Economic Impact Study of Clubs in NSW*. Allen Consulting Group, Canberra/Melbourne/Sydney.

The Allen Consulting Group. (2008). *Socio-Economic Impact Study of Clubs in NSW (2007)*. Final Report February 2008 Allen Consulting Group, Canberra/ Melbourne/ Sydney.

The Allen Consulting Group. (2009). *Review of Current and Future Trends in Interactive Gambling Activity and Regulation* Literature review June 2009. Report to the Australian Government, Department of Families, Housing, Community Services and Indigenous Affairs, Canberra.

The Columbia Encyclopedia. (2008). 6th Edition. Retrieved 14 July 2009 from http://www.encyclopedia.com/doc/1E1-parimutu.html.

The South Australian Centre for Economic Studies. (2003). *Measurement of Prevalence of Youth Problem Gambling in Australia: Report on Review of Literature*. Adelaide: The University of Adelaide.

The South Australian Centre for Economic Studies. (2005). *Problem Gambling and Harm: Towards a National Definition*. Adelaide: Department of Psychology, University of Adelaide.

Tuffin, A. and Parr, V. (2008). *Evaluation of the 6-Hour Shutdown of Electronic Gaming Machines in NSW*. A multi-method research report prepared for the NSW Office of Liquor, Gaming and Racing. April 2008. Blue Moon Research And Planning Pty. Retrieved 5 August 2009 http://www.olgr.nsw.gov.au/pdfs/ Evaluation_of_the_six_hour_shutdown.pdf.

Turner, N.E., Fritz, B. and Zangeneh, M. (2007). Images of gambling in film. *Journal of Gambling Issues*, 20, 117–43. Retrieved 28 July 2009 from http:// www.camh.net/egambling/issue20/02turner.htm.

Turner, N.E., Preston, D.L., Saunders, C., Mcavoy, S. and Jain, U. (2009). The relationship of problem gambling to criminal behavior in a sample of Canadian male federal offenders. *Journal of Gambling Studies*, 25, (2), June, 153–69.

United Kingdom Gambling Commission. (2005). *Licence Conditions and Codes of Practice*, UK Gambling Act 2005, enforced 1 September 2007. Retrieved 25 March 2009 from http://www.gamblingcommission.gov.uk.

United Kingdom Gambling Commission. (2009). *Survey Data on Remote Gambling Participation*, December 2008. Retrieved 31 March 2009 from http://www.gamblingcommission.gov.uk.

United Kingdom Office of National Statistics. (2007). *Consumer Trends*, Quarter 3. Retrieved 9 July 2009 from http://www.statistics.gov.uk/STATBASE/ Product.asp?vlnk=242.

United Kingdom Office of Public Sector Information. (2005). *Definition as Gaming, UK Gambling Act 2005, Explanatory Notes 2005*, Chapter 19. Retrieved 29 July 2009 from http://www.opsi.gov.uk/acts/acts2005/en/ ukpgaen_20050019_en_1.

United Kingdom Parliamentary Business. (2009). *V Gaming Machines*. Select Committee on Culture, Media and Sport Seventh Report. Retrieved 29 July 2009 from http://www.publications.parliament.uk/pa/cm200102/cmselect/ cmcumeds/827/82708.htm#n110.

United States Department of Justice. (2009). *Gambling Device Registration.* Retrieved 26 March 2009 from http://www.usdoj.gov/criminal/oeo/links/gambling.

Vander Bilt, J., Dodge, H. H., Pandav, R., Shaffer, H.J. and Ganguli, M. (2004). Gambling participation and social support among older adults: a longitudinal community study. *Journal of Gambling Studies*, 20, 373–90.

Veblen, T. (1899/1994). *Theory of the Leisure Class.* New York: Penguin.

Victorian Casino and Gaming Authority. (2001). *The Victorian Gambling Screen.* Gambling Research Panel, Victorian Commission for Gambling Regulation, Victoria Government, Melbourne.

Volberg, R.A. (2002). *Gambling and Problem Gambling in Nevada.* Report to the Nevada Department of Human Resources. Carson City, NV: Department of Human Resources. Retrieved 14 September 2008 from http://www.austgamingcouncil.org.au/images/pdf/eLibrary/911.pdf.

Volberg, R.A. (2003). *Gambling and Problem Gambling in Arizona.* Report to Arizona Lottery. Phoenix, AZ: Arizona Lottery. Retrieved 14 September 2008 from http://www.problemgambling.az.gov/statistics.htm.

Volberg, R.A. (2004). Fifteen years of problem gambling prevalence research: What do we know? Where do we go? *Electronic Journal of Gambling Issues: e-Gambling,* A festschrift in honour of Henry R. Lesieur, 10, February.

Volberg, R.A., Nysse-Carris, K.L. and Gerstein, D.R. (2006). *2006 California Problem Gambling Prevalence Survey.* Final report. Submitted to the California Department of Alcohol and drug Problems, Office of Problem and Pathological Gambling. Chicago: National Opinion Research Center.

Volberg, R.A., Rugle, L., Rosenthal, R.J. and Fong, T. (2005). *Situational Assessment of Problem Gambling Services In California.* California Council on Problem Gambling on behalf of the Office of Problem Gambling, Program Services Division, California Department of Alcohol and Drug Programs. March.

Walker, M.B. (1992). *The Psychology of Gambling.* Oxford: Pergamon Press.

Walker, M., Shannon, K., Blaszczynski, A. and Sharpe, L. (2004). *Problem Gamblers Receiving Counselling or Treatment in New South Wales.* Draft Report Eighth Survey 2004, A Report for The Casino Community Benefit Fund Trustees, University of Sydney Gambling Research Unit.

Walker, M., Matarese, K., Blaszczynski, A. and Sharpe, L. (2004). *Explaining the Attraction of Poker Machines: Cognition or Conditioning?* Gambling Research Unit, University of Sydney. Report to the Casino Community Benefit Fund Trustees. New South Wales Government, Department of Gaming and Racing, Sydney, March.

Wearing, B. (1998). *Leisure and Feminist Theory.* London, Sage Publications.

Wellman, B. (2001). Physical place and cyberspace: The rise of personalized networking. *International Journal of Urban and Regional Research*, 25 (2) June, 227–52.

List of References

Welte, J.W. (2008). The prevalence of problem gambling among US adolescents and young adults: Results from a national survey. *Journal of Gambling Studies*, 24, 119–33.

Welte, J.W. and Barns, G.M. (2004). The Relationship of ecological and geographic factors to gambling behavior and pathology. *Journal of Gambling Studies*, 20, 405–23.

Welte, J.W., Barnes, G.M., Wieczorek, W.F., Tidwell, M. and Parker, J. (2002). Gambling participation in the US: Results from a national survey. *Journal of Gambling Studies*, 18, 313–37.

Wiebe, J., Cox, B. and Mehmel, B.G. (2000). The south oaks gambling screen revised for adolescents (SOGS-RA): Further psychometric findings from a community sample. *Journal of Gambling Studies Special Issue: Youth Gambling*, 16, 275–88.

Wiebe, J., Mun, P. and Kauffman, N. (2006). *Gambling and Problem Gambling in Ontario 2005*. Responsible Gambling Council. Retrieved 14 July 2009 from http://www.responsiblegambling.org/articles/gambling_and_problem_gambling_in_ontario_2005.pdf.

Williams, R.J., Connolly, D., Wood, R.T. and Nowatzki, N. (2006). Gambling and problem gambling in a sample of university students. *Journal of Gambling Studies*, 4, (8), 1–14.

Winter, G. (2002). *Gambling: An Australian Tradition on the Up!* Department of the Parliamentary Library, Research Paper no. 14 2001–2002, Statistics Group, 14 May 2002.

Winters, K.C., Arthur, N., Leitten, W. and Botzet, A. (2004). Gambling and drug abuse in adolescence. In J.L. Derevensky and R. Gupta (eds) *Gambling Problems in Youth: Theoretical and Applied Perspectives*. New York, NY: Kluwer Academic/Plenum Publishers, 57–80.

Winters, K.C., Stinchfield, R. and Fulkerson, J. (1993). Toward the development of an adolescent gambling problem severity scale. *Journal of Gambling Studies*, 9, 371–86.

Winters, K.C., Stinchfield, R.D. and Kim, L.G. (1995). Monitoring adolescent gambling in Minnesota. *Journal of Gambling Studies*, 11, 165–83.

White, R.D. and Wyn, J. (2004). *Youth and Society: Exploring the Social Dynamics of Youth*. South Melbourne, Australia: Oxford University Press.

Wood, R.T.A., Derevensky, J.L., Gupta, R. and Griffiths, M.D. (2002). Accounts of the UK National Lottery and scratch cards: An analysis using Q-sorts. *Journal of Gambling Studies*, 18, (2), 161–84.

Wood, R.T.A. and Griffiths, M.D. (2008). Why Swedish people play online poker and factors that can increase or decrease trust in poker web sites: A qualitative investigation. *Journal of Gambling Issues*, 21, July, 80–97.

Wood, R.T.A. and Griffiths, M.D. (2005). *Problem Gambling as Coping: A Qualitative Investigation of Problem Gamblers and Their Coping Strategies*. Report prepared for the Responsibility in Gambling Trust.

Wood, R.T.A. and Griffiths, M.D. (2004). Adolescent lottery and scratchcard players: Do their attitudes influence their gambling behaviour? *Journal of Adolescence*, 27, 467–75.

Wood, R.T.A., Griffiths, M.D. and Parke, J. (2007). Acquisition, development, and maintenance of online poker playing in a student sample. *Cyber Psychology & Behavior*, 10, 354–61.

Wykes, A. (1964). *Gambling*. London: Spring Books.

Wynne, H.J., Smith, G.J. and Jacobs, D.F. (1996). *Adolescent Gambling and Problem Gambling in Alberta.* Edmonton, AB: Alberta Alcohol and Drug Abuse Commission.

Zaranek, R.R. and Chapleski, E.E. (2005). Casino gambling among urban elders: Just another social activity? *Journal of Gerontology: Social Sciences*, 60, (B:2), S74-S81.

Index

Figures and tables are indicated by **bold** page numbers.

AADs *see* approved amusement devices
Abbott, M. 65–6
acceptability of gambling 10, 25, 26, 162
accessibility of gambling 15, 16, 24, 25, 26, 27, 152, 161–3
advertising (gambling products) 1, 26, 27–8, 71–3
Africa **41**, 42, 45, 46, **48**, 49
age, and gambling 88, 144, 151–3
age restrictions 24, 27, 52–3, 61–3, 113–14
AGMMA *see* Australian Gaming Machine Manufacturers Association
alcohol 170, 173–6
America *see* USA
amusement with prize machines 45, 53
approved amusement devices 58
arcade games 118, **118**
Argentina **44**, 162
Aruba 47
Ashton, J. 12, 13, 14
Asia **41**, 42, 45, 46, **48**, 49, 186
astragals 1, 13
ATMs, availability of 69
Australia
    age restrictions 62
    casinos 45, 84
    gambler demographics 87–91, **89–90**
    gambling expenditure 19, 50, 95–8, **96, 98**
    gambling prevalence 22, 73–6, **83**, 91–100
    gambling regulation 28, 55, 56, 57–61
    gambling research 5–6
    gaming machines 38–9, 45, 46–8, **47**, 79–82, 91–5, **93, 94**, 186
    history of gambling 79–82, **80–81**
    horse racing 43, **44**, 79
    lotteries 2, **41**, 42, 79, 103

    responsible gambling 66–71
    sporting participation 35–6, 125–6
    sports betting 103–4
    see also New South Wales; Queensland survey
Australian Gaming Machine Manufacturers Association 66–7
AWPs *see* amusement with prize machines

Bellringer, M. 65–6
bereavement 157–8, 160
bingo 21, 124
Bittman, M. 32
Blaszczynski, A. 19, 72, 91
board games 12–13, 23, 112–13, 117–18
Boyer, R. 109
Brazil 43, **44**, 186

Campell, C.S. 30, 31
Canada
    casinos 45
    gambling expenditure 49
    gambling regulation 28, 55
    gaming machines 45, **47**, 48
    horse racing **44**
    lotteries 42, 55
    young gamblers 114–15
Canadian Problem Gambling Index (CPGI) 17, 73, 109
card games 1, 13–14, 23, 112–13, 117–18, 130
Caribbean **41**, 42, 45
case studies
    additional problems 173–6
    age of independent gambling 151–3
    cultural gambling traditions 161–3
    demographics of sample 144–8
    first wins 153–6

gambling expenditure 163–4
impact upon life 167–70
introductions to gambling 148–51
motivations for gambling 156–9
pathways to excessive gambling
    159–61, 193–6
research methodology 142–8
seeking help 164–7
social isolation 170–73
summary 191–6
casinos
    global statistics 45
    history of 14, 54, 84
    regulation 52
    and young people 24, 121–3, **122**,
        127
CDSE *see* Community Development
    Support Executive
Central America **41**, 42, 45
chariot racing 1, 13
Chile **44**, 162
China 1, 13, 42, 186
class 13, 14, 32, 34; *see also* socio-
    economic status
Club Safe program 68
clubs
    atmosphere of 4, 36–7, 72, 183–4
    and introductions to gambling 23–4
    lobbying power 71
    profits (NSW) 101–3, **103**, **105**
    role in community 4, 15–16, 36–7,
        83–7, 183–4
    use of gambling revenue 22, 85–6
    see also gaming machines
Clubs NSW 68, 71
communities, concept of 3–4
community clubs *see* clubs
Community Development Support
    Expenditure 7, 85–6, 100
competitiveness 10–11, 37–8
counselling *see* support services
CPGI *see* Canadian Problem Gambling
    Index
crane grab machines 46
crime 30–31, 161, 167
culture, and gambling 62–3, 65, 161–3
Cunningham, R.M. 110, 139

Delfabbro, P.H. 47, 59, 103
demographics of gamblers
    Australia 87–91, **89–90**
    case studies 144–8
    New Zealand 90–91
    Queensland survey 113
depression 25, 91, 158, 174, 175
Derevensky, J.L. 18, 23, 26, 110, 138–9
Diagnostic Criteria for Pathological
    Gambling (DSM-IV) 17
    Adapted for Juveniles (DSM-IV-J) 18,
        109
    Multiple Response-Adapted for
        Juveniles (DSM-IV-MR-J) 18
dice 1, 11–12, 13
Dickson, L. 110, 138–9
divorce 157, 160
dog racing 1, 21, 124–5, 153
domestic violence 169, 175
drug use 173–6
DSM-IV *see* Diagnostic Criteria for
    Pathological Gambling
Duan, L. 110, 139

education (about gambling) 184–5
education levels 88, 90–91
EGMs *see* electronic gaming machines
Egypt, Ancient 1, 12, 13
electronic gaming machines 45; *see also*
    gaming machines
employment status, and gambling 88,
    90–91, 145–7
England *see* United Kingdom
ethnicity, and gambling 62–3, 65, 145,
    161–3
Europe
    casinos 45
    gaming machines 46, **48**, 48
    lotteries **41**, 42, 186
excessive gambling
    as combined with other problems 76,
        91, 110, 158, 173–6
    compared to recreational gambling 38
    definitions of 20–21
    gaming machines as common path to
        152–3
    identification of 64

as individual problem 64–5
media coverage of 16
pathways to 5, 24, 159–61, 193–6
research on 5, 17–19
risk factors 24, 26
seeking help for 76, 164–7
see also case studies
excitement, as motive for gambling 25,
91, 158
expenditure (on gambling)
Australia 19, 95–8, **96, 98**
case studies 163–4
global statistics 49–51
Queensland survey 131–6, **132**

Fabiansson, C. 23–4
family
impact upon 15, 16, 21, 65, 75–6,
164–70
and introductions to gambling 15–16,
23, 117, 131, 138–9, 149
and seeking help 164–5
see also relationships
Feeney, D. 88
financial problems 167–71
Finnigan, F. 109, 136
France
gaming machines 45
history of gambling 14
horse racing 43, **44**, 45
lotteries 42, 186
France, C. 14
fruit machines 53, 118
Furstenberg, F.F. 33

Gamblers Anonymous 20 Questions 18
gambling, definitions of 8–11, 20
Gambling Act 2005 (UK) 52–4
Gambling Legislation Amendment
(Responsible Gambling Act) 1999
(NSW) 57
gaming industry, lobbying power of 50,
63, 71
gaming machines
Australia 38–9, 45, 46–8, **47**, 79–82,
91–5, **93, 94**, 186
design of 16, 91, 153
global statistics 45–9, **47, 48**, 186–7

New South Wales 57–61, 101–6, **103,
104, 105**
odds of winning 21–2, 66–8, **67**
as predominant gambling method 152–3
types of 45–6
Gaming Machines Act 2001 (NSW) 57,
60–61
Gaming Machines Amendment Act 2008
(NSW) 57, 60–61
Gaming Machines Amendment Regulation
2009 (NSW) 57, 58, 60–61
Gausset, Q. 21
gender, and gambling
in case studies 144, 152–3
and cultural restrictions 62–3, 162
history 14
and internet gambling 30
Queensland survey 137
research on 24, 30, 88, 90–91
Germany
gaming machines 45, **47**
history of gambling 14
horse racing **44**
lotteries 42, 186
Gibraltar 47
Gillespie, M.A. 26
Global Online Gambler Survey 29–30
global statistics
casinos 45
gambling expenditure 49–51
gambling regulation 51–63
gaming machines 45–9, **47, 48**,
186–7
horse racing 43–5, **44**, 186
lotteries **41**, 41–3, 186
Goldstein, A.L. 110, 139
Goodin, R.E. 32
Great Britain *see* United Kingdom
Greece 42
Greece, Ancient 1, 32
greyhound racing *see* dog racing
Griffiths, M.D. 24, 27, 28, 138
Gupta, R. 18, 23, 26, 110, 138–9

Hardoon, K. 138
Hartnagel, T. 30–31
HDI *see* Household Disposable Income
health 176; *see also* mental health

help, seeking 76, 164–7; *see also* support
services
history
of gambling 1, 11–15, 79–82, **80–81**,
182
of leisure 31–2
of youth construct 33–4
Hong Kong 43, **44**
horse racing
global statistics 43–5, **44**, 186
history of 12, 79
odds of winning 21
Queensland survey 124, 130–31, 189
hotels, profits (NSW) 101–3, **103**, **105**
Household Disposable Income 97–8, **98**
Hraba, J. 88
Huang, J-H. 109

Independent Pricing and Regulatory
Tribunal 57, 59, 61, 69–71
informal gambling 24
internet gambling 9, 11, 28–30, 55–7,
125–6
introductions to gambling 15–16, 23, 117,
131, 138–9, 148–51
IPART *see* Independent Pricing and
Regulatory Tribunal
Ireland **44**, 45
Italy
gambling regulation 182
gaming macines 46–7, **47**, 48, 186
horse racing **44**
lotteries 2, 42, 186

Jacobs, D.F. 23, 26
Jacques, C. 18–19
Jain, U. 31
Jansbøl, K. 21
Japan
gaming machines 45–6, 48
horse racing 43, **44**, 186
lotteries 42

keno 102, **123**, 123–4, 127, 129, 130, 188
knucklebones 1, 13
Korea 43, **44**, 186
Korn, D. 26, 69, 176

Ladouceur, R. 18–19
leisure, concept of 31–3, 35–7
licensing 51–2
loneliness *see* social isolation
losses
attitudes to 134–6, **135**
chasing of 91, 150, 157, 161
sizes of 163–4
lotteries
as fundraising 1, 41
global statistics **41**, 41–3, 186
high wins **2**, 2–3
history of 79
regulation 55
weekly purchase of 16, 23
and young people 119–21, **120**, 127,
130
luck, perception of 155–6

Macau 43, **44**, 47
Maki, T. 88
marital status 144–5
Marshal, D. 30, 31
Mcavoy, S. 31
media coverage (of gambling) 1–3, 16, 26,
27, 71–3
mental health 25, 91, 150, 158, 165, 173–6
Mesopotamia 12–13
Middle East **41**, 42, 45, 186
Mok, W.P. 88
Monaco 47
money *see* expenditure; financial problems;
losses; winning
Moodie, C. 64, 109, 136
Moore, S.M. 24, 109
motivations (for gambling) 25–6, 91,
156–9
MPGS *see* Multicultural Problem
Gambling Services
MTGMs *see* multi-terminal gaming
machines
Multicultural Problem Gambling Services
142–3, 145
multi-terminal gaming machines 58, 60, 61

Native Americans 14, 54–5
Netherlands Antilles 4

New South Wales
  gambling expenditure 104
  gambling regulation 57–61
  gaming machines 57–61, 101–6, **103,
    104, 105**
  prevalence survey 73–6
  responsible gambling 68–71
  see also Australia
New Zealand **44,** 45, 48, 50, 90–91
North America
  gaming machines 46, **48,** 49
  lotteries **41,** 42, 186
  see also Canada; USA
Norway 11–12, 48–9
Nova Scotia 176
Nower, L. 91

Ohtsuka, K. 24, 109
online gambling *see* internet gambling
Orford, J. 19

pachinko machines 46
pachislo machines 45–6
pari-mutuel betting 51
pathological gambling *see* excessive
    gambling
pathways, to excessive gambling 5, 159–
    61, 193–6; *see also* case studies
personality, and gambling 21
poker 21; *see also* card games; gaming
    machines
Portugal 48
Preston, D.L. 31
prevalence, of gambling 22, 73–6, 91–100,
    114–15
prevalence studies 15–20, 23, 73–6, 109
prizes *see* winning
problem gambling *see* excessive gambling
Productivity Commission 69, 73–4, 75,
    87, 88, 197
profit, as motive for gambling 25, 91, 161
protective factors 26

Queensland survey
  arcade games 118, **118**
  bingo 124
  board games 117–18
  card games 117–18, 130

casinos 121–3, **122,** 127
gambling expenditure 131–6, **132**
gambling intensity/or frequency?
    129–31, **130**
horse racing 124, 130–31, 189
internet gambling 125–7
keno **123,** 123–4, 127, 129, 130, 188
lotteries 119–21, **120,** 127, 130
older youths 127–9
overview 112–14, **128–9**
raffles 115–16, **116,** 130
research methodology 110–11
sports betting 125–6, **126,** 130
video games 118, **118**

race *see* ethnicity
racing *see* dog racing; horse racing
raffles 10, 52, 61, 113, 115–16, **116**
randomisation 21–2, 66–8, 155–6
recreation
  gambling perceived as 8, 10, 25,
    37–9
  as motive for gambling 25, 91
*Registered Clubs Responsible Conduct of
    Gambling Code of Practice* 68–9
regulation of gambling
  advertising 27–8, 71–3
  age restrictions 24, 27, 52–3, 61–3
  global overview 51–7
  history of 14–15
  internet gambling 28–9, 55–7
  New South Wales 57–61
  responsible gambling 28, 29, 54,
    63–71
Reith, G. 54, 65–6
relationships 157–8, 160, 165–70, 173–6;
    see also family
religion, and gambling 62–3, 65, 162
remote gambling *see* internet gambling
research on gambling 5–6, 7–8, 15–31,
    64–5, 197–200; *see also* case
    studies; Queensland survey
Resko, S.M. 110, 139
responsible gambling 28, 29, 54, 63–71
Rice, J.M. 32
risk factors 26
risk-taking behaviour 10–11, 21, 25, 26, 110
Rome, Ancient 1, 13, 32

roulette 21, 122
Russia 46, **47**, 186

St Kitts and Nevis 47
Saunders, C. 31
Saunders, P. 32
secrecy, and gambling 65, 167, 169
self-exclusion 65, 66, 69
separation *see* divorce
Shaffer, H. 26, 69, 176
slot machines *see* gaming machines
Smith, G.J. 20, 23, 26, 30–31
smoking 159, 173
smoking ban 58, 86, 159
social isolation 25, 73, 91, 158, 174–5
social networks, concept of 3–4
socio-economic status 147–8; *see also*
    class
SOGS *see* South Oaks Gambling Screen
South Africa **44**, 45
South America **41**, 42, 45, 46, **48**, 48
South Australian Centre for Economic
    Studies 64
South Oaks Gambling Screen(SOGS) 17,
    73
    Revised for Adolescents (SOGS-RA)
        18–19
Spain 42, 45, 46–7, **47**, 182, 186
sport
    and competitiveness 10–11
    and gambling sponsorship 28
    sporting participation 35–6, 125–6
    and young people 15, 35–6, 189
sports betting 21, 103–4, 125–6, **126**, 130,
    153
sports clubs *see* clubs
status, perception of 72, 156
Stebbins, R.A. 33
Stinchfield, R. 24–5
stress-relief, gambling as 25, 91, 158–9,
    174
support services
    funding from tax revenue 66, 50–51
    need for 5, 53–4, 61, 64–5
    role of 38, 50–51
    seeking help from 76, 164–7
Sweden 11–12

tarot cards 14
taxation 9, 50–51, 58, 63–4, 66, 86,
    98–100, **99**
theft 161, 167
totalizator systems 51
tourism 47–8
Turkey 43, **44**, 186
Turner, N.E. 31

underage gambling *see* age restrictions;
    Queensland survey; young
    people
unemployment 158; *see also* employment
    status
United Arab Emirates 43, **44**
United Kingdom
    age restrictions 62, 118
    casinos 52
    gambling expenditure 49
    gambling regulation 52–4
    gaming machines 45–6, **47**, 48–9, 53,
        118, 186
    history of gambling 14
    horse racing 43, **44**, 45
    lotteries 42, 52–3
    sports betting 52
USA
    age restrictions 62
    casinos 45, 54
    gambling expenditure 49
    gambling regulation 28, 54–5
    gaming machines 45, 46, **47**, 48, 186
    history of gambling 14
    horse racing 43, **44**, 186
    lotteries 42, 186
    young gamblers 115

venues
    design of 15, 26, 72, 153
    opening hours 27, 39, 152
    types of 22
video games 118, **118**
Video Lottery Terminals 45, 46
Volberg, R.A. 19, 65–6, 109

wagering *see* dog racing; horse racing;
    sports betting

Walker, M.B. 87
Walton, M.A. 110, 139
winning
  first experiences of 153–6
  as motivation for gambling 25, 91,
    161
  odds of 3, 27, 66–8, **67**, 153–4
  reinvestment of winnings 154–6
  sizes of wins **2**, 2–3, 162
Winters, K.C. 24–5
Wood, R. 27, 138
Wynne, H.J. 20, 23, 26, 30–31

young people
  access to gambling venues 24
  introductions to gambling 15–16, 23,
    117, 131, 138–9, 149
  and leisure 35–7
  prevalence of gambling 27, 114–15
  problem gambling 23
  research on gambling by 5, 15–31
  and sport 35–6, 189
  see also Queensland survey
youth, construct of 33–5

Made in the USA
Middletown, DE
06 January 2023

21570704R00137